Donald J. Raleigh, editor

A RUSSIAN CIVIL WAR DIARY

Alexis Babine in Saratov, 1917–1922

Duke University Press

Durham and London 1988

[redacted]

Printed in the United States of America
on acid-free paper ∞
Library of Congress Cataloging-in-Publication Data
Babine, Alexis Vasil'evich, 1866–1930.
Diary of Alexis Babine / Donald J. Raleigh, editor.
p. cm.
Bibliography: p.
Includes index.
ISBN 0-8223-0835-5
1. Babine, Alexis Vasil'evich, 1866–1930—Diaries. 2. Soviet Union—History—Revolution, 1917–1921—Personal narratives. 3. Saratov (R.S.F.S.R.)—History—Revolution, 1917–1921. 4. College teachers—Soviet Union—Diaries. 5. Librarians—Soviet Union—Diaries. I. Raleigh, Donald J. II. Title.
DK265.7.B3 1988
947.084—dc 19 88-3967

To Momcilo Rosic, Professor Emeritus, Knox College

CONTENTS

PREFACE

During the past two decades or so there has been a steady flow of scholarly writing on the Russian Civil War. More recently, heightened awareness on the part of Western historians of the importance of the years 1918–1921 as a formative experience for the fledgling Soviet state has resulted in a shift away from a focus on military developments, diplomacy, and politics at the top, to heretofore neglected questions of social and economic history.[1] With the exception of several published works and others in progress,[2] however, we still lack in-depth studies of the Civil War in the provinces, which would be valuable to the social historian in illuminating the events on which our understanding of the Civil War is based and in describing how central policies actually affected people.

1. See, for example, the collection of essays edited by Diane Koenker, William G. Rosenberg, and Ronald G. Suny, to be published by Indiana University Press under the title *Party, State, and Society in the Russian Civil War: Explorations in Social History* (Bloomington, 1988). See also Israel Getzler, *Kronstadt 1917–1921: The Fate of a Soviet Democracy* (Cambridge, 1983); and Silvana Malle, *The Economic Organization of War Communism, 1918–1921* (Cambridge, 1985).

2. Among published works I should mention Canfield F. Smith, *Vladivostok under Red and White Rule: Revolution and Counterrevolution in the Russian Far East, 1920–1922* (Seattle, 1975); Oliver H. Radkey, *The Unknown Civil War in Soviet Russia: A Study of the Green Movement in the Tambov Region, 1920–1921* (Stanford, 1976); Peter Scheibert, *Lenin an der Macht—Das russische Volk in der Revolution, 1918–1922* (Weinheim, 1984); Richard Sakwa, *Soviet Communists in Power: A Study of Moscow during the Civil War, 1918–21* (New York: St. Martin's Press, 1988); a study by Lars Lih, *Bread and Authority in Russia, 1914–1921* (Berkeley and Los Angeles, forthcoming); and works in progress by myself, Orlando Figes, and John W. Long.

The diary of Alexis Vasilevich Babine[3] is a unique historical source because it offers readers a rare glimpse into daily life during the Civil War in the provincial city of Saratov. Babine not only had an unusual story to tell, but also the ability to do so, and his writing casts fresh, if refracted, light on the Russian Civil War from an unfamiliar angle. As far as I know, his diary is the only non-Bolshevik book-length account that illuminates events in a provincial Russian town during the entire Civil War.[4]

Who was Alexis V. Babine?

Sometime in 1890 a twenty-four-year-old Russian made his way to Ithaca, New York, in the hope of working his way through Cornell University. He had the good fortune of asking directions of some adventuresome young men who happened to take a fancy to the outlandishly dressed muzhik they mistook for a "Polack or

3. Aleksei Vasil'evich Babin anglicized his name.

4. A spate of memoirs published in the twenties, far too numerous to cite here, sheds light on the White movement, the military campaigns, and escapes from Russia. Several memoirs dealing with provincial Russia can be found in *Arkhiv russkoi revoliutsii* (memoirs by Z. Iu. Arbatov, B. Shutskoi, and N. Voronich), and in the Inter-University Project on the History of the Menshevik Movement (e.g., the memoir of Iu. Grinfel'd).

There is also a fair amount of memoir literature on the Civil War in Russia's capitals, especially Moscow, by journalists and other foreigners. A few of the better-known examples are Margeurite E. Harrison, *Marooned in Moscow: The Story of an American Woman Imprisoned in Russia* (New York, 1921); Arthur Ransone, *Russia in 1919* (New York, 1919), and *The Crisis in Russia* (New York, 1921); Louise Bryant, *Six Red Months in Russia: An Observer's Account of Russia before and during the Proletarian Dictatorship* (New York, 1918); Alexander Berkman, *The Bolshevik Myth: Diary, 1920–1922* (New York, 1925); Emma Goldman, *My Disillusionment in Russia* (Garden City, N.Y., 1923); William A. Brown, Jr., *The Groping Giant: Revolutionary Russia as Seen by an American Democrat* (New Haven, 1920); Oliver M. Sayler, *Russia, White or Red* (Boston, 1919).

Chernov's daughter's memoir on the period provides interesting information on her travels throughout Russia (including Saratov province)—Olga Chernov Andreyev, *Cold Spring in Russia*, trans. Michael Carlisle (Ann Arbor, 1978). Nadezhda Mandelstam's *Hope Abandoned*, trans. Max Hayward (New York, 1974), offers some insights into provincial Voronezh during the Civil War, and Victor B. Shklovskii's *A Sentimental Journey: Memoirs, 1917–1922* (Ithaca, 1984) includes a staccato description of Saratov in 1918.

Western repositories (and Soviet archives) undoubtedly contain other documents of historical significance that have been neglected by or are unknown to historians. Terence Emmons, for example, has recently prepared for publication *Time of Troubles: The Diary of Iurii Vladimirovich Got'e. Moscow, July 8, 1917–July 23, 1922* (Princeton, 1988).

Magyar." Babine, his new acquaintances soon learned, spoke excellent but "foreign sounding English" as well as respectable German and French. He read the classical languages. Impressed by the "waif from Russia," Cornell student Edwin Emerson and his friends introduced Babine to Professors George Lincoln Burr and John Henry Comstock and his wife, Anna B. Comstock, through whose intercession Babine found employment in the Cornell University Library and was enrolled at the university. Babine had come to Cornell because he had read in a Russian newspaper that this new institution of higher education offered jobs to anyone willing to work his way through college. His reason for leaving Russia, according to the only report available, was that he had foolishly accepted the challenge of his closest friend to shoot a pine cone from his friend's head. Alexis, unfortunately, killed him.[5]

It was a long way between Ithaca and Babine's home town of Elatma, a sleepy old settlement founded by Mordvinians many centuries before and located in Riazan province southeast of Moscow. Babine was born there on March 22, 1866, to a builder (and fisherman), Vasilii Pavlovich, and Anna Stepanovna (née Artamonova). The fact that Babine graduated from the local gymnasium would suggest that his parents were modestly well off and educated.[6] The local gymnasium did an enviable job of teaching Babine English as well as other languages. His outstanding academic record secured him a place in the prestigious Institute of History and Philology in St. Petersburg, where he studied between 1885 and 1887. For the next two years he appears to have taught at and possibly served as librarian in the Okhta Trade School in the Russian capital. After the tragic shooting accident, Babine's parents purportedly exhausted their savings to pay blood money and send the young Babine away from Elatma. He worked his way to Riazan, to Moscow, and to the Baltic port of Riga, where he found a job as a stoker on a German steamer that took him to New York sometime in 1889.

And, so, this son of a builder, Alexis V. Babine, came to America to make a fresh start. That he was able to do so successfully is testimony to his many talents and also to the variety of opportunities

5. Edwin Emerson's reminiscences "Happy-Go-Lucky Groves of Academe," Cornell University Library Archives (hereinafter CULA), pp. 238–62.

6. Babine's family belonged to the provincial petit bourgeoisie. His father's social estate was that of *meshchanin*.

his new home made available to him. Babine also had a knack for impressing influential people with his seriousness of purpose. Welcomed into the cultural life of the Cornell University community, Babine was befriended by a group of kindred spirits who helped him secure employment later and who remained loyal to him, as he to them, in subsequent years.

Babine's Cornell years prepared him in a number of ways for a professional career and for his future adventures. Babine completed a B.A. and M.A. in American history at Cornell by 1894.[7] Apart from a short stint at the Sorbonne, he worked between 1891 and 1896 as a cataloger in the Cornell University Library, acquiring skills that, along with his knowledge of languages, would make his accomplishments highly marketable. In 1896 Babine accepted an appointment as librarian at Indiana University in Bloomington. In 1898 he moved to Stanford University, and in 1902, after causing a bit of a row at Stanford, to the Library of Congress, where he was employed until 1905, during which time he negotiated the purchase and transfer of the 80,000-volume library of the wealthy Siberian merchant G. V. Yudin, which remains at the core of the unusually rich Russian collection at the Library of Congress. After resigning from his position at the library he went to work temporarily for the Associated Press office in St. Petersburg.[8]

7. Babine's M.A. thesis, which he defended in 1894, is entitled "The Statesmanship of Daniel Webster."

8. The most complete biographical sketch of Babine is by Edward Kasinec, "Alexis V. Babine (1866–1930): A Biographical Note," in Kasinec's *Slavic Books and Bookmen: Papers and Essays* (New York, 1984), pp. 73–77. Additional biographical information can be found in the George Lincoln Burr papers in CULA, in Babine's papers in the Manuscript Division of the Library of Congress, and in Frederick B. Ashley's manuscript, also located in the Manuscript Division, "History of the Library of Congress, 1897–1939," chap. 34, pp. 1030–48. Babine's short stint at Indiana is discussed in correspondence between David S. Jordan and Indiana University President Joseph Swain and between Swain and Babine. The correspondence relating to Babine's stay at Indiana is held in the University Archives, Indiana University. Babine's tenure in Bloomington is also treated in "Reports of the I.U. President to the Board of Trustees (1896–98)" and in Mildred H. Lowell, "Indiana University Libraries, 1829–1942" (Ph.D. dissertation, University of Chicago, 1957), pp. 123–26. Babine apparently had been asked to resign his position at Stanford because of problems he had getting along with his colleagues. See Wojciech Zalewski, *Collectors and Collections of Slavica at Stanford University: A Contribution to the History of American Academic Libraries* (Stanford, 1985), pp. 4–5. Reference to Babine's acceptance of a position with the Associated Press can be found in U.S. Library of Congress, *Report*

For several reasons Babine decided to return to Russia to live in 1910. Little could he have realized at the time that fate would compel him to remain there for twelve years, during which he would live through revolution and civil war. We know that Babine's mother had been taken ill in 1910 and that Babine expressed his eagerness to see her before she died. He had also confided in a compatriot, historian S. M. Volkonskii, that he was bored with his adopted home and now wished to serve his native country.[9] Moreover, Babine was determined to fulfill a yearning he had harbored for some time: to publish, in Russian, a "popular history" of the United States. His two-volume *Istoriia Severo-Amerikanskikh Soedinennykh Shtatov* (History of the North American United States), begun while he worked in the Cornell University library, was published in St. Petersburg in 1912. In it, Babine revealed his strong sympathies for the American political system and for what his Russian reviewer called the country's "Anglo-Saxon" culture.[10] Although they have tended to dismiss Babine's non-Marxist approach, Soviet historians of the United States have read and continue to read and profit from Babine's pioneering work.

After publication of his history of the United States, Babine remained in Russia, where his connections helped him secure an appointment as a public school inspector in Kharkov province. In 1916 he assumed responsibility for the Vologda school district in northern Russia. Babine was serving in this capacity when bread riots and labor strikes in Petrograd set off the February Revolution of 1917 that toppled the reigning Romanov dynasty and inaugurated direct participation in politics by the heretofore disenfranchised Russian masses and by those who claimed to speak on their behalf. As the diary entries suggest, the new climate complicated Babine's relations with his subordinates, for whom Babine showed disdain. It is

---

of the Librarian of Congress and Report of the Superintendent of the Library Building and Grounds for the Fiscal Year Ending June 30, 1905 (Washington, 1905), p. 9. While working for the Library of Congress, Babine published a bilingual description of the Yudin Library. See *The Yudin Library, Krasnoiarsk (Eastern Siberia)* (Washington, D.C., 1905).

9. S. M. Volkonskii, *Moi vospominaniia*, vol. 1, *Lavry* (Munich, 1923), pp. 265–66.

10. A. V. Babine, *Istoriia Severo-Amerikanskikh Soedinennykh Shtatov*, vol. 1, *1607–1829*, vol. 2, *1829–1910* (St. Petersburg, 1912). The review by P. Fridolin' appeared in *Zhurnal ministerstva narodnogo prosveshcheniia* (September 1912), pp. 170–71.

 unclear how this problem was resolved. In May 1917 the Provisional Government abolished local school administrations and transferred their functions to zemstvos and town dumas. Babine may well have been dismissed at this time. In any event, what must have seemed like an opportunity to extricate himself from a difficult situation soon presented itself. In October Babine arrived in the Volga provincial capital of Saratov as an instructor of English and librarian at the local university, which had opened in 1909. Saratov University had established new departments of history and foreign languages in the fall of 1917. Although Babine's diary is silent about this episode, his correspondence reveals that he had actually applied to teach U.S. history in Saratov but had been voted down because he lacked a Ph.D. His efforts to obtain an honorary doctorate from Cornell for his two-volume history of the United States failed.

Before discussing Babine's diary and experiences in Saratov it would be helpful to comment briefly on his personality and political views. Unfortunately, much about Babine's personal life and personality remains a mystery, making it risky to attempt a confident character sketch. We can only imagine, for instance, the psychological impact of the shooting accident in Elatma. He never married and it is impossible to confirm any sustained amorous relationship. Bits and pieces of scattered evidence, however, mainly character evaluations by employers and long-term acquaintances, permit us to isolate several key traits, which Babine's own writings confirm. A gifted linguist and diligent, intelligent student, Babine has been described by those who knew him as sober, methodical, efficient, orderly, proper, and, on occasion, stubborn. He had a sense of adventure. He was bent on achievement. He was willing to indulge his interests. He could be charming in an eccentric way, loyal, and accessible, but, more important, he was private, elusive, secretive. Above all, he was a survivor.

This last point may also be the key to understanding his political beliefs. Despite the occasional nostalgic reference in his diary to the autocracy, he was not a monarchist *tout court;* the chaos and horror of the Civil War merely made him long for a return to the old way. Most likely, Babine had been a critic of the autocracy before 1917 who had sympathized with the political leanings of the Constitutional Democrats or Kadets. His fondness for American life-styles and for pragmatic, compromise politics had, over the

Alexis V. Babine in Saratov (Photo courtesy of the Library of Congress, Manuscript Division)

years, made him critical of his own country's backwardness and what he considered to be its political immaturity. The moderate socialist elements, who had won the sympathies of the majority of people and of the Russian intelligentsia, did not appeal to him because their all but blind yearning for change contributed, in his view, to the Bolshevik victory. Moreover, the middle-class liberals' inability to challenge the militant revolutionaries effectively during the Civil War made him lose respect for them, too.

Babine was too private a person and too impatient to unravel the complexity of Russian revolutionary politics to make his diary a classic of autobiography on the magnitude of N. N. Sukhanov's writings. Babine was not a major historical character or an exceptional social observer. In his own words, he "always diligently kept out of politics." When he chose to describe them, he did so with profound moral indignation. Moreover, he happened to be not in Petrograd or Moscow, the hubs of Russian revolutionary politics, but in Saratov, the woefully provincial town of Chekhov's "Lady with a Dog" which, despite its impressive expansion in the prewar period and its modern pretensions, remained, in the words of the Soviet writer Konstantin Fedin, a city "of gingham, retired generals, and flour kings."[11]

Paradoxically, the historical value and interest of Babine's diary lie in what appear to be these, its most obvious drawbacks. Babine's journal is a primary document of historical significance precisely because it takes us outside the Russian capitals and away from well-known political leaders. It describes daily life in a provincial Russian city that remained Red throughout the entire Civil War, and in so doing it calls attention to the rich diversity that lies behind historical generalizations. It also serves as an antidote for Soviet accounts: Babine had no sympathy whatsoever for the new order and was not an impartial observer. Lacking any understanding of the aspirations or motivations of the unscrubbed Russian masses, Babine rendered an account of a social milieu that despised, but did little to challenge, the Bolshevik order of things. His diary captures the distinct texture of civil war, showing us how a stratum of middle-class Saratov fared during five years of disorder, deprivation, and disillusionment. It focuses not on political ideas and causes, but on grubbing for food and staying alive. It is peopled not with faceless worker and soldier heroes, the darlings of Soviet historians, but with the good burghers of Saratov who lost their property and with the staff of Saratov University. They are the opponents of the new order who, for the most part, stayed in Russia and reached some sort of an accommodation with the Soviet regime. They were better equipped than the masses to tell their story, but conditions prevented them from doing so. Although Babine's diary is the record of how one individual responded to events, it is clear that the way in which he came to grips with this set of historical circumstances is not out of the ordinary. His diary sheds light on the collective experience of Babine's social class and is particularly valuable for what it tells us about provincial academic life.

Babine crafted his diary to serve as an indictment of Communist

11. Konstantin Fedin, *Early Joys*, trans. G. Kazanina (New York, 1960), p. 232. The second volume of Fedin's trilogy, *Neobyknovennoe leto*, provides an impressionistic view of Saratov during the Civil War.

brutality, but the strongest theme that the text conveys is that Russia had few heroes. Babine was certainly not a hero. And, as one early reader of the diary so succinctly—if unfairly—put it, Babine's friends at the university were "only a little less venal than their oppressors." Complete demoralization had seized hold of the population. "Fear overcame courage; decency submitted to indecency; selfishness abandoned the instinct for resistance."[12] Babine criticized the funk of his supine and cowardly colleagues, yet did nothing to risk his own safety. As the economic realities of War Communism took hold, and the old market forces were transformed and destroyed, Babine's activities were "confined exclusively to foraging for food and supplies, and to gossiping with similarly inclined friends and colleagues."[13] As the Civil War progressed and hunger destroyed life as it had been known, commentary on politics disappears from the diary; the entries become pithy and appear less frequently. Babine, like everybody else, was preoccupied with trying to stay alive.

Babine's diary reminds us that major historical events that attract historians' attention years after the events occurred may not have meant as much to those who lived during them and did not make them. To cite just a few examples, the journal tells us nothing about the Miliukov affair, the collapse of the successive provisional governments, elections to the Constituent Assembly, the establishment of an anti-Bolshevik government in neighboring Samara in the summer of 1918, the introduction of the New Economic Policy, etc. Instead, readers are fed a steady fare of second- and third-hand information and of rumors, some absurd, some remotely based on fact, some true. This is not to say that the unreliable entries or unsubstantiated reports are of little value. On the contrary, the reader senses that Babine recorded what was on the minds of those belonging to his social class, and that he observed and noted, and not unintelligently, that which affected his and their lives the most. Despair and anguish had made these people credulous and receptive to sustained rumors of Russia's salvation by Cossacks, Czechoslovaks, Germans, the English, French, and local soldiers—but never by Russians. Rumors of bitter tears streaming down the countenance of an icon of Our Lady and of Orthodox priests leading

12. Babine Papers, David C. Mearns's description of diary, August 21, 1951.
13. Babine Papers, B. Truscoe's discussion of the diary, August 23, 1951.

 armies of liberation took on significance for Babine because they were alternatives to reading the "illiterate sheet" put out by the local Soviet.

Babine kept his diary in the expectation that it would be published someday. He also wrote it for an American audience. Disgusted with what he called the "backwardness and barbarity" of his native country, Babine could be a myopic observer. He expressed longing for a return to the old regime that had become politically and morally bankrupt even in the eyes of Saratov's (and Russia's) middle class.[14] His understandable hatred of the leftist groups (Maximalists, as he called them) extended with little discrimination to everyone and everything that wanted to give Russia a fresh start—to Kerensky, the Socialist Revolutionaries, and the Russian intelligentsia in general. Babine was anti-Semitic. He disliked Poles. He showed contempt for the lower classes who had fallen victim to the seductive slogans flung at them from the political left. Readers of the diary encounter "ill-smelling peasants," the "rabble from nearby villages," the "blushing nobility and ignoble vulgar," and Babine's "unusually stupid maid." Babine could be arrogant, bigoted, and supercilious toward his subordinates. He dwelled on delays and inconveniences, and was impressed by the strength of his own will to cope and his ability to do so. He took pride whenever he resorted to manual labor or tapped some rural skill learned as a child. He expressed indignation when he had to deal with affronts to his sense of propriety.

Outsiders' descriptions of a culture are necessarily incomplete and often offer more of a reflection of the observer's own self-image. In this regard, however, Babine, as a trained historian who had spent almost twenty years in the United States, could assess his Saratov colleagues from a unique observation point. Even though Babine may not have pondered over the deep-lying causes of the revolution or the political cosmology of the Russian masses, he did understand middle-class Saratov. From the diary we learn how the class-oriented policies of the Bolsheviks, from housing and food supply to organizing the university janitors and giving them equal pay with the instructional staff, transmogrified the world of the former privileged. We learn about the "physical and moral flabbi-

14. See my *Revolution on the Volga: 1917 in Saratov* (Ithaca, 1986).

ness of . . . [Russia's] Christian citizens."[15] "The Russian tendency to protest against oppression and all sorts of barbarity by refusing to do any work," he tells us, "is, to me, as touching as the Russian incapacity to do anything to eliminate injustice."[16] Astutely, Babine realized that the common people felt alienated from Saratov's nonrevolutionary middle class, which was "corrupted by self-indulgence and physical idleness, disarmed and unfamiliar with the use of arms, incapable of resisting force by their own exertions, discredited in the eyes of a deceived people."[17] On this subject we get Babine at his best:

> The more I look at my university learned colleagues, the more I listen to their eloquent and animated or passionately subdued talks on the present state of affairs, the more disgusted I grow with their inability to do anything. . . . No rights whatsoever will or can they defend with their own flabby hands: they will much rather hire stronger hands than to expose their precious selves to the risks of a contest. Their chief end is life itself, and only life—under any conditions.[18]

In describing them he is describing himself.

Babine's diary likewise provides rich detail about daily life (*byt*) in Saratov and elsewhere in Russia. He describes how hunting for food made jobs secondary by 1918; the amazing growth of a black market; "bagmen" whose illicit activities kept people alive; behavior in lines. He describes conditions on trains and steamers, life in the villages, and in Babine's home town of Elatma, where his brother Peter was "reluctant to get involved." He describes the horrors of the famine and the operations of the American Relief Administration in Saratov. Apart from his moral outrage over the besotted ARA staff members and their succumbing to pleasures of the flesh, Babine sheds light on how the local Soviet authorities worked with their foreign benefactors. Even his escape from Russia offers insights into the bureaucratic nature of the Soviet state in the aftermath of Civil War. In drawing our attention away from

15. Babine Diary, October 27, 1917.
16. Ibid., December 1, 1917.
17. Ibid., November 18, 1917.
18. Ibid., February 2, 1918.

 the major political issues, characters, and places, Babine provides a rare portrait of how these very considerations affected everyday life in the provinces.

How credible is Babine's diary? Before addressing this question it should be noted that today Babine's diary can be found in his personal archive held in the Manuscript Division of the Library of Congress.[19] The archive, comprising six boxes of materials, contains a typescript and handwritten version of the diary covering 1917 to 1922, various documents, miscellaneous correspondence, and photographs. It also includes Babine's literary works, draft chapters of his history of the United States, and two historical-autobiographical essays based on information presented in the diary. The handwritten diary or journal begins on September 21, 1917, and ends on July 25, 1919. Babine most likely kept this journal during his stay in Saratov.[20] The more extensive typescript, covering the period from March 19, 1917, through November 18, 1922, may have been written shortly after his return to the United States,

19. Alexis V. Babine Collection, 3239. There is no published description of the materials in Babine's archive. The diary in its various forms and miscellaneous correspondence dating from 1901 to 1930 can be found in Box 1. Box 2 contains Babine's historical essays on the Russian Civil War, as well as draft chapters (in Russian) of his history of the United States. Box 3 includes various notebooks and address books, some of which list prices of foods and staples in Russia during the Civil War, and in the United States, 1923–29. Babine's notes on the diary as well as an English-language sentimental manuscript "Story of a Young Love" are to be found here. In Box 4 one finds diplomas, certificates, passports, photographs, and short stories probably written by Babine. Box 5 holds a manuscript "We the People," a play most likely written by Babine. Miscellaneous items are stored in Box 6.

One should consult the "Library of Congress Archives: Annotated List of Materials in the Library of Congress Archives, Manuscript Division (October 1982)." Additional Babine materials at the Library of Congress are located in the Acquisitions and Accession Records (correspondence concerning purchase of the G. Yudin collection); Correspondence and Memoranda (correspondence from Babine and Yudin); Other Library Officers' Correspondence (Babine's original correspondence regarding purchase of the Yudin collection); and in Frederick B. Ashley's "History of the Library of Congress," cited in note 8.

20. Elizabeth Rhodes Jackson (see note 10) claims that "Alexis Babine lived in constant fear of discovery and betrayal. He had a little hiding place in which he kept his diary." Letters he wrote from Saratov to G. L. Burr mention that Babine "shall have to write a book" about his experiences and noted that he had been collecting interesting newspaper material for four or five years.

from notes he had made in Saratov. This version expatiates upon the more laconic entries found in the written version and clarifies obscure points. Some entries are altogether new, such as those concerning Babine's activities before he arrived in Saratov in the fall of 1917. The added entries tend to moralize and criticize and may well have been omitted from the earlier version for fear of discovery. The published version presented here is a composite of the two documents.

Readers must learn how to read any diary or memoir. As is clear from observations made earlier, not all information in Babine's diary can be taken at face value. This fascinating primary source is most valuable for the picture of daily life it presents, for the sense of immediacy it conveys of the events described, and for what it tells us about the priorities of Babine's life. Having verified the major facts and chronology presented in the diary, I believe it to be a highly reliable, if personalized and incomplete, guide to Saratov during the Civil War. The categories of observations that tend to be less useful, not surprisingly, are those varnished by Babine's political attitudes and, of course, the rumors he was wont to repeat. Fortunately, Babine was careful in ascribing things he did not experience firsthand to rumor, and this should alert the reader to be on guard. It should be stressed as well that the rumor mill was an inseparable part of the Civil War: owing to the breakdown of transportation and communications, victors and vanquished alike hatched, spread, or made policies based on unverified reports.

As regards Babine's political biases, an astute reader of his diary back in 1951 realized that Babine had not told the whole story. "For if the Bolshevik supporters were so few in number, and so dishonest, ignorant, and ferocious as he suggests, and if they were so universally execrated, it is hardly credible that they should nevertheless have prevailed."[21] Much more work needs to be done on the Russian Civil War in order to understand the social underpinnings and constituency of Bolshevik power. (My related research would suggest a complicated picture in which support for the Bolshevik regime was constantly changing throughout the period, and was connected to availability of food rations as much as to ideological considerations.) Moreover, even though the diary ignores any analytical discussion of why the Bolsheviks were able to stay in power,

21. Babine Papers, B. Truscoe's discussion of the diary, August 23, 1951.

it does unwittingly suggest, at least in part, that the Bolsheviks did enjoy some popular support. On occasion Babine acknowledges that workers and soldiers backed the Communists (whose housing and other social policies mentioned in the diary surely were viewed by many as positive measures). Babine admits that the local soldiers were "as opposed to Kerensky as they are to a new monarch."[22] By September 1917 they had become mostly pro-Bolshevik, as had the garrison in Babine's home town of Elatma. Only once does the diary take us inside the Saratov Soviet of Workers', Soldiers' and Peasants' Deputies, but even this brief look at Saratov's revolutionary culture is instructive. An acquaintance of Babine's who attended a Soviet meeting reported that "a nervous person or a lady might get a fainting fit hearing what was said, and seeing how it was accepted by the audience, seeing the audience itself." The same report describes the Bolshevik leader V. P. Antonov as a charismatic speaker who reminded "you of pictures of Christ. . . . [When he spoke] the audience roared and applauded wildly. I never in my life saw such a collection of criminal and desperado types."[23] On another occasion Babine expressed shock that a friend of his (true, a "socially humble friend") had actually befriended Bolsheviks.[24] We also learn from the diary that the Whites were not always seen as liberators. Babine chronicles not only Bolshevik atrocities in the countryside, but also those of White bandits and Cossacks who robbed the peasants, too. Moreover, Russia's salvation from the Bolsheviks depended upon the victory of A. I. Denikin's Volunteer Army, whose officers, Babine concedes, deserted their men. Even some of Babine's conservative university colleagues occasionally found something complimentary to say about the Bolsheviks. Professor V. I. Veretennikov, a historian, spoke highly of a Bolshevik leader, Tsyrkin, who was killed by a political opponent. "Our ultra-conservative Professor [M. F.] Tsytovich," Babine notes, "spoke diplomatically well about the leading Bolsheviks as men of action today."[25] Like most members of the Saratov University faculty, Tsytovich eventually accepted the Soviet regime and went on

22. Babine Diary, October 28, 1917.
23. Ibid., May 25, 1918.
24. Ibid., November 22, 1918.
25. Ibid., December 12, 1918.

to become a member of the Soviet Academy of Sciences. Saratov had another political culture Babine did not understand.

Following his escape from Russia, Babine returned to Cornell, where he again took up work in the university library. In 1927 Herbert Putnam, Librarian of Congress, brought him back to Washington. When Babine died of an inoperable carcinoma on May 10, 1930, at the age of sixty-four, he was serving as assistant head of the Slavic Section of the Library of Congress. Apart from the sum of $500, bequeathed to his stepmother still living in Elatma, Babine left his entire estate to the Library of Congress. Monies from his investments and savings were to be used to purchase books for the library's Slavic collection. An old friend, Dr. Nan Gilbert Seymour, who visited Babine on his deathbed, urged him to entrust his diary to Putnam. Babine had been reluctant to do so earlier, for he considered the journal "too personal for publication" and he "feared reprisals from the Bolshevists [*sic*] on his few remaining relatives in Russia." Seymour, believing the diary to be "a document of . . . great historical value," eventually persuaded Babine to turn it over to Putnam.[26]

Several efforts to publish the diary at this time came to nought, undoubtedly owing to the underdeveloped state of Russian studies in America; ironically, by the time Russian studies had expanded after World War II, and particularly in the late 1950s, the diary had been forgotten. As executor of Babine's estate, Putnam had seen to it that Babine's remains were interred in his beloved Ithaca, and had set the diary aside for safe keeping. In the following years several of Babine's friends approached Putnam and President Edmund E. Day of Cornell University with proposals to publish the diary, but nothing ever came of these or similar efforts made later. Despite the sincere intentions of those close to Babine to commemorate the life of their eccentric Russian friend, their conception of what Babine experienced and described in his account, understandably enough, was confused, bungled, and so embellished over time that they could do little more than call the diary to the attention of someone such as Putnam who might be instrumental in getting

26. Burr Papers, CULA, Dr. Nan Gilbert Seymour to Burr, May 12, 1930.

 it published.[27] Putnam seriously entertained proposals to publish the journal ("with due regard for the possible inconvenience to any relatives of Mr. Babine surviving in Russia, or to persons mentioned in the text") but believed the project impractical "without extensive editing."[28]

Rich in experience, accomplishment, and adventure, Babine's life had become intertwined with some of the most disruptive events of the twentieth century. His diary is a fitting tribute to the man: in keeping it, he tapped his knowledge, experience, and professional training to explain his native but now alien land to his adopted and vastly different America. As a historical source used with the appropriate measure of caution, Babine's diary illuminates events, behavior, and attitudes that take on significance precisely because they were ordinary. In this regard, we are fortunate that Babine was, as a colleague at the Library of Congress described him, "scholarly, methodic, industrious, punctilious. . . . [His] peculiar uprightness of mind, character, and bearing gave him distinction and inspired confidence and liking."[29]

Babine's diary presents some peculiar problems to the editor. Babine wrote the diary in English. Although fluent in English, he frequently made mistakes in syntax, spelling, and diction. In editing the diary, I have corrected errors, restructured sentences, modernized spelling and usage to conform with contemporary usage, and deleted repetitive and tedious passages. However, I have endeavored to retain the quaint flavor of the original as much as possible. Dates in Babine's diary are given according to the Julian calendar,

27. See, for example, Babine Papers, Manuscript Division, Library of Congress, letter of Elizabeth Rhodes Jackson to Edmund E. Day, November 11, 1940. Another attempt to publish the diary was made in the early 1950s, but it, too, never amounted to anything, probably because no one could be found to edit the manuscript. In 1951 Mr. George Groce favored publication over the Library of Congress imprint. The chief of the Manuscript Division, David C. Mearns, believed the diary might attract attention "if thoroughly edited and published anonymously by some commercial house." Although his written evaluation of the diary is less than a ringing endorsement in favor of publication, he verbally strongly favored seeing the diary in print. See Office Memorandum of Mearns to Groce, August 21, 1951.

28. Ibid., Herbert Putnam to Dr. Madison Bentley, February 20, 1941.

29. Ashley, "History of the Library of Congress," p. 1047.

which was thirteen days behind the Gregorian calendar of the West, until February 1918, when the Gregorian calendar was introduced into Russia. Transliteration from Russian is based on the Library of Congress system, but for stylistic considerations I have deleted the soft sign from place names and proper nouns (e.g., Kazan rather than Kazan'). In some surnames *ii* is rendered *y* to conform with common usage: Kerensky, Trotsky. To make the diary more accessible to the general reader, I have annotated the text extensively, with the aim of identifying people and places, clarifying obscure points, correcting errors, and calling attention to Babine's most obvious biases. I have also taken the liberty of dividing the diary into six chapters by year, and I have prefaced each chapter with a thumbnail sketch of the major political developments in Saratov during the period under discussion. Finally, I have appended a selected bibliography of sources I used in connection with this project and related research, which have helped me annotate the text and which illuminate developments in Saratov during the Civil War. Many of these sources were consulted in the Soviet Union during the first half of 1986, where, thanks to the support of the Fulbright-Hays Faculty Research Program and the International Research and Exchanges Board, I was able to conduct research on the Civil War in Saratov province.

It is a pleasure for me as well to acknowledge the assistance of those who helped me with this project. I am especially indebted to Edward Kasinec, chief, Slavonic Division, New York Public Library, for calling Babine's diary to my attention and for facilitating publication of this work in a variety of ways. I regret that Mr. Kasinec did not have time to collaborate with me on this project. John M. Thompson and Michael S. Melancon read Babine's typescript version of the diary and encouraged me to proceed with my plans to publish it. Kevin Moore provided many hours of careful clerical assistance. Patricia Polansky, Russian bibliographer at the University of Hawaii's Hamilton Library, helped me obtain materials and track down elusive references. Frederick Marcham, professor emeritus of Cornell University, kindly responded to my inquiries in regard to Babine's Cornell days. David L. Arans of the Library of Congress shared his vast bibliographical knowledge of the Russian Civil War with me. David W. Doyle offered some valuable suggestions for improving the introduction. I also wish to acknowledge the professional assistance I received from Professor Everett A. Wingert, who prepared the maps published in this book, and to Dr. Sara Sohmer, who compiled the index. Thanks to N. N. Bolkhovitinov of the Institute of History of the USSR Academy of Sciences, I now have a copy of volume one of Babine's history of the United States.

I wish to record my indebtedness as well to Richard C. Rowson and the staff at Duke University Press; to the staff of the Manuscript Division of the Library of Congress; to the Hoover Institution, particularly to Mr. Ronald M. Bulatoff; to Nancy Dean at Cornell University Library Archives; and to Mr. Bruce Harrah-Conforth, University Archives, Indiana University. The Hoover Institution and Library of Congress must be acknowledged for providing some of the photographs reproduced here. Cornell University Press permitted me to reprint photographs and maps that appeared in my *Revolution on the Volga: 1917 in Saratov* (Ithaca, 1986). As ever, I wish to record my appreciation to my wife, Karen, for her enthusiastic support of my projects, and my son, Adam, for putting the world in better perspective.

1917

Babine was serving as school inspector of Vologda province when news of the fall of the autocracy reached him. Although Babine records his reactions to the political events of the day, the diary entries from the start suggest that politics per se concerned him less than the impact they had on his own world of letters. In this regard the revolution exacerbated Babine's already strained relations with his subordinates and probably led to his dismissal from his post of school inspector. What this indicates, of course, is that in the popular view Babine had become too closely associated with the old regime and its officials.

The journal becomes detailed with Babine's arrival in Saratov in the fall of 1917, to begin an assignment as instructor of English at Saratov University. Although for generations of educated Russians Saratov was the stereotype of a provincial town, many contemporaries in fact found Saratov more attractive and culturally exciting than other Volga cities. Founded in 1590 as part of a chain of fortresses built to defend the Muscovite state's commercial interests, Saratov remained an insignificant provincial outpost until the eighteenth century, when it acquired some commercial importance and became the administrative as well as the commercial and cultural center of newly created Saratov province. By the beginning of the nineteenth century Saratov's future had become vitally linked to the rich black earth of the northern part of the province and to the processing and shipping of grain and agricultural products. The introduction of steamships and railroads and completion of the Volga–Baltic Sea Canals contributed to Saratov's commercial importance.

Like many Russian urban centers, Saratov had registered dramatic population growth and progress in connection with the boom years of Russian industrial expansion in the 1890s and again after 1910. By 1914 the city had become the eleventh largest in the Russian empire, with a population

SARATOV PROVINCE
Simbirsk Province
KUZNETSK
Penza Province
Tambov Province
SERDOBSK
PETROVSK
KHVALYNSK
VOLSK
VOLGA
RIVER
ATKARSK
BALASHOV
Voronezh Province
SARATOV
POKROVSK
Samara Province
Don Region
KAMYSHIN
RIVER
VOLGA
TSARITSYN
Astrakhan Province
0 30 60 120
kilometers
Barents Sea
Baltic Sea
ST. PETERSBURG
MOSCOW
SARATOV
Black Sea
Caspian Sea
EUROPEAN RUSSIA (1917)

Saratov in the early twentieth century

of 242,425. According to a local census carried out during World War I to ensure better distribution of food supplies, slightly more than half of the population belonged to the working class, of whom only about 25,000 could be considered members of the industrial proletariat, employed in approximately 150 factories in town. The remaining part of the population classified as working class included large numbers of artisan workers, domestics, dock hands, and other unskilled types. As a sign of the times, it should be stressed that refugees made up the second largest social group in town. Saratov's middle class—merchants, factory owners, professionals, university personnel, and a large number of office workers—constituted one-fourth of the population in 1917.

Saratov's downtown area, bordered by Moscow, Ilin, Konstantinov, and Nicholas streets, made a favorable impression on many visitors. It was here that shops catered to the affluent, where, as one 1911 guidebook boasted, expensive food items, jewelry, cosmetics, musical instruments, and rich pastries were displayed, "just like in the capital." It was here that the university was located and here that Babine found lodging. The poorer sections of town, the working-class neighborhoods and factory districts, stretched along the riverfront, the two ravines that divided the city into three districts, and the town's outer perimeter. Few streets were paved in these areas and indoor plumbing and electricity were rare. The very outskirts of town differed little from the surrounding countryside.

Well before 1917, Saratov had acquired a reputation as one of the most

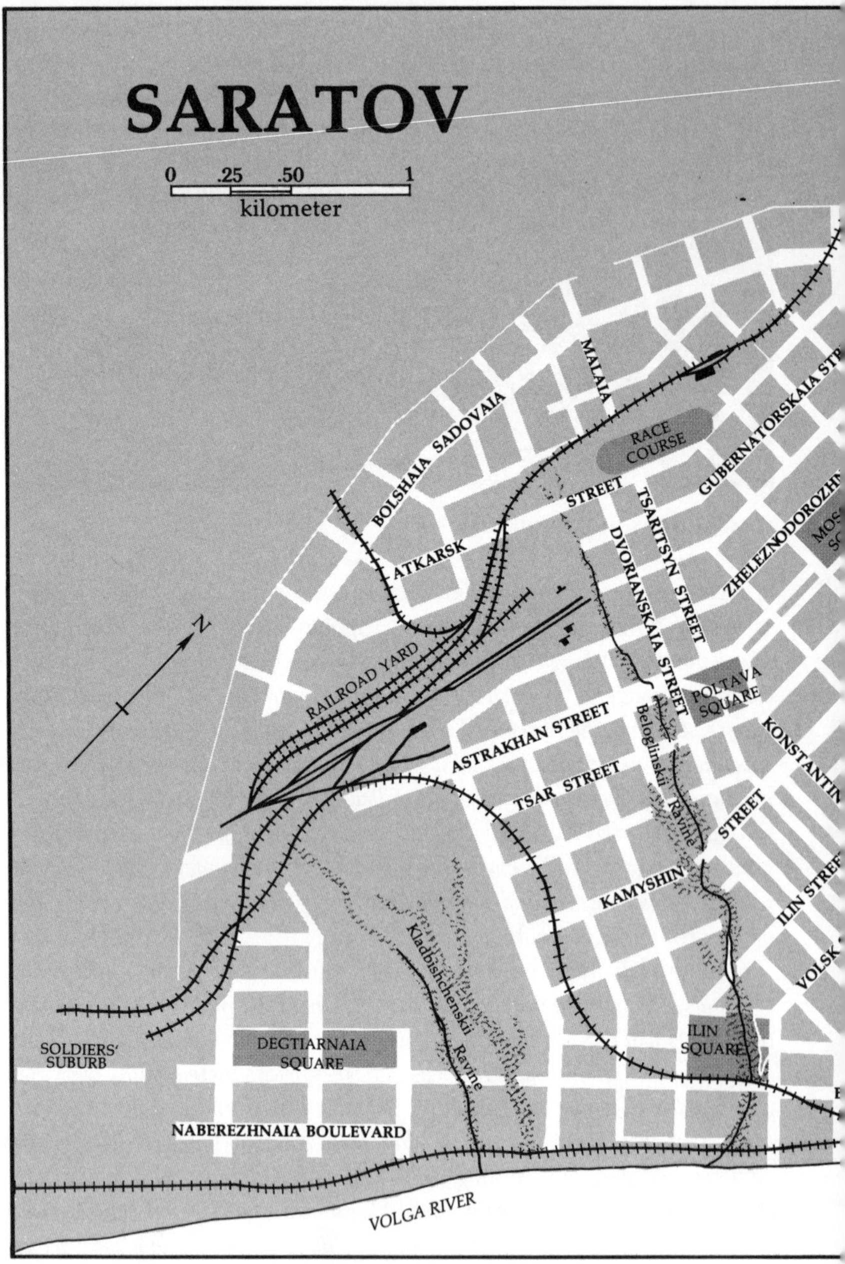
SARATOV
0 .25 .50 1
kilometer
N
MALAIA
BOLSHAIA SADOVAIA
RACE COURSE
STREET
ATKARSK
TSARITSYN STREET
DVORIANSKAIA STREET
RAILROAD YARD
POLTAVA SQUARE
ASTRAKHAN STREET
TSAR STREET
STREET
Beloglinskii Ravine
KAMYSHIN
Kladbishchenskii Ravine
ILIN SQUARE
SOLDIERS' SUBURB
DEGTIARNAIA SQUARE
NABEREZHNAIA BOULEVARD
VOLGA RIVER

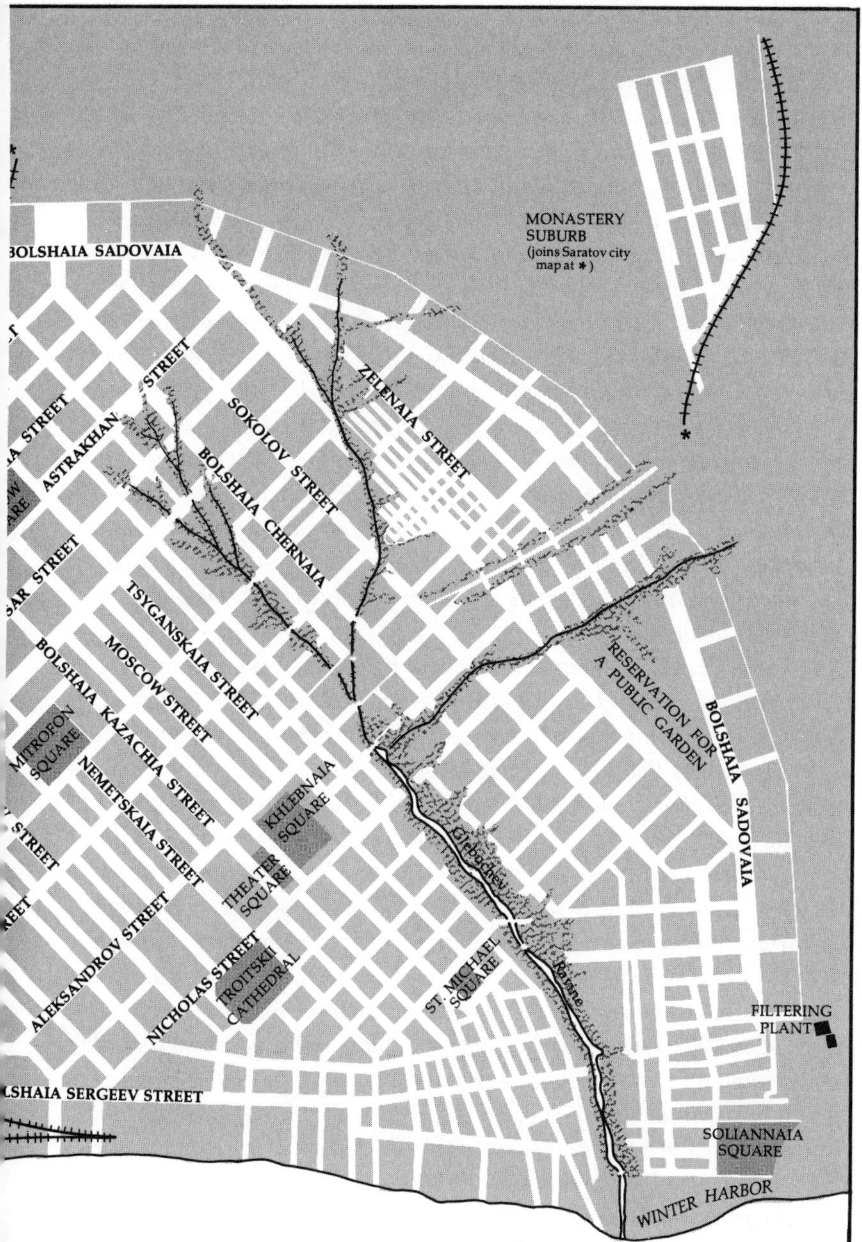
BOLSHAIA SADOVAIA
MONASTERY
SUBURB
(joins Saratov city
map at *)
ZELENAIA STREET
SOKOLOV STREET
ASTRAKHAN STREET
BOLSHAIA CHERNAIA
TSYGANSKAIA STREET
MOSCOW STREET
BOLSHAIA KAZACHIA STREET
MITROFON SQUARE
NEMETSKAIA STREET
KHLEBNAIA SQUARE
THEATER SQUARE
ALEKSANDROV STREET
NICHOLAS STREET
TROITSKII CATHEDRAL
ST. MICHAEL SQUARE
Glebuchev
Ravine
RESERVATION FOR
A PUBLIC GARDEN
BOLSHAIA SADOVAIA
FILTERING
PLANT
SOLIANNAIA
SQUARE
WINTER HARBOR

radical Volga provinces. Soviet historiography links Saratov in the seventeenth and eighteenth centuries with peasant rebels Stenka Razin and Emilian Pugachev, whose leveling appeals struck fear into the hearts of Russia's landowning class. The pantheon of local radicals includes Aleksandr Radishchev, author of the famous Journey from St. Petersburg to Moscow, *published in 1790, and N. G. Chernyshevsky, whose* What Is to Be Done?, *published in 1863, long appealed to the country's alienated youth. Such prominent populists as Vera Figner, M. A. Natanson, A. A. Argunov, Viktor Chernov, and Stepka Balmashev all spent time in the Saratov underground, as did a variety of prominent Bolsheviks, some of whom, such as V. P. Miliutin and V. P. Antonov (Saratovskii), achieved national stature. During 1905 and again in 1917 peasant disorders, punctuated by occasional paroxysms of violence, swept across the local countryside, securing for the province a reputation for rural unrest. Not surprisingly, Saratov emerged as a center of the Socialist Revolutionary party when it was founded at the turn of the century and was to remain a center of Russian populism. Throughout the period before 1917, Saratov revolutionaries maintained cordial relations with local liberal circles, forging a strong liberal-radical alliance.*

Babine arrived in Saratov in the wake of the Kornilov adventure, which had radicalized politics throughout Russia and had brought Bolshevik majorities to power in many local soviets. Contemporary newspapers openly discussed rumors that the Bolsheviks were planning to seize power in conjunction with the Second Congress of Soviets, slated to open in Petrograd in late October. Nevertheless, Babine, like many others, was distracted by the immediate problem of coping with everyday life. Widespread demoralization locally, linked to a dismal economic situation and to a glaring decline in public services, gave no sign of easing off. Three years of war had taken their toll: food and housing shortages, labor unrest, typhus epidemics, a breakdown in law and order, and peasant disturbances in the countryside had exacerbated popular discontent. Saratov itself, now swollen with refugees and other transients, also housed a large garrison which in 1917 ranged in size from 30–70,000 men. The strong liberal-radical alliance that had been forged in Saratov during the political and social unrest at the turn of the century had broken down as Russian society became polarized. The local Soviet had held de facto power in Saratov since spring, and now, in early September, elections to the Soviet had brought the Bolsheviks stunning success. Nonetheless, the Saratov Soviet's victory in October over the forces of the city duma, mainly composed of moderate socialists, touched off a rash of opposition to what soon amounted to Bolshevik rule. Civil war was in the making.

March 19, 1917. I was waiting for my relay horses to rest before taking me to my next school, when an excited traveler suddenly broke into the dirty station room and gleefully announced the new millennium: Nicholas II has abdicated in favor of his brother Michael.[1] A free constitutional rule, perhaps even a republic, is assured. The man's accent bespoke a Pole. The stationmaster and his peasant help looked at him sourly. One could read in their eyes: "What joy can there be in a tsar's abdication—except for an infidel like you?"[2]

It was now questionable whether I should hurry home by rail and cut short my school inspection program, or disregard the change of rule and carry out my plans as though nothing had happened. I chose the latter course.

March 20, 1917. My next school was found closed on account of a smallpox epidemic. Only the principal was in the school building and she did not seem to take any interest in what was going on outside her school.

The relay station office was the cleanest I saw during my trip. The gray-haired keeper was quiet, dignified, and courteous. The horses were served on the dot; his unusually clean and bright-looking boy of sixteen acted as a driver. "What do you think about the tsar's abdication?" I asked him after we got started on our way. "I don't know much about it," the boy answered in a clear, musical tone, "but my father says there's gonna be mass confusion now." "Why should there be any confusion?" I wished to know. "When the

1. At first Nicholas II abdicated in favor of his son, Aleksei, but on March 2 he decided to transfer the crown to his brother, Grand Duke Mikhail Aleksandrovich (1878–1918). After consulting with prominent political leaders, however, Mikhail Romanov learned they could not guarantee his safety or that the monarchy would survive. He therefore elected not to accept the Russian throne.

2. The historical enmity between Poles and Russians can be traced to both religious and political causes. Almost all Poles were and are Roman Catholic whereas most Russians (including Babine) were Orthodox. In his remark Babine is already showing his displeasure with the new order as well as his hostility toward Poles, many of whom welcomed the formation of a democratic republic in the hopes that it would grant greater autonomy if not independence to the empire's Polish minority, formed when Russia, Prussia, and Austria partitioned Poland in the late eighteenth century.

Constituent Assembly[3] meets the people will decide what kind of a government they want." "I do not know," the boy repeated, "but my father says there'll be total confusion."

March 21, 1917. At Nikolsk[4] the liberals—social revolutionaries[5]—are forcing themselves to the fore in matters of local administration. Old government officials are beginning to feel pressure from the oncoming disorderly tide. Teachers feel their positions threatened by anarchist inroads and do not know where to turn. I calmly ignore the new developments and attend to my work in utter disregard of what has happened in St. Petersburg.[6]

March 24, 1917. No bear having been located in the wilderness

3. The new "provisional" government was to govern Russia until a constituent assembly, elected by the entire people, was convened to decide the country's future political structure. Elections to the assembly actually took place in November, after the Bolsheviks had already come to power. More than 41 million citizens took part in the elections, 50 percent of whom voted for the SRs (see note 5 below) and other populists. The second-place Bolsheviks captured roughly 25 percent of the popular vote. The Constituent Assembly met on January 18, 1918, and was immediately shut down by the Bolshevik government. As justification, Lenin argued that the lists of nominees represented a "relationship of political forces that no longer existed," for they had been compiled back in September. Although the Constituent Assembly became the rallying point of many opposed to what soon amounted to Bolshevik rule, it is important to note that right-wing forces in Russian society also hailed the closing of the assembly. For an analysis of the election results, see Oliver H. Radkey, *The Election to the Russian Constituent Assembly* (Cambridge, 1950).

4. (Nikol'sk), a district center in Vologda province located on the Iug River and founded in 1780.

5. Babine is referring to the Socialist Revolutionaries (SRs), Russia's largest political party. It is interesting that he considers them liberals, a term usually assigned to the Constitutional Democratic or Kadet party (Party of People's Freedom). What this rightly suggests is that the moderate socialist elements (mainstream SRs, Mensheviks, and Popular Socialists) composed the political center in Russia at this time. In fact, in view of the political alignment of various parties in Russia after the February Revolution, the Kadets became a conservative force in Russian politics. On the SRs, see Oliver H. Radkey, *The Agrarian Foes of Bolshevism: Promise and Default of the Russian Socialist Revolutionaries, February to October 1917* (New York, 1958), and *The Sickle under the Hammer: The Russian Socialist Revolutionaries in the Early Months of Soviet Rule* (New York, 1963). The most comprehensive study of the Kadets is William G. Rosenberg, *Liberals in the Russian Revolution: The Constitutional Democratic Party, 1917–1921* (Princeton, 1974).

6. St. Petersburg had been renamed Petrograd during the war. Babine's use of the old name tells us something about his personality and attitudes.

around Nikolsk, I started on my way to Totma[7]—a relay after relay for countless miles—stepping out of my sleigh at stations to take a cup of tea and to change horses, and sleeping in my sleigh at night, snug in my fur coat, my dog robe, and a big dog fur blanket, with my inseparable clumber spaniel buried in at my feet. Habitations are scarce, and I am almost the only traveler in this primeval forest, leafless, silent, buried in deep, fluffy snow.

March 27, 1917. Meetings have been held in the auditorium of the Totma Manual Training School by revolutionary agitators who would not have even dreamed two weeks ago of entering the school premises without proper—i.e., my—sanction.

The master of the relay station tells me that German prisoners living in a house nearby claim that the war will soon be over. "And they know everything."

March 29, 1917. Straggling, worn out, shabbily clad soldiers are beginning to line the road, trudging wearily along, with half empty knapsacks on their backs, homeward bound.

March 30, 1917. For the first time on my two-thousand-mile sleigh trip I came upon an impudent relay station keeper who finally refused to give me horses. With a teacher's help, I hired a team to Kadnikov.[8] The same weary soldiers keep adding a new feature to the monotonous winter landscape.

March 31, 1917. The Kadnikov school principal is just back from a revolutionary campaign trip in the country, and looks sheepish and contrite, not knowing how much I know about his exploits—and what I may do about it later on.

April 2, 1917. Back in my office in Vologda.[9] During my absence the governor found it best to leave the city. The vice-governor, a charming man, beloved by all, is moving to his country place, a few miles from Vologda. My turn is coming, says he, since the revolutionary rabble now in power intends to oust all old government officials.[10]

7. (Tot'ma) the administrative center of Totma *uezd* (district), Vologda province, located on the left bank of the Sukhona River approximately 215 kilometers northeast of Vologda. Totma became a district center in 1796.

8. A district center in Vologda province. It became a city in 1780.

9. Russian province lying in the northern part of European Russia. The population of the capital city of Vologda was 58,000 in 1926.

10. Across the country, newly elected soviets and public executive commit-

According to a current report, Miliukov,[11] at a secret meeting of the Provisional Government, acknowledged the fact that German money had powerfully contributed to the overthrow of the Russian imperial government.[12] The revelation of this important secret made Kerensky[13] perfectly wild with rage. But people who claim to know Kerensky insinuate that he is the last person to shun money no matter whence it came.

April 3, 1917. A verbal message came today from the new, self-appointed revolutionary governor asking me to call at his office at my earliest convenience.

April 4, 1917. Having ignored yesterday's invitation, I was reminded of it today. Instead of going to see the new pharaoh,[14] I telegraphed to my department in St. Petersburg for instructions.

April 5, 1917. The "governor's" messenger grew impatient today when I told him about my telegram to the only authority I was bound to respect.

---

tees replaced tsarist officials with more popular ones. The leaders of these new institutions born of revolution were far from the local rabble. Most were well-known, respected members of their communities. They had, however, supported the February Revolution, and this reduced them to rabble in Babine's mind.

11. (1859–1943) leader of the Constitutional Democratic or Kadet party who served as minister of foreign affairs in the First Provisional Government set up in March 1917. P. N. Miliukov's reassurance to the Allied governments that Russia would honor obligations contracted by the Romanov dynasty (and not press for peace) contributed to the collapse of the First Provisional Government in April.

12. Although Germany financed the return to Russia of revolutionaries who had been living abroad, it is a distortion of the historical evidence to conclude that such efforts caused the February Revolution. See Tsuyoshi Hasegawa, *The February Revolution: Petrograd 1917* (Seattle, 1981), and E. N. Burdzhalov, *Russia's Second Revolution: The February 1917 Uprising in Petrograd*, trans. and ed. Donald J. Raleigh (Bloomington, 1987). Émigré historians are the most likely to emphasize the importance of German money in the revolution. See George Katkov, *Russia, 1917: The February Revolution* (London, 1967), and S. P. Melgunov, *Zolotoi nemetskii kliuch k bol'shevistskoi revoliutsii* (Paris, 1940).

13. (1881–1970). Minister of justice in the First Provisional Government and member of the Petrograd Soviet. Kerensky, a Socialist Revolutionary, became head of the government in July 1917 and was still in that position when the government fell to the Bolsheviks in October. For a sympathetic account of Kerensky's role in the Russian Revolution, see Richard Abraham, *Alexander Kerensky: The First Love of the Revolution* (New York, 1987).

14. Russians colloquially referred to police and other unpopular officials as pharaohs.

April 6, 1917. A report has reached us from St. Petersburg that a mixed band of thirty anarchist agitators, with one Lenin at their head, has landed in St. Petersburg, after a trip from Switzerland through Germany in a sealed car and under German guard.[15] On his way to Russia Lenin stopped in Stockholm for a conference with German agents. At that conference a plan was worked out to overthrow the Provisional Government of Russia, to destroy the Russian army, and to make a separate peace with Germany.

Speaking before the [Petrograd] Soviet of Workers' and Soldiers' Deputies, Lenin was met with exclamations: "Get out," "You are not wanted," "Go back to Germany," "German spy," "Provocateur," "William's messenger."[16]

April 7, 1917. I attend to my official duties as usual. But after my regular office hours I called on the new "governor" late this afternoon in order, informally, to state my position to him—and to see what kind of man he was.

He does not look as though he had been cut out for a governor's business at all. When he attempted to inveigh that I did not appreciate the general situation, I frankly confessed that that was exactly my opinion regarding him, and bowed myself out.

April 10, 1917. A fairly clean-looking individual appeared in my

15. Shortly after Lenin's return to Russia on April 3, the conservative Petrograd press had charged that he was working for the German General Staff. Lenin's "guilt" was in accepting safe passage through Germany in order to return to Russia to subvert the government and Russia's war effort. Accusations that Lenin was working for the German General Staff multiplied during the summer political crisis known as the July Days. See note 12 above.

16. Lenin's militant stance did miff many revolutionaries. Upon his return to Russia, Lenin enunciated his controversial April Theses, which sharply separated him from the mainline Kamenev-Stalin group that had gained control over the party leadership. Rejecting the "revolutionary defensism" of the Petrograd Soviet as unacceptable, Lenin called for fraternization at the front. He argued that the events of February had represented the bourgeois-liberal stage of the revolution, and that Russia had entered a transitional period and already was moving toward social revolution. He opposed any expression of support for the "bourgeois" government and ridiculed the prospects for reunification with the Mensheviks, advocating instead an immediate transfer of power to the soviets. Lenin's theses shocked his Petrograd comrades, as well as Bolshevik committees throughout Russia. Yet despite the initial sensation the theses had caused, by the end of April Lenin had swung the party over to his side. Its adoption of the theses provided the party with tactical guidelines that ultimately resulted in the drawing of hardened class and party lines within political institutions.

 office this morning, claiming some connection with the new local administration, and demanded my resignation. I informed him of the fact that my only authority was the national Ministry of Education, and that I knew no other. He looked disgruntled when I saw him to the door.

April 14, 1917. Food shortages are beginning to be felt. Only a limited quantity of bread is sold to the public, although my old baker lets me have all I ask for. Prices are going up very steadily.

April 18, 1917. A public meeting was held last night by the Vologda teachers in one of the school buildings in denunciation of my official activities under the old regime. A notice was served to me to appear as defendant. I could only ignore this piece of impudence on the part of my subordinates.

Among my crimes was mentioned the fact that I was nearly always accompanied by my spaniel while inspecting schools, that a year or two ago I had brought him to an examination and so scared the children that many of them failed and the woman teacher fainted. One detail in this connection was, however, omitted by my accuser, namely, that when I majestically ordered a whole bucket of cold water brought at once and emptied on the teacher's head, the sufferer came to before anybody had started after my medicine, and sat through the rest of the examination like a true Christian.

May 3, 1917. At the government bank the cashier refused to honor my order for my monthly salary.

May 7, 1917. I got my salary today, and an informal explanation. Owing to my refusal to recognize the new local government and to resign my office without instructions from the Ministry of Education, a special agent was sent to St. Petersburg to expedite my expulsion. To the agent's surprise, he was advised to leave me alone and warned that in case I was molested, all educational appropriations for Vologda province would be withdrawn.

May 15, 1917. The Provisional Government has a poor reputation not only among the masses, but even among the intellectuals. Rumors are rampant of its incapacity to run the immense country, and sensibly to carry out its protestations of fidelity to the Allies. There is no doubt that if the Constituent Assembly were called together soon and were given a real chance to represent the country instead of the revolutionary theorists, the people would pronounce in favor of a ruler that could rule instead of make speeches.[17]

May 20, 1917. Work at the office having grown slow, I left one of my inspectors in charge and went to see my friend the vice-governor on his estate near Vologda. In addition to my suitcase and my spaniel I took forty loaves of white bread, and carried it all about five miles from the station in my hands and on my back, there being no other means of transportation to his out-of-the-way place, as all the peasants were busy with plowing. The ground was wet and soggy. There being practically no road to speak of, I cut across the country and reached the house by noon, through the woods back of the house, much helped by my hunter's instinct. My friend's little Eskimo dog speedily announced my arrival. I found the family at lunch.

After lunch my friend resumed his daily task, which at present is plowing. There is only one servant at the family's disposal, a female cook, and therefore the vice-governor has to do the plowing himself. Being a man of wiry physique, he acquits himself of this task splendidly. Mrs. V. and the cook attend to the dairy, while the novel plowman's son, a boy of about seventeen, a promising artist, makes himself useful around the house and the stables. To me was assigned the harrowing of such parts of the field as were ready for it.

May 22, 1917. [There are] fifteen inches of soft, fluffy snow on the ground this morning. Being short of firewood, we immediately put our best horse to work and brought two loads of wood from the park in a sleigh. The day was spent chiefly in the stables that had not been cleaned for something like fifteen years. The dung was so compact that we had to cut it into strips with an ax before handling it at all. No help was to be had: most of the younger villagers were

17. Although citizens across Russia welcomed the fall of the monarchy and establishment of the Provisional Government, the latter's inability to solve the vexing problems facing the country or at least to mollify popular discontent made the government an object of criticism. Moreover, the war was growing increasingly unpopular; those leaders, revolutionary or otherwise, who continued to support the war effort soon found themselves discredited. The Provisional Government may well have postponed calling a constituent assembly because it feared an even more radical solution to Russia's political impasse.

 fighting Germans or Turks, and the old men had to see to their own farms.

May 29, 1917. The fieldwork finished, we are repairing fences and barns. I am specializing mostly in carpenter work and stable cleaning. I look with pride at a very creditable job on one of the barn doors I have just finished, for which I have received at first an incredulous, then admiring glance from one of our peasant visitors. Vestiges of my high rank—my official uniform—preclude even the slightest suspicion of my accomplishments as a graduate cabinetmaker.

Mrs. V. stays all day long in her vegetable garden where she works barefoot like a real woman.

In the evening, just before sunset, we men often take an hour or so woodcock hunting. I seldom return from these hunts without a brace of birds. The surrounding countryside—an otherwise lost one with us at large—is paradise for them.

June 3, 1917. My friend and I went on horseback to see his sister and niece on their farm about eight miles from us. They, too, are short of help, and have their causes for anxiety before the coming year, in face of rather disquieting reports from St. Petersburg. The Provisional Government has so far shown very little executive ability, and mere hot air carries little weight with the people.

June 7, 1917. A long drought fills us with worry about the fate of the seeds we have put in the ground through the sweat of our brow—so novel to us. Just before sunset today we carried water in buckets from an adjacent brook to our wheatfield.

June 12, 1917. Spent most of the day cleaning one of the stables. Since the day was very hot, I shut the stable door, stripped myself to the waist, and did the Herculean work with ax, spade, and pitchfork. Semidarkness drove out the flies, which evidently pestered the horses I had driven out, for the wise animals broke in several times, insisting on keeping me company, behaving like gentlemen, and placidly watching my work.

June 26, 1917. At home in Elatma[18] again. Here, in the heart of Russia, in a small country town, away from the turmoil of the capitals,

18. (Elat'ma), a settlement in Kasimov district, Riazan province, located on the left bank of the Oka River.

life goes on as quietly as it did before the war. But to the masses the overthrow of the monarchy seemed like the subversion of a time-honored and tried regime by a class of selfish and unscrupulous individuals of whom the humble have always been, and perhaps justly, distrustful. The delay in calling the Constituent Assembly is interpreted as trickery on the part of the Social Revolutionists, who seek to pack it with birds of their own feather regardless of the masses of the tillers of the soil who consider themselves the real salt of the earth, ever trodden down and selfishly exploited by the gentry and the intelligentsia.[19]

June 28, 1917. I had to pay four and a half rubles for a pound of the commonest laundry soap that used to cost from ten to fifteen kopecks a pound at most. The high price of provisions is very much felt by everybody, and especially by the common people. To keep the latter supplied with their staff of life, black rye bread, a millionaire lady, who has always been known for her charities, bought at a high price a store of flour in Nizhnii-Novgorod[20] that will keep the city [Elatma] in bread for at least a year. She now sells it to citizens at a nominal price, and keeps the wolf from their doors.

July 8, 1917. The news has come of the failure of the Bolshevik attempt to overthrow the Provisional Government.[21] The connection of the Bolsheviks with Germany has been fully exposed, some of the Bolshevik leaders have been arrested, a number of Bolshevik orators have been roughly handled by the irate public. But Lenin

19. A far more accurate description would read "Kadets" instead of "SRs." The SRs, it will be recalled, captured the largest number of votes cast in elections to the Constituent Assembly in November.

20. Now Gorky, a major river and industrial center located at the confluence of the Oka and Volga rivers.

21. On July 3–5 Petrograd workers and soldiers, exasperated by the government's renewed prosecution of the war and by their deteriorating standard of living, poured into the center of Petrograd. The demonstration, which threatened to topple the government, was also the result of weeks of Bolshevik agitation. Rank-and-file party members had played a leading role in organizing the movement, while local committees encouraged it against the wishes of both Lenin and the Central Committee. As the eruption subsided the rightist press launched an attack on the Bolsheviks, while the government closed down Bolshevik newspapers, arrested a few key leaders, and drove Lenin and others underground. See Alexander Rabinowitch, *Prelude to Revolution: The Petrograd Bolsheviks and the July 1917 Uprising* (Bloomington, Ind., 1968).

 has managed to escape—probably with the secret cooperation of Kerensky, whom hardly anybody would be willing to trust as far as he could see him.[22]

September 4, 1917.[23] St. Petersburg. Newspapers find Kerensky's part in the Kornilov affair dastardly and contemptible, and demand his resignation.[24]

September 8, 1917. St. Petersburg. General Krymov, Kornilov's right hand, whose "suicide" was announced by the government papers after his interview with Kerensky, is said to have slapped Kerensky in the face, and to have been shot by Savinkov,[25] Kerensky's satellite with a bloody record.

September 16, 1917. St. Petersburg. One of the heads of the Ministry of Education told me: "We do not know how long we ourselves are going to last—the minister and all." This confirmed my previous information about the inroads of total obscurities, overflowing with the most liberal ideas, on the business and the administration of the ministry.

22. Babine's dislike of Kerensky leads to distortions once again. Kerensky would gladly have arrested Lenin if he had not gone into hiding.

23. Babine meanwhile had traveled to Petrograd, ostensibly to receive a new assignment.

24. After the abortive July uprising in Petrograd, conservative Russian statesmen, including prominent leaders of the Kadet party, encouraged Kerensky's commander in chief, General L. G. Kornilov, to assume a political role to arrest the growing anarchy in the country. Kerensky supported Kornilov's efforts to curb the local revolutionary organs in the country, but was suspicious of Kornilov's political designs. Their relationship deteriorated at the end of August. Convinced that Kornilov had double-crossed him, Kerensky ordered the general's resignation on August 27, just as troops were preparing to march on Petrograd. To Kerensky's surprise, socialist forces in the capital rallied behind the government. In the wake of the Kornilov affair soviets across the country elected Bolshevik majorities and often demanded a transfer of power to the soviets.

25. A. M. Krymov (1871–1917) was a military commander who had advocated a palace coup against Nicholas II before February and who later became a supporter of Kornilov. When Kornilov's forces refused to march on Petrograd and Kerensky reprimanded him, Krymov committed suicide. B. V. Savinkov (pseud. V. Ropshin, 1879–1925) was an SR leader who, before 1906, directed the party's notorious battle organization. During 1917 he served as a go-between for Kerensky and Kornilov. The SR party expelled Savinkov in September for his duplicitous role in the Kornilov affair. After October he took part in various oppositional activities against Soviet power.

September 21, 1917. St. Petersburg. Have been formally notified by the Ministry of Education that I, director of public schools of the province of Vologda, have been temporarily detailed to teach English at Saratov University. Am purchasing necessary books and making other preparations. The railway strike may prevent my starting off for Saratov immediately.[26]

September 24, 1917. A friend of mine, who attended one of the public meetings addressed by Kerensky, tells me that Kerensky had acted on the platform like a maniac. There was very little substance in what he said, and his removal from the government, according to my frend, is certainly imperative.

The newspaper headlines demanding Kerensky's resignation seem only too natural.

September 25, 1917. Received my traveling expenses to Saratov—six hundred rubles.

October 5, 1917. Vologda. Barely managed to pack my things and small baggage toward evening. At 9 P.M. I was ready for my cab. But the cab question was a serious one. The drivers are simply robbing their customers at such hours of the night. I went and hired one myself for three rubles, took one load to the station, then returned with the same man for another. By purchasing three third-class tickets, I was able to ship my baggage in spite of its considerable bulk and weight.

The first-class car was not at all crowded, and I had a compartment all to myself and Boss, my beloved spaniel, all the way from Vologda to Moscow. The train was over four hours late.

October 6, 1917. Following a porter's advice to take only a through train to Saratov, I left all my baggage in the parcel room and went to look for a night's lodging. Finding none, I decided to spend the night at the Northern Railway Station. Although the lights were put out toward midnight, I stuck to my chosen hard bench, chained Boss to my wrist, put my gun where it would be handy in an emergency, and stretched out on my new bed. Before I went to

26. A national railroad strike, prompted by workers' demands for higher wages, broke out on September 24. When the strike ended on other lines on September 26–27, Saratov workers voted to continue the strike, ignoring the role of Vizkhel (the All-Russian Executive Committee of Railway Workers).

 sleep, however, I saw an old man making a round of the benches, a lantern in hand and a guard following. I sat up when he came near me, and showed my passport to him. The old man—he wore a general's uniform—quietly wished me goodnight, and departed without any comment about my quartering myself in an empty station.

October 7, 1917. After a very common breakfast of bread and tea, I went to my (the Riazan) station and hunted up yesterday's porter. My train was not to leave until that afternoon. But seeing the immense crowd filling the station—entrance, benches, floors—I began to look for a chance to get into my car before it came to the platform. This could not be done without a special permit from some high authority. Having tried several officials within easy reach without any success whatever, I tried an agent recently appointed by the new regime, the "commandant" of the station, on whom, according to my porter, everything depended but who was sure to refuse my application. I succeeded in finding the man in his unapproachable office, showed the notice of my new appointment to him, and explained to him the importance of my reporting on duty good and early. In less than a minute I had a scrap of paper in my hands with which I immediately rushed back to my porter. My suitcases were redeemed in a hurry, and I soon was following him to my car. It took us about a quarter of an hour to find it on a siding some distance from the station, and standing all by itself.

Having reached the car, my porter tried first one door, then another, but found them both locked. In response to his hammering on one of them, the guard raised a window and emphatically refused to admit me. But the word "commandant" at once made him my obsequious servant. To my surprise, there already were several passengers in the car. I found six in the compartment he took me to, which normally was to hold only four passengers. My predecessors cast inquiring looks at Boss, but all smiled broadly when I introduced him as a native English citizen (which he was), and a corner on the upper berth was assigned to him without any protest.

Our car was three hours behind time getting to the platform. When we got there, passengers immediately began to take it by assault. Owing to immense crowds of deserting "tovarischi" it would have been utterly impossible for me to have gotten into the car with my luggage and Boss. Some passengers were dragged into the car through the windows, since it was impossible to enter it in the regular way. There were now ten of us jammed together in a compartment intended for four. Fortunately, half of the passengers had very little baggage. It was torture to use one of the restrooms, especially for ladies.

The conversation was confined chiefly to the political situation in general and to the Kornilov affair in particular. The general jist of it was unfavorable to Kerensky, and only a young subaltern sided with the accidental man of the hour—whose manhood many were inclined to question.

October 9, 1917. The train reached Saratov at 3 A.M.—fifteen hours behind schedule. We considered ourselves fortunate to have reached our destination without an accident, since the car axles took fire several times during the trip because of the overcrowding.

My attempt to find lodging was unsuccessful, and I spent the rest of the morning at the railway station. At about 9 A.M. I called at Professor Birukov's[27] house, had a cup of tea with him, and left Boss in a cold backstairs closet—since my host and old schoolmate was in mortal fear of microbes that surely must infest my prize spaniel's rich coat—and started on a room hunt. Having been told that some professors were camping at the university, I went to the so-called "second building," and found there a colony of some five members of recently established departments,[28] and their families, who had arrived in Saratov about a week earlier and still had not succeeded in securing homes for the winter. I was given possession of one of the vacant rooms on the top floor, put two rings and a padlock on the door, brought my luggage from the station, moved in a bedframe (with M. M. Boldyrev's[29] assistance), borrowed a mattress from N. K. Piksanov,[30] rescued Boss from his seclusion, and established myself in the spacious empty room camp fashion, the bed being my only piece of furniture, windowsills serving as tables, and my Primus burner as a kitchen.

27. B. I. Birukov, professor of biology at Saratov University, 1909–22.

28. History and foreign languages.

29. Babine may have been mistaken. An N. V. Boldyrev taught at Saratov University at this time.

30. A philologist who taught at Saratov University, 1917–25. He later became a corresponding member of the Soviet Academy of Sciences.

October 12, 1917. Last night I rented a room on Nemetskaia (German) Street,[31] after a long hunt. My landlady, Mrs. V. V. Krasulina, widow of a local millionaire, rented a spare room in her house for fear of its being requisitioned by one of the "tovarischi" with whom the city is infested.

October 13, 1917. At 2 P.M. attended our dean's opening lecture[32] devoted to the importance of "humanities" to a community. He is a dull speaker. The lecture was fairly well attended and courteously applauded. Its purport was healthy and conservative—calling for broader culture in order to save the country from conditions similar to the present ones.

October 14, 1917. Today Burtsev's *Common Cause*,[33] no. 17, gives a list of the twenty-nine traitors who had arrived with Lenin in St. Petersburg, April 3, 1917, after their journey in a sealed car through Germany. Everybody is indignant seeing Kerensky leaving nearly all those rascals at large, and the general conviction grows stronger and stronger that he is a secret member of the same disreputable, criminal anarchist gang.

October 24, 1917. At a meeting of the University Council last night, I was elected instructor in English at Saratov University, a vote standing twenty-five for and five against my election.

October 26, 1917. I gave my first English lesson at 5 P.M. About twenty-five students were present, all of whom had some knowledge of Latin, Greek, or French.

October 27, 1917. An appeal has been published in the local papers to all good citizens to resist the expected Bolshevik attempt to

31. A major thoroughfare in "downtown" Saratov, popularly known as the Nevskii Prospekt of Sartov (Nevskii was the major street in Petrograd).

32. The unnamed dean was the well-known religious philosopher S. L. Frank (1877–1950), who taught at Saratov University 1917–21. He moved to Moscow in 1921 and was exiled the next year, owing to his opposition to the ideals of the Soviet government. A one-time legal Marxist who gradually came to embrace religious idealism, Frank had contributed to the renowned symposium *Vekhi* (Signposts) in 1909, which denounced the efficacy of violent revolutionary change.

33. V. L. Burtsev (1862–1942) was a Russian publisher known for his exposure of tsarist police provocateurs (especially E. F. Azef and R. V. Malinovskii). Burtsev returned to Russia in 1915 and after the February Revolution began publishing *Obshchee delo* (Common Cause) (September–October 1917), which supported General Kornilov and denounced the left.

Saratov University (Photo courtesy of the Hoover Institution)

overthrow the existing government in Saratov. Owing to the unpopularity of Kerensky and his rule and to the physical and moral flabbiness of our Christian citizens, only 150 persons are said to have answered the call to defend the city and to have entrenched themselves in the city duma building.[34]

October 28, 1917. Some patriot has written on one of the macadam sidewalks of the Linden Park in chalk: "Down with the Jew Kerensky." It is rumored that the soldiers[35] are planning a Jewish pogrom. Last night and the night before, crowds were gathering around the newsstands awaiting and discussing the latest telegrams. The crowds behaved in an orderly way. This morning streets were full of dirty-looking workers[36] armed with foreign muskets, and of armed soldiers. Soldiers are as opposed to Kerensky as they are to a new monarch.[37] My landlady's lawyer reports that all city banks are closed. She sent her jewelry and other valuables to some poor

34. On October 27 the supporters and opponents of a transfer of power to the soviets took measures to ready themselves for an armed struggle. The local Menshevik newspaper, *Proletarii Povolzh'ia* (Proletarian of the Volga Region), that day informed readers that the Petrograd Soviet, demanding a transfer of power to the soviets, had declared the Provisional Government deposed.

35. The Saratov garrison was the second largest in the Kazan Military District. The garrison fluctuated in size throughout the year; one source puts the number of soldiers at 60,000 in October, though I suspect this figure may be too large.

36. "Dirty-looking workers," Red Guardsmen and soldiers defended the transfer of power to the soviets.

37. This is one of the few times Babine is willing to admit that the old order had been discredited.

 relations of hers for safekeeping. As a local millionaire, she fears an attack from the Bolshevik mob. She has no weapons and hardly a decent hatchet in the house. The front door was locked for the day, and an order has been given to the janitor to keep the iron yard gate securely barred. In case of need the house could make a good fortress and be defended against any number of the common rabble by spirited, well-armed inhabitants.

General Kaledin is reported to be marching toward Saratov with his Cossacks from Atkarsk.[38]

At 6 P.M. several rifle shots were heard. People moved away in a stream from the monument at the end of Nemetskaia Street, first at a walk, then on a run. Reports of rifle volleys and of cannon began to be heard. The street soon emptied, and lights were turned off everywhere. Only soldiers passed our windows during the entire evening. We found out by telephone that the Bolsheviks were besieging the city duma building, that there were wounded and killed on both sides.[39] A rumor was also transmitted to us of the arrival of Cossacks. The children were put to bed about 9 P.M., but did not sleep for some time. My landlady, her sister, and myself watched the street from our darkened house until 2 A.M., when I decided to go to bed without undressing. The doors and the iron gate were securely fastened against a possible attack from the armed and other rabble. My wealthy landlady was sorry she had no firearms, and tried to procure some through a Jewish tenant of hers, but without any success.

October 29, 1917. Our street was not by far as lively this morning as usual. Dirty armed "pals" were to be seen marching back and forth with tired looks and extremely unmilitary bearing. A party paper, published by the new Saratov powers that be,[40] a worthless,

38. District center in Saratov province, located ninety-two kilometers northwest of Saratov at the confluence of the Atkara and Medveditsa rivers. Local opponents of the transfer of power to the soviets pinned their hopes of salvation on the Cossacks. This was particularly true because Ataman A. M. Kaledin, elected leader (ataman) of the Don Cossacks in July, had been accused of siding with Kornilov in August.

39. Fewer than 400 junkers, officers, and private citizens had taken up arms to defend the city duma against the forces of the Soviet. The duma casualties were one dead and eight wounded; the Soviet lost two men and another ten were wounded. For a discussion of the October Revolution in Saratov, see my *Revolution on the Volga: 1917 in Saratov* (Ithaca, 1986), pp. 262–91.

40. The official publication of the Saratov Bolshevik organization, *Sotsial-Demokrat* (The Social Democrat).

illiterate sheet without any news and with an outline of the party's social policy, was brought by our maid. In the afternoon I went in a circuitous way to see Birukov. The artillery seems to have been placed the night before on Gornaia Street, from whence it bombarded the city duma building. There is no sign of the arrival of Cossacks. One of our maids saw artillery posted at the railway station and along the riverfront—expecting government troops and Cossacks from these quarters. At precisely 6 P.M. rifle shots began to sound again, and our street was empty once more. I went to bed early to make up for the lost sleep last night.

While I was at Birukov's a notice had come from the president of the university to continue instruction until further notice.

October 30, 1917. My baggage shipped from Vologda on the 5th of October has not yet arrived.

Streetcars are running from the depot only as far as Ilin Street, below which trenches are being built in expectation of an attack by government troops. Windows have been shattered to pieces by cannon fire on the corner of Moscow and Ilin streets. Some buildings bear bullet marks on Moscow below Ilin. Saratov is said to be surrounded on all sides by government troops and Cossacks. The Bolsheviks seem to have abandoned post and telegraph offices at the approach of the government forces. It is rumored that Kerensky has returned to Petrograd and that the Bolsheviks have been defeated in Moscow and Kazan.

October 31, 1917. Government alcohol stores were looted at 8 P.M. last night, and most of the liquor emptied into the gutter. Some of the soldiers succeeded, however, in getting drunk. The night passed quietly.

5 P.M. A telegram is being circulated to the effect that Kerensky is back in Petrograd and that the Bolsheviks have been cornered at the railway stations in Moscow. A rumor has hanged both Lenin and Trotsky—to the general satisfaction.[41]

November 1, 1917. Mr. A. A. Arnaud returned to Saratov last Sun-

41. Rumors that the Bolsheviks had been overthrown in Petrograd and that their leaders had been hanged or fled the country continued circulating in early 1918. The rumors most likely got started owing to the prompt appearance of armed opposition to the October Revolution immediately after the Bolsheviks had come to power. In general, it was widely held at this time that Bolshevik power could not survive.

 day from his farm on a train with 700 Cossacks who disembarked before reaching the city. The besieging force is said to be working on the morals of the rebellious soldiers, and hopes to take the latter without fighting.[42] The city is said to be full of spies, and the Jewish population is in fear of a pogrom.[43] Jewish shops, cafes, etc., close immediately after dark.

November 5, 1917. I called on a lawyer friend of mine today, in search of information as to the present political situation. Coming to the door on the second floor of his house, I saw my friend standing at the door, and another gentleman just in front of him, conversing with two extremely untidy individuals armed with muskets of Austrian pattern, with mounted bayonets. "Are you at home?" I asked my friend with a knowing smile. He smiled in return: "Not only at home, but not even allowed to step out anywhere." I walked in and was shown to his workroom while he attended to his guests.

In about five minutes he appeared and explained the situation. In the morning his maid informed him that their lodging was guarded by armed men. My friend immediately telephoned to the Military Section [of the Soviet—Ed.]—which knew nothing about it. Later it was discovered that the lodging above him had been searched by an armed ragged band that had no search warrant to show and that, under pressure, explained that it was searching for sugar and flour. My friend invited an acquaintance, a commissioned army officer, to his quarters to parley with the rabble on the strength of his uniform. The officer was walking up and down the hall and tugging nervously at his incipient moustache when I came in. When I left my friend, his exit was free. But one of the knights of the Austrian musket was standing at the door of a first-floor apartment, palavering with a crowd of common women—through which I walked unconcernedly.

42. Ironically, just the opposite took place. Soviet agitators convinced the Cossacks to withdraw. The possibility of direct Cossack intervention helped solidify the anti-Soviet opposition; from the end of October until the last days of December the Orenburg Cossack Division, under orders from Ataman Dutov, maneuvered along the Lower Volga.

43. More than 6,000 Polish Jews had been evacuated to Saratov during the war; several thousand more Jews had lived in the city since the nineteenth century and had been subjected to a violent pogrom during the Revolution of 1905–7.

November 8, 1917. Mrs. Fasmer reported a search at their house by a party of eight armed men furnished with a warrant from the Military Section. The party claimed that they had received a report to the effect that a person armed with a saber and a revolver had stood at their front door and fired several shots. The search was directed against their landlord, whose son, an army officer, was ordered, but refused, to surrender his sword and revolver that had been entrusted by military authorities to his keeping. The search party carried away two baskets—of wine and other things. The search was conducted rudely. The men entered Professor Fasmer's[44] room, too, asked if he had any weapons (he had no revolver—"fortunately"), looked around, but made no search.

This morning all local papers were confiscated—some say because they contained a report of the approach of Cossacks to Saratov, others, because of a telegram divulging the fact of a surrender of thirty-five army divisions to the Germans without a fight on one of our western fronts.[45]

The Cossacks are said to be near the city, and their representatives to be negotiating with the rioters. Some Cossacks are credited with having quietly carried away two cannon and several machine guns while entrenched rebels enjoyed their tea.

November 9, 1917. Although I had shipped my baggage from Vologda on October 5, I received it only today. It came five days ago, and I was charged forty kopecks for storage. One satchel was tampered with—with a loss of some clothing costing at present prices about nine hundred rubles. I am exceedingly happy to get what has come, since I began to fear that my baggage might have gotten lost entirely.

November 10, 1917. Moscow papers sell here for fifty kopecks, and for one and two rubles a number. Local papers are still under the Bolshevik ban. There is widespread dissatisfaction with the sup-

44. M. R. Fasmer, a philologist, who taught at Saratov University, 1917–18, perhaps best known for his four-volume classic work on the etymology of the Russian language.

45. The papers, more likely, were suppressed because they called for an end to Soviet power. "We are living under the power of darkness," cautioned *Saratovskii listok* (Saratov Sheet) (no. 238) when it resumed publication on November 5.

 pression of free speech.[46] There is also every reason to believe that people would prefer even monarchy to the present state of anarchy and wanton oppression. A formerly extreme "red" wife of a professor last night expressed her perfect readiness to accept a monarch in order to get rid of Kerensky, Lenin, Bronstein, Rosenfeld & Co.[47]

November 12, 1917. Last night I called on Professor Chuevskii[48] and met Professor Pavlov[49] there. When the latter left, the conversation drifted toward the abuses of the Bolshevik domination, and my host told me of a recent experience of Professor Pavlov's with the Bolshevik Military Section. His son-in-law, a young, gushy officer, happened to express his opinion rather freely about the Bolsheviks in a remark addressed to a young lady passenger when he landed in Saratov. The latter, a Bolshevik, made a scene, had him arrested, and taken to the Military Section. There she loudly denounced the young officer (to whose rescue Professor Pavlov went) for speaking disrespectfully about her party, even about Lenin and Trotsky themselves. According to the infuriated female, it was a pure case of lèse-majesté. "Are these your convictions?" inquired the presiding powers that be (two noncommissioned officers). "They are," announced the captive. "Then we cannot hold anybody for his convictions," declared the court and set him free "for the time being." At one point the examination of the prisoner was interrupted by the arrival of another victim of the new disorder of things in the person of a respectable old colonel and a whimpering girl about nine years old, brought in by the soldiers. The girl accused the colonel of threatening to kill her and to make sausages out of her. The respondent explained to the court that the girl belonged to a washerwoman. Not receiving his laundry for some time, he went to the washerwoman's house, found the door bolted, and, asked by the child who he was, told her he was a burglar. The case was dismissed. The "court" told Professor Pavlov about several other

46. The moderate socialist opponents of the Bolsheviks and conservative elements challenged the Bolshevik ban on publishing, as did some local Bolshevik leaders who lamented the deterioration in relations with their fellow socialists. On the other hand, some rank-and-file Bolsheviks and more militant local leaders supported such hard-line measures.

47. Babine reveals his anti-Semitism yet again. Trotsky's real name was Bronstein; L. B. Kamenev's real name was Rosenfeld.

48. I. A. Chuevskii, professor of medicine at Saratov University, 1909–26.

49. V. A. Pavlov, professor of medicine at Saratov University, 1910–30.

arrests on ludicrous charges by the newly constituted guardians of our peace.

This evening, returning from Professor Piksanov's at about 7:35 P.M. on Volsk, just beyond Moscow Street, I ran into a soldier fully armed with a musket and a fixed bayonet who in the dim light of a house lantern rather insolently demanded documents from a young man. "Don't you understand plain Russian?" quoth the armed scum while I hurried home. On reaching my room I telephoned Professor Piksanov to change my lecture hours from 5 P.M. to 3 P.M., as this would enable me to return home by daylight.

The Cossacks are said to have been hoodwinked by the Bolsheviks, and instead of occupying the city, in accordance with their telegraph orders, to have moved away from it—according to some reports a distance of two days' march. These Cossacks were of the Orenburg variety—mere impoverished, indolent peasants without any military spirit—entirely unlike those of the Don, who surely would have had Saratov in their hands long ago.[50]

November 14, 1917. This morning, armed with a notice from the president of Saratov University, I called on my new chief, the librarian, I. A. Busse.[51] I remained in the library until 3 P.M., the closing hour, and left under the impression of a very dense ignorance of Mr. Busse in library matters, from an American standpoint. From our conversation it became clear that he has not received university training—and is not much in the way of temper and manner.

50. The privileged elite cavalry units of the tsarist forces, the Cossacks were organized into eleven "hosts" (*voiska*) by 1917. The Don and Kuban Cossacks were the most populous, followed by the Orenburg host. Although Babine's assessment does not do justice to the complexity of the issue here, the Don Cossacks did enjoy the best military reputation. Although often considered the most determined military opponents of the Bolsheviks, the Cossacks were not entirely committed to the White cause, and the Bolsheviks actually organized special Red Cossack units composed of poorer Cossack elements. Moreover, Cossack regionalist sentiments clashed with the centralist views of the White generals. In early 1920, when it appeared that Red fortunes had improved considerably, the Bolsheviks convened a Congress of Cossacks in Moscow at which the hosts were disbanded and integrated into the Soviet state. Other Cossack elements continued to fight against the Bolsheviks, especially in the Far East. See Philip Longworth, *The Cossacks* (New York, 1969).

51. I. A. Busse, formerly of Kazan University, became librarian of Saratov University in September 1909. During Babine's stay in Saratov the Soviet government confiscated the private libraries of wealthy landowners and merchants, adding an estimated 177,000 volumes to the university collection.

 November 15, 1917. The Soviet's general and indiscriminate amnesty of all political and criminal prisoners, with all jails thrown open and court records burned, has filled the country with dangerous elements. The younger and the more enterprising jailbirds immediately after their liberation joined the Communist party.[52] In many cases they were given responsible administrative positions and furnished the Bolsheviks with the fittest possible material for fighting and exterminating the enemies of the party, i.e., all idle and flabby lovers of law and order.

November 18, 1917. The air and the local Soviet's newspaper are full of soldiers' threats of a St. Bartholomew's Night[53] for the bourgeoisie, the well-to-do, the liberals in general, and the non-Bolshevik socialists in particular. The condemned victims, corrupted by self-indulgence and physical idleness, disarmed and unfamiliar with the use of arms, incapable of resisting force by their own exertions, discredited in the eyes of a deceived people, are utterly helpless, and merely shudder at the prospect of the impending doom.

November 21, 1917. A dense crowd of citizens gathered on our street corner this afternoon and discussed the Bolshevik oppression, abuse of power, and the general betrayal of the people's interest. But the meeting did not last long.[54] A detail of Red soldiers came and ordered it to disperse. When the crowd refused, the sol-

52. It should be pointed out that most political prisoners had been freed by popular action during and after the February Revolution, and that numerous criminal elements and opportunists had joined the Bolshevik party, whose membership soared from 115,000 in October 1917, to 750,000 by the time the Civil War drew to a close. Aware that large numbers of uncommitted, unsavory, and ideologically unacceptable sorts had joined the cause, the party carried out frequent purges of its membership. See T. H. Rigby, *Communist Party Membership in the USSR* (Princeton, 1968).

53. Refers to an episode during the religious wars in sixteenth-century France. On the night of August 23–24, 1572, a general massacre of Protestants took place in Paris and in the provinces, sparked by the marriage of Henry of Bourbon, king of Navarre, to the sister of Charles IX, Margaret of Valois.

54. That day an estimated 10,000 people held a demonstration inspired by the SRs in Theater Square to condemn one-party rule and to demand freedom of speech and of the press. Emphasizing the legitimacy of the upcoming Constituent Assembly, the meeting called for the creation of a new national government, but one excluding the bourgeoisie. This episode indicates that Saratov's political center opposed the capitalists as well as the Bolsheviks (and the latter for violating revolutionary camaraderie).

diers fired several shots in the air as a warning. The crowd scattered at once. The Bolsheviks know the herd of sheep they are driving.

November 25, 1917. The long oppressed members of the university —janitors, messengers, laboratory hands, and such—have raised their heads under the Bolshevik regime; they are demanding economic equality with the teaching body and, holding frequent meetings at the university, are discussing their wrongs and elaborating ways to dispose of them.

The university library closes at 2 P.M. every afternoon to enable the staff to attend the rabble's "emancipation" meetings.[55]

December 1, 1917. This morning I found the doors of the high school where I give English lessons locked. In response to my ring a porter explained that the night before an order had been given by the principal not to let anybody in on account of a one-day strike of all public institutions, declared as a protest against the high-handed policy of the Bolsheviks with regard to the city council and the local press. The porter, though he let me and several members of my English class in, refused to open a classroom, and we had to go home, to our general disappointment.

From the school I went to the university library, intending to spend my morning there. But that was closed, too. There was a notice on the bulletin board signed by the president of the university (posted late last night) to the effect that he appreciated the sentiments that had prompted the students to declare the strike, and on his part supported them by ordering an interruption of university classes for one day.

The Russian tendency to protest against oppression and all sorts of barbarity by refusing to do any work is, to me, as touching as the Russian incapacity to do anything to eliminate injustice.

There are no newspapers in town except the Bolshevik slanderous, lying sheets which nobody wants to read. Moscow's *Russkoe slovo* (Russian Word) has been suppressed and looted. *Utro Rossii* (Russian Morning) and the *Russkie vedomosti* (Russian Gazette) sell for two and three rubles a number. The library copies could not be found this morning.

55. The new government made an effort to enroll into unions those elements of the proletariat that had not yet been organized.

December 6, 1917. A search party cleaned out an old widow's apartment in our neighborhood last night.

December 8, 1917. The contents of safes have been declared national property. My landlady was ordered to be present while an inventory was taken of her safe. During the process she managed to "steal" her own gold watch.

Peter's Cocoa costs twenty rubles a pound now. Fearing further increases, I bought five pounds of it at once—my dealer's supply coming to an end and there being none to be found anywhere else, to my knowledge.

December 9, 1917. Got up at 6 A.M., and by 6:30 was on my way to the nearest bakery. At a street crossing I saw a man with a basket on his arm start for the shop at a brisk run. When I came near the place I saw the reason for his haste: there was already a line of some seventy-five persons, chiefly women, in front of the shop door. We all had to wait until 7 A.M., the opening hour, and shiver in the early morning air to our hearts' discontent. While we stood waiting for the door to open, an old Jewess tried to break into line and get in front of my plucky predecessor. But he protested and threatened so emphatically to throw her out of line that she left for another place—the line behind us being too long to give her any hope of obtaining her ration of bread when her turn came.

My neighbor said that the end of the Bolsheviks was in sight: the Ural Cossacks were expected in Saratov next week. Reports of the Bolsheviks' discomfiture in the Don region and elsewhere make people hope for a speedy end to their wanton and rascally rule. A young woman told the company that only a few days ago three or four Bolshevik "guardsmen,"[56] dirty, ragged fellows, at gun point "requisitioned" twenty-one thousand rubles' worth of rifle and revolver ammunition at one of the sporting goods stores in Saratov.

December 10, 1917. At the committee meeting of the People's University of Saratov (a starveling night school with a big name) the chairman, a one-eyed, drawling, untidy schoolmaster, dropped casually: "As far as this goes, we cannot be sure that we shall be

56. Red Guardsmen, that is. For their role during 1917, see my *Revolution on the Volga*, especially pp. 241–45, and Rex A. Wade, *Red Guards and Workers' Militias in the Russian Revolution* (Stanford, 1984), pp. 208–38.

alive tomorrow, considering the present condition of the country."
There was a general unbusinesslike quality about those present—from the one-eyed chairman to the elderly treasurer. There were not enough chairs in the room for all present. The room was so cold that some of us had to put on our overcoats. In one corner of the room there stood a red flag with "Long Live Socialism" on it. It was resolved to hold a regular reelection of instructors for the year at 5 P.M. next Sunday, "to prevent all sorts of Black Hundred sympathizers[57] from remaining in our midst," explained the one-eyed chairman before the adjournment.

December 11, 1917. Got up at 4:45 A.M. and at 5 A.M. was at the bakery door, only to discover that even at that early hour I was already fifteenth in the line for bread. The door opened only at 7 A.M., and at 7:30 I was at home with two loaves of bread weighing about ten pounds and costing two rubles sixty kopecks, instead of the usual twenty kopecks for the same quantity of bread. During the vigil, women squabbled with a puny soldier who also had come after bread: he had no business there, since he was boarded at the barracks. A doubt was frankly expressed of his ever having been at the front, and even of his being a soldier. It was openly averred that the present occupation of soldiers consisted of attacking and robbing peaceful citizens, breaking into houses, murdering and agitating.[58] The member of the God-beloved army bore the taunts and charges of the women quite mildly. Of course, there were charitable females who tried to defend the army. But their voice was rather weak.

December 12, 1917. Was up at 6 A.M., had a lesson at the high school at 8 A.M., put in the rest of the time at the library until another lesson on my schedule which came at 3:15 P.M. and lasted until 6:45 P.M.

57. Ultraconservatives who were pro-monarchy, anti-Semitic, and nationalistic. Back in 1905 they had organized a branch of the Union of the Russian People, one of several right-wing organizations formed in Russia at that time and commonly known as Black Hundreds. For a discussion of anti-Semitism and right-wing politics in Russia, see Hans Rogger, *Jewish Policies and Right-wing Politics in Imperial Russia* (London, 1986).

58. Indeed, in a practical sense, the city was at the mercy of the soldiers. Sources present a shocking scenario of besotted soldiers, responsible to no one, sauntering about the city, subjecting the civilian population to indiscriminate violence. Even working-class attitudes appeared to be turning against the armed soldiers who seemed to be the cause of the city's woes.

 I had to go without my dinner today and get by on cocoa, bread, and cheese.

December 13, 1917. Up at 4:45 A.M. and to the line for bread. I was about twentieth in line: the white bread that was being distributed this week is not going to last long, and draws large crowds. The usual squabbles took place with those who came late and tried to get in among the early risers.

December 14, 1917. The white bread we have been getting up to this time came from eight carloads of wheat flour intended for Moscow and intercepted in transit by the Saratov Bolsheviks.[59]

A large store of calico is said to have been recently discovered by the Bolsheviks in a quiet place, and is going to be sold to inhabitants at a low price.

A notice is posted all over the city of the coming distribution of wheat and rye flour and sugar.

The Ural Cossacks are reported to be stationed at Urbakh,[60] within a day's march of Saratov. This makes all university employees hope that they will receive their unusually belated salaries in full and in due time before Christmas.

Local Bolshevik leaders, Lebedev[61] and Vasil'ev,[62] have disappeared. In Tsaritsyn[63] the Cossacks are said to have hanged all the

59. As Russia broke apart into separate economic units, local authorities often seized grain and other supplies en route to other cities, in order to ward off hunger locally.

60. A nearby junction on the Riazan-Uralsk railroad line.

61. P. A. Lebedev (1877–1952), professional revolutionary and Bolshevik activist since 1901, with broad experience in the local revolutionary movement. Upon his return to Saratov from Siberian exile in March 1917, he was elected to the presidium of the Saratov Soviet. During the October Revolution in Saratov Lebedev assumed the responsibilities of provincial commissar (and replaced the old governor). He tended to be a moderating force within the local Bolshevik organization.

62. M. I. Vasil'ev (Vasil'ev-Iuzhin) (1876–1937), another local Bolshevik with a rich revolutionary past. Vasil'ev had worked in the St. Petersburg and Baku party organizations and had taken an active part in the Revolution of 1905 in Moscow. In 1917 he served as an outspoken, extremist deputy chairman of the Saratov Soviet. He was one of the leaders of the October transfer of power and remained active in Saratov until recalled to the center at the end of 1918.

63. Saratov province's "second" city, known during Babine's time as Russia's Chicago because of its rapid growth in the decade after 1905. The most important industrial center in southeastern Russia, Tsaritsyn had a larger per-

Red Army men on lantern posts, and this has set the Saratov Red rabble thinking.[64]

December 16, 1917. Receiving no news through the accustomed channels (now hopelessly clogged), the public feeds on rumors. In the line for bread this morning a well-informed woman stated that the Cossacks were approaching Saratov from two sides, that the battle was to take place outside the city, that the artillery, a machine-gun and another regiment, had refused to support the Bolsheviks. She had it from the commander of the garrison "for whom we have made a winter cap." Other sources supported her statements. The Ural Cossacks are said to be in Pokrovsk,[65] just across the Volga, which they can easily cross on ice. Railway passengers have reported that St. Petersburg is entirely isolated from Moscow, that the Semenovskii and Preobrazhenskii regiments had risen against the Bolsheviks and besieged them in Smolnyi;[66] that Smolnyi is on fire, that Lenin and Trotsky have disappeared, that they are dead. Two of our Bolshevik ringleaders, Vasil'ev and Lebedev, have also disappeared and, according to some reports, with large sums of money from the local branch of the National Treasury. Cossack delegates are said to be in Saratov, demanding unconditional surrender of the troops in town. An attempt was made last night at the city theater to disarm a Ural Cossack officer, but totally failed.

Cossacks are expected here tomorrow.

Our baker remarked this morning that the supply of flour in town would last only through December.

---

centage of industrial workers than other Volga cities. Events there had taken a more radical turn than in Saratov. From the spring of 1917, Bolsheviks and Left SRs came to control local politics. See my "Revolutionary Politics in Provincial Russia: The Tsaritsyn 'Republic' in 1917," *Slavic Review* 40, no. 2 (1981): 194–209. Owing to the role Stalin played during the siege of Tsaritsyn in 1918–19, which has been greatly embellished and distorted by Stalinist historiography, the city was renamed Stalingrad in 1925 and, during the anti-Stalin campaign after 1956, renamed Volgograd in 1961, which it is still known as today.

64. An exaggerated rumor.

65. Now Engels, a rail and river port on the left bank of the Volga across the river from Saratov.

66. In August 1917 the All-Russian Central Executive Committee of the Petrograd Soviet moved to the Smolnyi, formerly known as the Smolnyi Institute for Wellborn Girls. It later became the administrative center of events during the October Revolution, for Lenin went there to direct the uprising in Petrograd.

This morning I heard that a government machine gun had been offered for sale by soldiers at the town market. One could buy there any number of muskets and amount of ammunition, not to speak of army clothing and accoutrements.

December 17, 1917. A peaceful demonstration was announced yesterday by various city and private organizations in favor of the Constituent Assembly, to take place today. The Bolsheviks replied by sponsoring an armed demonstration, turning out all their artillery and infantry, which have just defiled past our house, carrying red flags with the usual inscriptions and howling revolutionary songs as far as today's bitter cold allowed. Many ugly faces turned up toward the upper story of our house. One armed scoundrel shook his fist at the spectators at a window, and another made a show of slipping in a cartridge, with a suggestive gesture.

The peaceful demonstration, under the circumstances, was indefinitely postponed.

December 19, 1917. Lines for bread became shorter when the wheat flour ran out. This morning I ventured to get up at six o'clock, and found only nine persons ahead of me in front of the bakery. Returning home from the university at 2 P.M., I stopped at another shop kept by a Jewish refugee family, and learned that they were going to issue white bread two hours later in the day. It was an unexpected piece of good luck. I hurried home for my bread tickets and by special favor obtained ten pounds of white bread on tomorrow's and several other days' accounts.

Today I lost two English lessons at my high school, owing to the fact that four upper classes had declared a twenty-four-hour strike to protest the election of an unacceptable principal by the Teachers' and Parents' Board. The teachers found themselves entirely helpless and incapable of coping with the situation—but, doubtless, shall hold their positions.

December 22, 1917. 10:30 P.M. Just as I got into my bed, the telephone rang vigorously. My landlady answered the call, which was for our maid. Since the latter could not make out what the other person was talking about, my landlady took the receiver and explained that the call was from the maid's sister employed elsewhere. My landlady's exclamations made me get up and peep through the door. It turned out that at six o'clock that very afternoon robbers came to a Dr. Brod's house and shot him in the stomach. The "militia" (police) was called—and shot the doctor's cook dead: taking the "militiamen" for another set of robbers (they looked like armed highwaymen, to be sure), the cook and the maid ran to the attic for safety, were mistaken for robbers, pursued and fired at, with a fatal result for the cook.

The doctor's condition is considered hopeless. His wife happened to be away from home at the time, and so escaped injury.

Owing to the fact that the self-organized vigilance guards[67] report on duty only at 7 P.M., burglars and all sorts of murderers begin and transact their operations before that hour of the day.

A strict order has been given to our rather unusually stupid maid not to open the doors without first securing them with chains, and to admit no strangers.

December 23, 1917. 10 A.M. The telephone reports Dr. Brod dead.

It was his [Dr. Arapov's] firm opinion that Brod's murderers were soldiers and not civilians in soldiers' uniforms.

At about three o'clock this afternoon as Birukov and I approached the Military Section on Volsk Street, we saw two sleighs heading for it. In the first sleigh there was seated an individual in a mixed Caucasian and European costume, while to his left stood another individual who looked like a Red Army man and who cursed for all he was worth, as only Russians can curse. "Do you know how we shoot? . . . We shoot through the windows," we heard him shout. In the second sleigh there sat two men armed with foreign muskets. As the first sleigh emptied in front of the building, the cursing individual explained something to the armed rabble that came out to meet him. "Killed a man," I heard him say when he took his charge into the building. "Kill him," suggested one of the rabble persuasively. "Let us move away from here," suggested Birukov anxiously, "lest we catch something, too."

December 24, 1917. A detail in connection with Dr. Brod's murder. Answering a doorbell, the doctor opened up as far as the safety chain allowed. Outside there stood a civilian wearing a painful look

67. In middle-class neighborhoods citizens organized their own street militias to protect themselves against mob rule and to ward off frequent robberies and assaults. See Babine's entry for December 28, 1917.

 and begging for medical help. When the doctor let the sufferer in, five soldiers walked in from behind the door, and the sick man put his gun up to the doctor's temple.

On the fatal day the doctor had cashed a check for three thousand rubles to be used for the Deaf and Dumb Asylum. A local paper a day or two before the doctor's murder called attention to the close connection of similar attacks on, and robberies of, other citizens who had withdrawn money from local banks.

December 25, 1917. Dr. Brod is further said to have freely expressed his opinion to his uninvited guests about them and to have tried to turn them out by force. He was wounded in the scuffle that ensued. Mr. Brovarskii, a neighbor of ours, a baptized Jew, credited with having been a secret service man under the tsarist regime and now a pronounced Bolshevik, speaks disparagingly about Dr. Brod's temper and manners.[68] He thinks his murder had something to do with his having been a prison physician—none too courteous to his patients of the poorer class.

The murderers are said to have been apprehended.

This afternoon, at about five o'clock, an attempt was made to enter a doctor's residence on our (Nemetskaia) street. A man that had asked to be admitted was told by a lodger that the doctor was not at home, and would not allow the patient to wait for him inside in spite of his insistent request. On dismissing the visitor, the lodger, a porter pro tem, immediately stepped out into the street and saw four men at the front door, one of whom was informing the rest that the doctor was out and that the man inside was no fool.

December 28, 1917. 11:30 A.M. Constant burglaries and murders and the inadequacy of police protection under the new demoralized anarchical regime compelled citizens to organize civil vigilance companies with compulsory attendance on the part of all able-bodied males. Last night I performed my duty as a guardsman for the first time. Aside from a big fire somewhere beyond the city

68. Babine is referring to the tsarist political police, the *Okhranka*. Soviet authorities executed many Okhranka agents exposed after October. Babine is once again suggesting that all sorts of rabble and opportunists had flocked to the Bolshevik party. Perhaps what is more important to call attention to here is that the poorer class was hostile to people like Brod, who were associated with the old regime.

limits, nothing of notice happened during the night. Relieved of my duties at 7 A.M., I hurried to the bakery with the intention of taking advantage of my guardsman's privilege and of getting my loaf ahead of the bread line, but found a notice on the door to the effect that there would be no bread before 9 A.M.

On returning home I took Boss out for a walk, went to bed and did not get up until nearly eleven o'clock. When my maid failed to answer several of my bells I went to the kitchen, but found it empty. The landlady, whom I approached on the matter, explained to me that the maid had gone to see a lynching. It turned out that at about 10 A.M. three robbers got into a house nearly opposite ours. The inmates managed to raise an alarm, one of the robbers was killed outright, one ran away, and one was caught by soldiers. The crowd that had assembled in front of the house roared for the last named—and our maid hastened there to see the execution.

Our servant soon returned with her story. When she got to the scene, soldiers were killing the second man with their bayonets. The body was put on a sleigh, and the face covered with a piece of fiber matting. But the matting would slip off and expose the blood-covered head and the face pierced with bayonets. That victim was a young man, almost a boy.

The robbers wounded their man in the hand, but his wife flung herself into the backyard through a window—glass and all—cutting herself considerably. Both of them were taken to a hospital.

At this point in the maid's story our janitor was let into the kitchen and reported the capture of the third malefactor.

The crowds are said to become perfectly frantic on such occasions and invariably demand immediate execution. A pious and charitable old lady who happened to be present at the lynching of a housebreaker goaded on the crowd, though under ordinary circumstances she would not hurt a fly. "Everybody is so tired of them," our old janitor explained. He, too, saw no other way out of it.[69]

December 29, 1917. Yesterday's execution of the housebreakers was the work of women, exclusively, who surrounded the building after the alarm had been raised. They got hold of heavy sticks of wood and pounded the captives on their heads, even after they, dead, had been placed on a sleigh.

69. Saratov newspapers reported numerous cases of mob justice, or *samosud*.

40 December 31, 1917. This morning I read a Bolshevik notice on a board fence (the usual way in which the Bolshevik rulers announce their will in Saratov ever since the involuntary death of local newspapers) to the effect that searches of private residences will be made all over the city for concealed stores of provisions. The searches are to be conducted under certain regulations between the hours of 9 A.M. and 5 P.M.

The demonstration, which had been planned for December 17, and which so ignominiously failed, was announced again for today—to fail again. But crowds gathered on some street crossings and listened to speeches condemning the existing misrule. The meetings and the speeches were evidently not to the Bolsheviks' taste, and the crowds were encouraged to disband by the firing of muskets in the air and by strong armed patrols.[70]

I overheard a workman murmur to his companion on the street: "Soldiers are worse than dogs nowadays."

70. See Babine's entry for January 1, 1918.

1918

Babine's entries for 1918 provide a fascinating glimpse into the human experience of the zigzag course of social upheaval. Russian institutions had collapsed in 1917 and all power relationships had become voluntary. The underdeveloped social structure, now under siege, could not prevent the country's plunge into chaos.

Hostility to Bolshevik rule, expressed in many quarters, colored the first year of Soviet power locally. In early 1918 opposition was encouraged by the possibility of direct Cossack intervention in Saratov, by news of conflict within the Bolshevik top leadership in Petrograd, by a host of rumors that exaggerated hopes of salvation, and by an anti-Bolshevik uprising in neighboring Astrakhan. It first found expression in boycotts by the majority of Saratov's officials and professionals, who hoped to undermine Soviet power by refusing to cooperate with it. Financial collapse, unrest in the villages, turmoil among the once pro-Bolshevik soldiers who had served at the front, sporadic peasant disturbances, an anarchist uprising against Soviet power in May 1918, a revolt of Czechoslovakian troops against Bolshevik rule, and formation of an anti-Bolshevik government in Samara, located up the Volga from Saratov, were all expressions of civil war. Moreover, by summer the eastern and southern fronts had moved in on Saratov as the armies of the White generals reached the Volga and seized nearby Volsk, where they executed local Communists. In August strategically important Tsaritsyn, situated in the southern tip of the province, was under siege. Local authorities now directed all of their energies at warding off the military threat. Although in September Soviet troops were on the offensive across the eastern front, a new danger had emerged behind the front lines: food brigades arrived from the outside to wrest grain from the countryside and this embittered many elements within the local peasantry against Soviet power.

Developments within the Saratov Bolshevik party organization should be noted in brief, particularly since Babine does not appear to know much about them. During the year the lines had become blurred between party organs and Soviet institutions, especially in the wake of the uprising in mid-1918, after which the Mensheviks and Right SRs were driven out of the Soviet and other institutions. Frequent mobilizations of party members and of those social strata who had supported the party now led to a visible decline within the organization. V. P. Antonov (Saratovskii) and M. I. Vasil'ev (Iuzhin) continued to orchestrate and inspire local party activities. Again and again, they followed an independent course, from refusing at first to accept the Brest-Litovsk Peace, to pursuing an independent economic policy and advocating the formation of a Lower-Volga Republic. By the end of the year local-born leaders had come under fire from newcomers and district party officials as well as from Moscow, ending in the center's recall of Antonov and Vasil'ev. Their departure marked the beginning of a new period for the Saratov party organization, as it came to be headed by outsiders who had few ties if any locally.

Under Antonov's and Vasil'ev's leadership, the Saratov Soviet took the first steps to create new institutions of Soviet power; the early months of 1918 witnessed the introduction of policies aimed at disenfranchising the former privileged. The old judicial system was dismantled, workers' control was extended to most enterprises (even though many old managers were retained), banks were nationalized, land reform was introduced, and, as Babine's diary graphically shows, housing was nationalized and the unscrubbed poor and good burghers of Saratov now often found themselves sharing quarters.

These measures were enacted as the strains of civil war manifested themselves in strong relief. Lack of raw materials and fuel and the disruption of transportation wreaked havoc on the local economy, which was already in shambles owing to a severe lack of revenue (apart from confiscations). Crime soared as criminals flooded the province, forcing the civilian population to arm and defend itself against hardened criminals, those driven to crime out of necessity, and besotted soldiers. Hostilities increased between the local population and the estimated 120,000 refugees and prisoners of war who had flooded the province. Scarcities of all sorts forced people to reorient their priorities.

His diary entries reveal how Soviet power intruded upon Babine's life. Despite all of the disruption and deprivations, middle-class Saratov still was able to cling to many of its privileges. By the end of 1918, for example, few substantive changes had come to the university, and members of the faculty could still claim a fair measure of autonomy. As we shall see, though, what

Hungarian prisoners of war who joined the Red Army in Saratov (Photo courtesy of the Museum of the Hungarian Labor Movement, Budapest)

shocked Babine in 1918 would be viewed with some nostalgia in the not too distant future.

The diary also depicts the growing hostility toward the middle class following the events of the summer of 1918. When he left Saratov for his native Elatma in June, for instance, Babine found that civil war had already begun in earnest. His description of the terror unleashed after an attempt to assassinate Lenin and the murder of M. S. Uritskii, head of the Petrograd Cheka, shows how far the frightening arm of the Red terror reached into the backwaters of Russia.

January 1, 1918. While on my regular walk this afternoon, about two o'clock, I again heard several rifle shots in the direction of the Volga, where the toughest of our free citizens congregate. The public seems to pay no attention to the shooting.

There is again a large crowd today on the corner of Nemetskaia and Ilin streets, where proclamations may be read regarding the abolition of private property in real estate.

3:20 P.M. A caller, Professor Arnol'dov,[1] tells me that a peace-

1. V. A. Arnol'dov was a member of the faculty of medicine at Saratov University, 1912–30. He served as rector of the university from May 7, 1918, to September 28, 1918.

 ful demonstration did take place yesterday. At about 4 P.M. the demonstrators reached the city jail, held a meeting, and demanded liberation of several unjustly imprisoned public men. The crowd was ordered to disperse and, when it refused to obey the order, several shots were fired in the air. The crowd lay down in the snow. On rising, it repeated its former demand, but it was at once fired upon. A coed was shot dead, a student is on the point of death, four others were severely wounded and taken to the Aleksander Hospital. The total number of wounded is about twenty.[2]

An army officer, a friend of Professor Arnol'dov, just back from the Caucasian army, told him about an experience of his at the Groznyi Railway Station. An army officer was eating his soup at the general table. A private beside him, apparently through carelessness, flicked the ashes of his cigarette into the officer's plate. Without a word the officer ordered another plate of soup. When that was brought, the private got up, deliberately spat into it, and stood staring at the officer. The latter threw himself back in his chair, stared in return, pulled a revolver out of his side pocket and shot the offender. With a second shot the officer killed himself.

January 2, 1918. 3:12 P.M. Returning home from the library I overheard a rowdy say to his companion: "I took my revolver along hoping to get a chance to punch a hole through somebody at the demonstration."

At the boarding house an officer greeted a new arrival: "I have just relieved one of your pards from guard duty, So-and-So. . . . A prisoner was found missing. . . . 'Oh, he always goes out for a walk,' your man said reassuringly." "Curious things are going on," quoth the other, a youth of not over twenty. "Imagine a trooper taking a government horse from the stable and selling it on the market for eighty rubles. . . . The general's horses were sold the same way. . . . There were 250 revolvers in our squadron store: only 12 of them remain now. The rest have been stolen and sold at 250 rubles apiece. . . . If the Cossacks come now, they will take us

2. According to reports in *Izvestiia Saratovskogo Soveta* (News of the Saratov Soviet) (no. 1, January 3, 1918), Right SRs and Mensheviks planned the demonstration against Soviet rule. Members of the intelligentsia, officials, students, and middle-class Saratovites assembled to protest conditions. Workers and soldiers baited them, and a clash broke out in which several people were killed and wounded.

bare-handed." The first youngster believes that it will all end in a bloody orgy, that the leaders are having a hard time keeping down the armed rabble.

January 2, 1918. 10:30 P.M. An eyewitness has given Professor Chuevskii another story of the demonstration. The demonstrators started from the jail for their homes. A crowd of only about five hundred persons marched down Moscow Street. Shouts were heard of "Down with the Bolsheviks." At that a post office guard rushed out of the building and began to shoot. A young woman carrying one of the flags was wounded. A student ran to her support when she tottered down. "Ah, you, too, are with her," shouted a soldier, and shot him dead. Altogether, two students were killed. Their funeral is to take place tomorrow. "The three hundred thousand inhabitants of Saratov are at the mercy of three or four thousand armed ruffians. Our so-called intelligentsia are flabby. Their brains, their will power are as flabby as their muscle. No resistance can be expected on their part in case of a St. Bartholomew's Night, which is promised by the soldiers for January 5."

January 3, 1918. There were nine caskets at the funeral of the victims of the shooting that took place on December 31. But more than nine persons were killed: many were buried privately. The funeral procession was immense, the public's gloom deep. Even grown men could not help weeping. A story has been told to me of a shooting near a tram park. When a student fell, a coed with her two brothers rushed toward him and put her muff under his head. (The three were a park mechanic's children, and watched the procession together with Mrs. DeWilde,[3] the head manager's wife.) "Where are you going?" shouted Mrs. DeWilde to them. As the girl leaned toward the fallen student, a soldier ran up to her and fired his musket at her face, tearing off her nose completely. "Oh, what are you doing! What cruelty! What brutality!" moaned Mrs. DeWilde. "This is no place for a woman. . . . She is just a woman, and she should have known her place," coolly remarked a car conductor.

The Bolsheviks have arrested a number of prominent businessmen after failing to extort eighteen million rubles from the Saratov Exchange members (all of whom have fled the city).

3. DeWilde was the manager of the Belgian-owned tram company, which the new regime nationalized in 1918.

 January 4, 1918. Yesterday a man dressed like a worker and wearing rubbers without any shoes and accompanied by an armed soldier rang our bell. My landlady opened the door as far as the guard chain allowed and in response to his questioning informed him that Mr. Krasulin had died about a year ago and hence could not be seen on short notice. The man apologized and went away together with his companion. In the early part of this afternoon, when one of our women tutors was going out, a well-dressed man forced his way into the hall and informed "Mrs. Krasulina" that the Executive Committee[4] wished to see her. He explained that he was a detective—and the same man who called yesterday. In support of his statement regarding the pleasure of the Executive Committee, he fumbled in his hands a penciled note with my landlady's full name and signed, according to him, by Antonov,[5] Lebedev, and Vasil'ev. But their signatures could not be seen, and their presence in town was improbable, since Vasil'ev is known to be in Petrograd at present. Mrs. Krasulina declared that the note did not refer to her, since her name was Dukhanin, a mere penniless guardian of her and Mr. Krasulin's children, and refused to go to any committee (she, with a brilliant town career in her youth, had never been legally married to Mr. K.). The man wanted to know who the other guardians of the children were and, somewhat disconcerted, went "to arrest A. I. Arnaud." Until late tonight, when the story was told

4. Of the Saratov Soviet.

5. V. P. Antonov-Saratovskii (1884–1965), a Saratov-born revolutionary who, along with Lebedev and Vasil'ev-Iuzhin, was one of the major leaders within the local party organization during 1917–18. A graduate of Moscow University's law faculty, Antonov was active in the local and Moscow undergrounds in 1905 and again during World War I. He was elected chairman of the Bolshevized Saratov Soviet in September (after the Kornilov affair) and was one of the leaders of the armed uprising in October. After leaving Saratov in early 1919, he served in several local military revolutionary councils. Following a short stint as rector of Sverdlov University (1921–23), Antonov's career became closely linked with the country's judiciary system. Between 1923 and 1938 he served as chairman of the commission that prepared legislative proposals for the Council of People's Commissars. From 1939 until his retirement in 1952 he worked in the People's Commissariat of Justice. See Antonov's memoirs on 1917, *Pod stiagom proletarskoi bor'by* (Moscow-Leningrad, 1925), and the much less reliable *Krasnyi god* (Moscow-Leningrad, 1927), which deal with the 1905 Revolution. A sanitized Soviet biography of Antonov is also available. See B. Barkov, *Zhizn', izbrannaia serdtsem* (Saratov, 1967).

to me, my landlady has been in ignorance as to Mr. Arnaud's fate, and asks me to call at his house tomorrow.

January 6, 1918. Last night I had to attend to my duty as a street watchman. I reported at our office (in the Astoria Hotel building) at 7 P.M. and found the door locked. Our messenger boy who stood in front of a store window nearby informed me that "he" had not yet returned. In about ten minutes the door was opened and I got in. The head of the watch was absent. Nobody even knew who was to be the head of the watch for the night. By general consent, Mr. Knaube was sent for and soon appeared at the desk. Even he could not determine whose place he came temporarily to fill. Looking around, he counted only seven heads instead of eighteen, necessary for the night, and wondered why so few were present. One of our paid watchmen called Mr. Knaube's attention to eleven notices that had not been delivered to the Astoria guests (assessed for the benefit of our organization) who were no longer in town. Protests rose against such a way of managing things, and the person to blame for it was found, namely our vice-president, who is too much given to gambling even while on duty. Then it became known that there was altogether too much card playing at our headquarters, and that it was necessary to put an end to it. The gambling was attributed to the disappearance of one of our revolvers (costing no less than 250 rubles) while Mr. Imenitov (a Jew), the vice-president, was on duty—and deeply absorbed in a game of cards. It was stated that one evening a young student had lost at the green table in our office 7,000 rubles—4,500 rubles in cash, and the balance in notes.

Mr. Mittel'man, an elderly Jewish gentleman, stepped in, quietly took a chair, and calmly remarked that he had been shot a little while ago (rifle shots had been heard outside shortly before). Everybody wanted to hear the details. Mr. Mittel'man quietly opened his winter overcoat and showed a hole torn in his sackcoat just below the right breast. Then he took a large square pocketbook from his pocket, also with a hole through half of it—through all the papers and his passport in it. "And this is what saved me," he said, pointing to a tiny metal clasp, somewhat mangled, on the inside of the pocketbook. "And here is the bullet. It stuck in the pocketbook." It was a .45 Colt automatic bullet. "A junior officer came to my store this evening just about closing time and offered a big Colt revolver to me for 600 rubles. He took out the clip and showed me how to open the action. As the barrel struck home—a shell in the barrel did its work, struck the desk that was between us, and glanced in my direction. Here is a little piece of wood that was in the pocketbook, too, together with the bullet." We congratulated the old man on his escape and did not refrain from appropriate reflections.

"Why aren't you on duty?" somebody asked a youngish Hebrew in the company. "Oh, I am an invalid," he replied, pointing to his bandaged left hand. It was Mr. Levikov, the watchmaker, whose shop had been attacked on December 28 and who had been shot through the palm of his hand while timidly emptying his Browning at the robbers. I found out later that only two robbers had been killed, that the ringleader had escaped and had not yet been found. One of our paid watchmen confided in me that it was not unreasonable to suspect a certain drunken lout called "Mikishka," who has not been seen for some time, but who had passed by the other night with a woman, limping somewhat. I asked him to describe the man: the description fitted that of the fellow who had called on my landlady the other day and who once had attracted my attention on our street.

When I returned to our office after my first watch (about 10 P.M.), I was told that Doctor Murashev had just brought a report that a general massacre of capitalists was under discussion at the Military Section;[6] that some of the members insisted on the necessity of an immediate extermination of the hated capitalists and merchants, while others opposed that wild measure, carrying the discussion very nearly to the point of an armed conflict. While on my next beat, I heard shooting in the direction of the Military Section. However, the night passed without an outbreak. But a search was made in the Astoria: some said the police were looking for a certain band of burglars who were guilty of several murders perpetrated recently; others said arms and ammunition were sought under the cover of a search for provisions. Several machine guns had been stolen and sold by soldiers with full equipment. Two cartloads of hand grenades are said to have been removed by unknown persons from

6. No sources confirm that this was ever seriously considered. Such rumors were common at this time, however, probably because the Saratov Soviet discussed the role of the local revolutionary tribunal and measures to take against "enemies of the people."

a government storehouse. The Bolsheviks apparently suspect a conspiracy against their rule. They certainly can count on no friends among the general mass of the people.[7]

January 6, 1918. It is denied that a pogrom is planned against the well-to-do and the educated classes, against those who are opposed to Bolshevik theories and practices. But among the soldiers there is said to exist a tendency to slaughter their officers.

In connection with Dr. Brod's murder, a woman aroused suspicion of a local vigilance league and was tracked to the Rossiia Hotel (corner of Aleksandrov and Nemetskaia streets). A search of her room disclosed many interesting documents and led to the capture of thirty-two criminals who had committed about seventy murders in Saratov and Kharkov.[8] The woman alone had slit four men's throats.

At a dance given January 3 by the Saratov Intermediate Training School, five or six drunken army officers made themselves at home in the ladies' room, driving out its lawful occupants. When an attempt was made to remove the drunkards, the latter pulled out their guns. Then the military was called from a nearby station. The Red Army men, ten or fifteen of them, ran into the building. Everybody rushed to the cloak room and the clicking of loaded muskets filled the air, while the ragged defenders of law and order philosophized: "Here is a good place to get clothes." In the meantime the drunkards escaped by the back door to a parallel street, were pursued, and fired upon. A bullet whistled past Mr. Moskvichev and his company on Astrakhanskaia Street.

January 9, 1918. 11:30 P.M. At 7:30 P.M. I dropped in at our vigilance league headquarters, where a small company was already arranging its watches for the night. An elderly, respectable-looking

7. Although there was much opposition to the Bolsheviks, Babine cannot explain why they were able to stay in power and survive the Civil War. Despite all, the Bolsheviks still enjoyed the support of large numbers of workers and soldiers.

8. A major industrial and administrative center and capital of Kharkov province in the Ukraine, founded in 1655–56 by Cossacks. Until 1934 Kharkov was the capital of the Soviet Ukrainian Republic. During World War I, large numbers of people were evacuated to provinces located at the rear. In the spring of 1918 several sizable factories were evacuated from Kharkov to Saratov. It appears that criminals also flocked to Saratov, not only from Kharkov but from Moscow and Poltava as well.

 gentleman came in and told some of us, who gathered around him, that an old customer of his had just told him that at 7 P.M., only half an hour ago, four soldiers had deliberately shot two prisoners in their charge on Tsaritsyn Street, near Volsk. When the public protested against the murder, the soldiers threatened to shoot the protesters. The bodies of the dead men were loaded on a sleigh, and one of the soldiers went with them to the university. The rest of the soldiers went their way. Another gentleman came in who corroborated the story and stated that there was considerable excitement at the scene of the murder. "An excited young Jew expressed his belief that the Bolsheviks would shoot us and do with us anything they pleased as long as we did not repel them in kind. He was sure that somebody in the crowd had a gun. Why did he not kill the scoundrels? . . . The orator got no reply whatever from his audience: we were too wise for that."

At about 8 P.M. a meeting opened at the Astoria in connection with the Bolshevik decree abolishing the right of property in real estate in Saratov.[9] Several persons spoke, mostly Jews and other aliens in broken, poor, illiterate Russian. Mr. Maizul' opened the meeting, proposing to ignore all the decrees of "this band of highwaymen." His resolution carried. He then explained why he called the Bolsheviks highwaymen. That very evening two soldiers came to his store from the Military Section and wished to purchase a typewriter. They selected one costing 900 rubles and asked him to take the machine to the Section, where he would be paid. Mr. Maizul' took a cab and delivered the machine. After he placed the typewriter on a desk he was told that he might go. "But I want my money," he declared. "We have no money: we requisitioned the machine for public use," was the reply. In the end, the purchasers gave Mr. Maizul' a scrap receipt with the letterhead (a rubber stamp which one of the men had pulled out of his pocket) of the "Northern Army for the Counterrevolutionary Struggle."[10]

9. In late November 1917 the new government had abolished the right of private ownership of large houses, transferring them to town soviets. Housing committees, elected by residents, were to administer the property.

10. Probably the Eastern Army of the Counterrevolutionary Struggle, led by S. I. Zagummenyi, which the Saratov Soviet had formed to defend Saratov from the Cossack threat. Kaledin's forces, which had seized Rostov in December, marched against Saratov, Tsaritsyn, Balashov, and Atkarsk in January. Astrakhan Cossacks supported Kaledin and raised a revolt against the As-

A committee of seven was appointed to deal with the supplies question that is becoming quite acute. The committee was instructed, and it promised to go to work immediately.

It was privately stated after the meeting that sailors and marines had come to Saratov for the express purpose of exterminating the army officers in Saratov. It was also explained why the few soldiers that remained in Saratov did not return to their homes: they stay here in hope the city will be looted and that they will have a chance to take home nice presents of jewelry etc. for their sweethearts.

Armenian students are leaving the university to defend their homes from the Turks, since the Russian army of the Caucasus has entirely fled the front and allowed the enemy to reoccupy his lost territory.[11]

January 10, 1918. The victims of last night's shooting are lying at the university morgue. They are said to have been noted criminals with a glorious record of murderous exploits. They had been caught across the river, in Pokrovsk, brought to, and examined at, the Saratov Detectives' Bureau and forwarded to the Military Section, which they did not reach.

January 11, 1918. 11 P.M. The shooting took place in front of the house belonging to Mr. Yust, a lawyer. When he and a neighbor of his ran out to the street, the murderers were ordering some cabmen to take away the bodies. When the cabmen refused, they

---

trakhan Soviet on January 11, 1918. In response, the Saratov Soviet appealed for volunteers and two days later reported that more than 200 persons had already responded to the Soviet's call to arms. Although the Eastern Army suppressed the Astrakhan uprising at the end of January, a new threat was posed by the Ural Cossacks under Dutov, who rose up in March. In April the *Osobaia* (Special) Army was formed in Saratov and was soon renamed the Fourth Army and subordinated to the headquarters of the eastern front. (V. I. Chapaev [1887–1919] and his unit, a Red Army commander and Civil War hero whose reputation assumed near legendary proportions, joined the *Osobaia* Army.) As the Civil War unfolded, Red Guard units were transferred into regular military units and in June Soviet authorities introduced a draft. The vicissitudes of the Civil War in South Russia are chronicled by Peter Kenez, in *Civil War in South Russia, 1918: The First Year of the Volunteer Army* (Berkeley and Los Angeles, 1971) and *Civil War in South Russia, 1919–1920: The Defeat of the Whites* (Berkeley and Los Angeles, 1977).

11. For a discussion of the complicated history of the Armenian people during this turbulent period, see Richard G. Hovannisian, *Armenia on the Road to Independence, 1918* (Berkeley and Los Angeles, 1967).

 threatened to shoot them. When the corpses were finally placed on a sleigh, the soldiers disappeared, and a meeting of citizens was held around a pool of blood on the white snow. An orator said: "A great struggle among the classes is in progress. . . . There will be a sea of blood. Why should you wonder at this little pool?"

The victims were dressed in students' uniforms, hence their removal to the university morgue.

January 12, 1918. The president of our vigilance league, having dropped in at the headquarters about midnight on his return from a birthday party somewhere uptown, told us that on every blessed corner of the city's streets he had found groups of four or five watchmen with army muskets, who not only looked him and his wife over but accompanied them from corner to corner. There are about four thousand armed men on watch every night—many more than there are Red Army men at the present moment, with the departure of some three thousand of them for the Don.[12]

January 14, 1918. Martial law was proclaimed in Saratov today,[13] evidently in view of the anti-Bolshevik movement among citizens and of meetings at which the brainless Bolshevik confiscatory measures had been freely discussed and condemned.

Our house was searched for provisions yesterday afternoon—quite leniently, according to my landlady's statement. She declared some 100 lbs. of flour in her possession, and had her bread tickets clipped in consequence, to keep her from getting more than her share of the Bolshevik bounty. They let go two tickets intended for the janitor and his family. As I was absent, one of the searchers tried my door, found it locked, and seeing my professional card on it connecting me with the university, decided that I could not have anything.

The search party carried no muskets: weapons have scared some housekeepers quite out of their wits. An old lady is said to have fainted at the sight of soldiers, who left her half-dead without searching the house at all.

Because a meeting of householders could not be held this afternoon, the president of our vigilance league called at the Military

12. Babine is referring to the Eastern Army; see note 10 above.

13. Martial law was proclaimed, owing to the Cossack uprising against Soviet power in neighboring Astrakhan, which was liquidated on January 25.

Section. But Antonov was out, and others would give no information and were somewhat restless and uneasy, probably owing to a reported approach of Cossacks, who are said to have destroyed the railroad bridge at Krasnyi Kut.[14]

Professor Chuevskii, in connection with Shingarev's assassination[15] and the assassin's (Basov, a sailor) stealing his leather jacket, told another story of the Russian peasant's economic propensity. Two soldiers strongly imbued with Bolshevik ideas came to a village from the western front on furlough. They were greatly wrought up over the fact that a lady landowner living near their village had not yet been killed and went to her residence in order to kill her. At her house they found out that she had gone away, and they killed only her foreman, a Kirghiz, his wife, and five children. But the old Kirghiz woman only feigned death, ran to her folk, and brought some two thousand excited Kirghiz to the village where the murderers resided. The village elders had no sympathy with the murder, and at once surrendered the criminals. One of the Kirghiz immediately stuck his knife into one of the murderers, but was stopped by the rest, who preferred to belabor both men to death with their nagaikas (heavy quirts). When the execution was over, the villagers pulled the boots off the bloody corpses, not to let the good stuff go to waste.

Mrs. Chuevskii remembered a story her father used to tell to illustrate the Russian peasant's practical turn of mind. A young peasant killed his young paramour's husband and was sentenced to Siberia for life. After the sentence had been read, the young fellow's father, one of the witnesses, asked the court's leave to let him have the substantial wooden pole with which his son had committed the murder. To the court, wondering what he wanted the pole for, the old man explained that a substantial piece like that could certainly be put to some good use around the house.

In another case a gang of peasants murdered a whole family,

14. A settlement located in the trans-Volga region (Novouzensk district) approximately 117 kilometers southeast of Saratov.

15. A. I. Shingarev, Kadet leader who served as minister of agriculture in the Provisional Government. In response to an anti-Bolshevik demonstration in the capital, the Soviet government declared the Kadets "enemies of the people" and their leaders subject to arrest. Shingarev and F. F. Kokoshkin were among those arrested and imprisoned in the Peter-Paul Fortress. Later transferred to a hospital, they were murdered in early January by a band of soldiers.

 and among the bodies strewn all over the house feasted on plain black rye bread and other spare food. To the court's question why the accused ate plain bread when there was plenty of rich meat pie and other pastry in the dining room, one of the murderers replied in a matter-of-fact tone: "It was Friday," a day when no true Russian Orthodox Christian would defile himself by eating meat, eggs, butter, or milk. And the court understood.

January 15, 1918. The well-to-do people are being expelled from their residences to unsanitary basements and to hovels on the outskirts of the city, while the poor are encouraged to occupy the rich men's "palaces."[16] But the benighted beggars prefer to remain in their izbas (huts) and leave the promised "palaces" to Bolshevik princes and their hirelings.

Landowners, priests, physicians, rich merchants, and businessmen are daily reported shot in cold blood and without even a semblance of a trial.

Searches for weapons without any warrants have been especially frequent recently. Cases are reported of citizens shot in the yards of their residences when only an empty revolver cartridge had been found among their effects, it being taken for granted that the owners of cartridges had owned weapons, but refused to surrender them.

January 16, 1918. The report of a Cossack approach to Saratov is being substantiated. One of our members stated at the vigilance league headquarters this afternoon that he had seen with his own eyes three carloads of wounded Red soldiers brought from Balashov.[17] Mr. Brendel said that two ladies of his acquaintance had told him today that their father had just returned from Krasnyi Kut, where the day before he saw some eight hundred Red Army men so badly cut up and mutilated by the Cossacks that he hoped never to see the likes of it again. The Cossacks would not even fire: "We shall need ammunition elsewhere," they said. They simply drove

16. In connection with this, *Izvestiia Saratovskogo Soveta* (no. 12, January 17, 1918) announced that beginning on February 1 apartment rental rates would be reduced.

17. A district center in Saratov province that served as an important railroad junction, located on the Khoper River. In fact, a division of Ural Cossacks equipped with machine guns and artillery had passed through Atkarsk, and this prompted the Saratov Soviet to form a special defense staff.

the panic-stricken defenders of the Bolshevik revolution for over twenty miles, belaboring them with cold steel. The Bolsheviks do not trust regulars any longer. They have disarmed the 92d Regiment by a ruse. But the 91st Regiment refused to surrender its arms.[18] Something is brewing, and a hope is hovering in the air that the Bolshevik reign of ignorance and terror will soon be over.

January 17, 1918. The three and five carloads of badly maltreated Red soldiers from Balashov grew to six carloads today. A rumor has it that machine guns have been placed on housetops along Nemetskaia Street.

Antonov, one of our Bolshevik leaders, is reported to have been caught in Tambov with a foreign passport on his person.[19]

January 18, 1918. After my lecture at the People's University, I dropped in at the headquarters of our vigilance league to tell Ryvkin, our secretary, to slate me for Saturday night. But Ryvkin was not in and was expected to be away for some time. Our president, however, was present, but acted in a somewhat nervous way. I soon was informed about the cause of his nervousness: some ten armed soldiers sacked our headquarters this afternoon and carried off several revolvers belonging to the league, as well as our muskets. The locks of several cupboards were broken by the uninvited visitors in their search for weapons. The president swears that he will have his guns and muskets returned: Antonov has given his word—a word of honor. At the same time he mentioned the fact

18. The Saratov Soviet at this time was trying to demobilize the local garrison. The radicalized soldiers, armed and angry, were facing unemployment and extreme difficulties in being integrated back into civilian society. Taking advantage of the Soviet's efforts to discipline the garrison, anti-Bolshevik elements within the officer corps sowed discontent against the Bolsheviks. Riley soldiers in the artillery units (where certain SR leaders had remained popular after October) on several occasions had planned to disband the Soviet by force. In December 1917 the Soviet had abolished the organization of soldiers who had been at the front (*frontoviki*), but to no avail. By early 1918 the volatile *frontoviki*, returning from the front to find themselves unemployed, posed one of the greatest problems for local leaders.

19. Early in 1918 rumors circulated in Saratov, ostensibly floated by anti-Bolshevik elements, that Antonov, Vasil'ev, and other Bolshevik leaders had fled town with large sums of money. In response to rumors about his leaving Saratov, Antonov announced that he was going to Petrograd for a few days in connection with his work in the Executive Committee.

 that Antonov had been brought back under guard:[20] he was no longer trusted by his faithful tools.

Yesterday and today Mr. Mittel'man's store was visited by armed men who, on the strength of a scrap of paper from the Executive Committee, by force of bayonets compelled him to admit them into his store and carried away several bundles of merchandise without taking the trouble of paying for it.

A gentleman from the Rossiia took advantage of this occasion—the robbery in broad daylight—to tell of what happened last night at his hotel. An armed band of soldiers entered the hotel in order to occupy some thirty rooms for the Bolshevik telephone girls. But the soldiers were set upon by the hotel waiters, who upbraided them most violently for the existing misrule and for the starvation to which the waiters were brought after the Bolsheviks had come to power. Hearing the heated discussion, members of a military band that was playing at the hotel joined the waiters and said to the soldiers: "You have come with fixed bayonets and think you are smart. But we will meet you with bayonets too." "But," said the gentleman in conclusion, "what the waiters said and the way they did it was better than any bayonets. If more people feel like those waiters, we may hope for better times soon."

Is it a tiger's spirit rising in the people?[21]

January 20, 1918. In the line for bread this morning a woman said that a peasant this same morning was offering wheat flour at fifty rubles a pood[22] to the patrons of Center Market. The flour was

20. Antonov had traveled to Petrograd to attend the Third All-Russian Congress of Soviets. While there, he met with Lenin twice, in part to complain that N. I. Podvoiskii, who chaired the "higher military inspection," refused to release funds for financing the Saratov Red Guard. Saratov Bolsheviks also needed money to start up a volunteer army and to improve the vile conditions in the local garrison. Returning to Saratov on January 30, Antonov announced that he had brought back 20 million rubles to be used for the above causes and a radio transmitter, needed to keep in direct contact with the center. During this period Vasil'ev publicly denounced rumors that he had absconded with 2 million rubles.

21. Not exactly. On January 19 the post and telegraph workers' strike against the Bolsheviks was liquidated. (That very day the student body of Saratov University met to discuss a proposed boycott of Soviet power. Instead, however, the students disbanded, fearing that a detachment of worker Red Guards would break up any assemblies, as Saratov was under martial law.)

22. A unit of weight used in Russia, equal to about 36.11 pounds (16.38 kg.).

nearly confiscated by Cossacks, eight squadrons of whom are stationed at Trofimovka.[23] Having escaped the Cossacks, the man was not allowed to enter the city by the usual road near the depot, but was compelled to take a circuitous track since machine guns were posted in the depot in expectation of the Cossacks' arrival.

It is now averred that when Antonov was arrested three foreign passports were found on his person together with a million or even a million and a half rubles in money.[24]

After a meeting of our house committee (organized for the express, though secret, purpose of defeating the Bolshevik confiscatory measures), I reported on duty at the headquarters of our vigilance league. As I was late for the first beat, I lay down on a bench to take a nap. Before I fell sound asleep, however, Mr. Trzecak strolled in and remarked that the Cossacks were advancing toward Pokrovsk and that a special meeting of the Bolshevik Executive Committee was in session. In the earlier part of the evening I was told by a member of the league present that five squadrons of Cossacks—about seven thousand men—were stopped at Trofimovka by the Bolsheviks, who insisted on disarming the Cossacks. The latter refused to surrender their arms and demanded free passage home (from the western front), explaining that they had not come to fight the Bolsheviks. Thus it seems that there are Cossacks on two sides of Saratov. Those at Trofimovka are said to have brought their dead and wounded comrades along with them. Tapers are said to be constantly burning in the cars where the dead bodies are lying.

Listed for the second beat, I, at about 10 P.M., was conducted to my post on the corner of German and Aleksandrov streets, and received an old Berdan rifle with a fixed bayonet, a certificate, a wooden badge of office, and three cartridges from my predecessor. It was wet under foot, and the northwestern wind blew a perfect gale on the street that seemed to me altogether too crowded considering the martial law proclamation. At about 11 P.M. a bill was posted on the board fence near my house: it was a new Bolshevik decree proclaiming (again) martial law in Saratov on account of the approach of Cossacks, abolishing all vigilance leagues and

23. Babine may have been referring to a small settlement in Tambov province.

24. See notes 19 and 20 above.

 entrusting their functions to the military, demanding surrender of all arms by the league as by everybody else, and declaring thieves and robbers national enemies.

About ten minutes later a fellow in a leather jacket walked across the street toward me, while another fellow alighted from a sleigh, and thrust a gun into my face. "What's up?" I asked indifferently. They wanted to know if I belonged to a vigilance league, and to my affirmative explained to me that the leagues were abolished and demanded my Berdan. As I hesitated, the fellow in the leather jacket pulled the musket from under my arm by the rusty old bayonet, and the other, with a revolver under my nose, ordered me to throw up my hands—which I did in a rather leisurely way, wondering whether it was worthwhile to make the northwestern wind blow through the men in absence of the sun. "Got a revolver?" the one in the leather jacket wanted to know. "We have not been given any revolvers," I answered truthfully, without mentioning my own .38 hammerless I was holding above the fellow's head and out of his sight. "Let me have the cartridges," the man with the revolver proposed next, and without waiting for me to comply with his demand —I was uncommonly slow of motion and understanding and not at all dangerous—he turned to the sleigh and engaged in a hurried talk with a fellow who had brought one more musket. Seeing that nobody was paying attention to me, I walked quietly to our stout iron gate, slipped through it, locked it behind me, found my landlady up and watching the street ("They have been running back and forth all evening long"), and went to bed.

The commissar of the Volga-Kama Bank, an untidy, dirty, pimple-faced fellow, irritably declared yesterday in an altercation about a check in everybody's presence: "Antonov has not arrived at all. . . . I know better than you do. . . . Vasil'ev has shamefully deserted us. . . . And I tell you that he had not been commissioned to go to Petrograd, but shamefully ran away."[25]

January 21, 1918. 2:30 P.M. Mr. Knaube, whom I met on the street a few minutes ago, told me that our headquarters had been sacked last night and nearly all the weapons carried away by Anarchists, who left a receipt on paper with their own letterhead and who took Mr. Imenitov, the vice-president, a Jew, to the Saratov Exchange

25. Vasil'ev had left for Petrograd to attend the opening of the Constituent Assembly.

Building, which at present has a sign above its main entrance reading: "Anarchist Club."[26] A meeting of the Central Committee of Vigilance Leagues of the city is to be held this afternoon and their future policy considered.

6:30 P.M. Six sleigh loads of wounded Red soldiers are said to have been brought in today, with five wounded men in each sleigh. Enough wounded soldiers cannot come to please everybody, since the defeat of the army spells the downfall of the hateful regime. "A battle somewhere near Saratov must be in progress."

January 22, 1918. Red soldiers lying in the government liquor warehouses have their backs so badly cut with nagaikas that they can lie only on their stomachs. In some cases flesh is cut to the bone and hangs in shreds. Many will not survive the execution wrought by the Cossacks.

Eighteen murders took place in the city last night.[27] Vigilance leagues have been reestablished by a new Soviet decree.

January 23, 1918. The Ural Cossacks that had come from the west and scared our Bolsheviks to the extent of declaring martial law in Saratov are said to have slipped away to their home in a circuitous way across the Volga.[28]

January 26, 1918. 6:15 P.M. "Anything new, doctor?" "Just a tiny bit of news. Last night our committee discussed the question of closing four local Red Cross hospitals, and decided in the affirmative. But word was received from the Military Section to postpone the action, since a transport of wounded Red Army men was expected from the front."

January 28, 1918. 10 P.M. A great religious procession took place

26. Various Anarchist groups had played an increasingly destabilizing role in Saratov politics as 1917 unfolded. Following the Kornilov affair, three Saratov Anarchist factions had formed a Free Association of Anarchist Groups of the City of Saratov. They called for an armed uprising against the Provisional Government and briefly put out a newspaper, *Golos anarkhii* (Voice of Anarchy).

27. Although crime was certainly on the rise at this time, I was unable to verify Babine's claim that eighteen murders had taken place.

28. The Saratov Soviet had set up a special department back in December to carry on propaganda among Cossacks, and met with some success, especially among younger Cossacks, who proved highly susceptible to Bolshevik reasoning. In fact, local authorities lifted the state of siege in connection with the withdrawal of the Cossack division.

 today, with plenty of church banners and icons. Services at the cathedral continued from 10 A.M. to 9 P.M. In the evening, meetings were held on main streets at which the Bolsheviks' church policy was strongly condemned.[29] Soldiers are said to have turned against the Bolsheviks.

January 29, 1918. 9 P.M. As I approached the Linden Park, musket shots were heard in the direction of the Exchange Building, and people ran hurriedly toward and into the park or under the protection offered by house walls. At 6:30 P.M. a lively musketry fire exploded under the very windows of my English class in the Khramstov School. A male student jumped up and leaned against the brick wall between two windows. I ignored or pretended to ignore the unusual noise, continued the lesson, and after it safely reached my lodgings.

January 30, 1918. A decree has been posted all over the city prohibiting under severe penalties all impromptu meetings, promiscuous shooting, and unauthorized possession of firearms—on account of the "antirevolutionary propaganda."

February 2, 1918.[30] The more I look at my university-learned colleagues, the more I listen to their eloquent and animated or passionately subdued talks on the present state of affairs, the more disgusted I grow with their inability to do anything, with their theoretic worship and advocacy of all sorts of "rights" and with their practical inability to defend these rights, with the weakness of their brawn and the consequent weakness of their brain and willpower. No rights whatsoever will or can they defend with their own flabby

29. The trouble this day was caused by two separate but related events. As background, the Russian Orthodox Church had anathematized Bolshevik power for its harsh policies toward religion. Local church leaders then organized a religious march that turned into a demonstration against the government's decree separating church and state and forbidding religious instruction in schools. The next day (see Babine's entry for January 29) Black Hundred and other conservative groups attacked the local Anarchist Club, which had earlier issued appeals, "Down with religion." The Soviet rightfully believed "if a pogrom broke out, it would not be limited to attacking Anarchists."

30. This date cannot be correct. February 14 followed January 31 because Russia switched from the Julian to the Gregorian calendar. All dates hereinafter, however, are given in New Style, which took effect at this time. In switching calendars Russia "lost" two weeks.

hands: they will much rather hire stronger hands than to expose their precious selves to the risks of a contest. Their chief end of life is life itself, and only life—under any conditions, however oppressive and humiliating. Can this be accounted for by the presence among the university teaching body of so many members of a nation which through centuries of persecution has stood away from all physical struggle against oppression, which has always purchased for money what pittance of an existence it could get, or hired others, or inspired them, to stand the brunt of armed conflicts? Or is it purely the Slavic unmorality, immorality, and the physical and moral decrepitude of the polished and so-called educated and intellectual classes?

February 17, 1918. As I was dozing on a sofa at our vigilance league last night, waiting for my beat, Mr. Nashivochnikov, one of our members, came in and told those present that just a few minutes before the Bolsheviks, by force of bayonets, had taken possession of his drugstore in the name of the government and generously offered him a clerk's job in his own store. Everybody was duly indignant, and duly acknowledged the convincing power of the bayonet argument.[31]

At about 2:15 this afternoon I saw a body of armed soldiers cross Aleksandrov Street marching up Nemetskaia Street. "Where are they from?" I asked a veteran journalist friend of mine. "Devil knows," quoth he in a tone of great disgust.

February 23, 1918. Returning from my walk with Boss at 6 P.M., I saw groups of people standing around central figures reading aloud the latest telegram. I addressed a young gentleman on the corner who was scanning his by himself. "They say St. Petersburg is occupied by the Germans. . . . I do not find it in this telegram . . . but a friend of mine, my colleague in the Riazan-Ural railway office, has just told me about a telegram to that effect which is being transmitted along the line."[32]

31. As justification for nationalizing drugstores, the local soviet noted that the measure was prompted by the fact that proprietors were sending their stocks to other cities and thereby threatening the city with grave shortages. That same day, incidentally, university students, by a vote of 252 in favor, 54 against, and 26 abstentions, approved a 100 percent tuition increase so as to avoid turning to the Bolshevik authorities for financial assistance.

32. Fed up with the Soviet government's slowness in agreeing to peace

 February 24, 1918. Dr. Kadykov, a local vet, returning from Razboishchina by train fell in among a band of riotous soldiers and felt somewhat uneasy. By and by the crowd began to sing:

Renounce the old world,
Shake off the Bolsheviks' remains from your boots.
We don't need an idol like Lenin
Nor a mansion like Trotsky's.[33]

The vet's spirits rose. "How do you like this occupation of Dvinsk by the Germans?" he asked, pulling an orthodox Bolshevik paper out of his pocket. The company knew nothing about it, and the cursing that followed was terrible to hear. The soldiers claimed they had followed the Bolsheviks hoping for an honorable peace; they did not follow them in order to rob churches.

In a crowd on our street corner citizens freely and openly spoke last night in favor of driving the Bolsheviks away from the power they have been so basely abusing.

February 25, 1918. All open-air meetings have been prohibited under severe penalties.

February 27, 1918. The grocery woman informed me this morning that I was getting my coal oil from her for the last time, since the Bolsheviks had declared coal oil a government monopoly together with salt, flour, and other vital necessities. "How I shall make my living is more than I can tell. . . . Being a widow, I have had hard enough time supporting my children. . . . And now those Bolshevik curses."

Last night the Hotel Rossiia was searched by order of the Military Section. Under the pretext of looking for firearms the searching party confiscated all the cash it could lay its hands on. The proprietor is said to have lost 215,000 rubles, and the guests had to fork out several thousand to satisfy Bolshevik appetites. It is believed that in view of the German advance local Bolsheviks intend to flee the country, and make every effort to obtain cash for that purpose.

---

terms, the German Military Commander on February 16 announced his government would end the armistice and attack Russia. Two days later Germany launched a full-scale invasion along the entire Russo-German front.

33. The first line comes from the opening measures of the "International."

March 3, 1918. At about 1 A.M. I was awakened from my sleep at our vigilance league headquarters, after my beat between 8 and 10 P.M., by a rush of our men to the street. In a minute or so they returned, announcing that a body of cavalry had come to search the Astoria. Our night captain went to attend the search as a witness in his official capacity and did not return until 5 A.M. Not all the rooms were searched. One of the guests lost about four thousand rubles: he tossed a wad of bills from a window to the roof of the building, but was caught in the act, and his money was confiscated. Only our captain saved him from arrest. Another guest was relieved of some eight hundred rubles.

There is much discontent among soldiers who have recently returned from the front, shabbily dressed and shod and underfed, with the refusal of the Bolsheviks to furnish them necessary clothing. Among the office employees of the Military Section, the *frontoviki*[34] found many who never smelt powder nor risked their lives, but who are drawing handsome salaries for doing nothing. The discontent among the *frontoviki* has apparently been bred and fed by local businessmen wronged by the Bolsheviks.[35] It is rumored that two merchants have given two million rubles to the *frontoviki* to meet their most crying needs. The *frontoviki* seem to favor driving the Bolsheviks from power and letting local government organs resume their lawful positions. Last night several *frontoviki* leaders were arrested by the Bolsheviks, with three Red Army men killed during the operation. One of the leaders was Mr. Deterre, whose house on Krapivnaia was peppered with machine-gun fire. Another was Colonel Medvedev, taken at the Rossiia. An armed conflict is expected at any moment between the *frontoviki* and the

34. Other sources confirm this report that the city expected an uprising on the part of the *frontoviki* against the Soviet. A meeting of the Union of Front Soldiers criticized the Soviet Executive Committee, and, according to *Izvestiia*, there was a sharp difference of opinion "between the former officers and the lower ranks." On March 1 the Saratov Soviet resolved to create a department to assuage unemployment, especially among former soldiers. Moreover, the Soviet abolished the Military Section in view of the demobilization of the garrison. By mid-February relations between the Union of Front Soldiers and Soviet organs had deteriorated further. Representatives of the *frontoviki* demanded clothes and boots and later recognition of their organization, but the Executive Committee turned down their request.

35. Other sources substantiate this rumor.

 Bolsheviks.[36] The former are said to number over six thousand men, well armed and supplied with machine guns and ammunition.

March 4, 1918. 6 P.M. The *frontoviki* held a meeting at the Hall of the Nobility in the morning, having protected the building with their machine guns. At the Passage Market a Red Army man was shot dead by a *frontovik* and remained in the street for several hours, nobody caring or daring to remove the body. There was some shooting in the evening.

March 5, 1918. 10 P.M. Leaving my high school after a lesson, at 4 P.M., I asked a porter if there was any shooting in town. He answered in the negative, but called my attention to the fact that no electric cars [trolleys] were running for some time: a fight was expected. When I was out in the street I heard several shots in the direction of the Exchange Building and received a warning from a passerby not to go that way. I then turned from Moscow to Great Kazachia, but on the corner of Ilin and Nemetskaia streets saw a crowd moving from Volsk, with a man driving it toward Ilin. It was impossible to cross Volsk and to get home. It was also impossible to get home or to take food to Boss confined to a cage at the Bacteriological Station with rheumatism. With much hesitation I begged Professor Pavlov for shelter (readily granted) and remained at his house until 9 P.M. We knew through phone messages that machine-gun fire was covering Volskaia, and that it was impossible to cross it without risking one's life. At 9 P.M. I safely reached my home, having met a few men on my way and a number of armed soldiers. Reports of rifle shots reach my ear at this writing (apparently from Moscow Street).

March 6, 1918. 7:50 P.M. This morning at 6:30, housewives, maidservants, and early risers began to appear on our street. I went to see Boss at the Bacteriological Station. People went about as usual. At the government warehouse on Work Lane there stood guard two workers armed with muskets, one of them a mere boy of about eighteen who amused himself by breaking the morning ice with a long stick. Formerly I saw only soldiers at the warehouse in question.[37]

36. See note 34.

37. This indicates that the Bolsheviks relied more heavily on the working class than the soldiers and that workers still supported the Soviet.

Electric trolleys are running as usual. At 7 P.M. rifle shots could be heard from various directions.

March 7, 1918. 3:40 P.M. At about 5 P.M. yesterday I saw on the corner of Nemetskaia and Aleksandrov streets a number of Red Guardsmen rather energetically ordering the crowd assembled there to disperse. I had barely time to return home from Tiedeman's music store when sharp firing was heard from the same corner, and people rushed up Nemetskaia Street. A few minutes later the howl of what sounded like a wounded boy filled the air. From my window I saw two soldiers driving the crowd and brandishing their muskets on the opposite side of the street. But the street was full of people again in a few minutes.

This morning I was told that a number of people had been killed and wounded on Aleksandrov Street. My informant with his own eyes saw a wounded man.

In front of the post office building a young man came up to the crowd assembled there and without any warning shot a man dead. The crowd made a rush at the murderer and killed him on the spot. Mr. Luchinkin told one of our janitors that on his way to the university library this morning he saw on one of the streets the body of a man killed apparently last night, and by ten o'clock this morning not yet removed.

March 10, 1918. No Moscow or Petrograd papers have been received here for the last few days. Our local Bolshevik paper is evidently hoodwinking its benighted readers as to the peace situation.[38] A letter a friend of mine received from Petrograd states plainly that Petrograd (and the writer) is in direct communication with Reval, and that a German lieutenant had informed him recently that the German government had no intention to make peace with the Bol-

38. On March 6 the local Executive Committee instructed delegates to the Fourth All-Russian Congress of Soviets to reject signing a peace with Germany. On March 6–8, at the Eighth Party Congress, the majority of delegates from throughout Russia agreed to accept the Draconian peace offer; however, the Saratov delegates voted against it on March 14 at the Fourth Congress of Soviets. Among local leaders, Vasil'ev advocated a revolutionary war against Germany; Antonov supported Trotsky's "neither war nor peace" formulation; Lebedev, like Lenin, favored signing the treaty. As elsewhere in the backwaters of Russia, delegates from the district towns of Saratov province tended to favor the peace. Interestingly enough, the local Left SR committee carried a resolution that was similar to Trotsky's "neither war nor peace" platform.

 shevik rabble; that it would take over Moscow, assemble the Fourth Duma,[39] call a Constituent Assembly to decide upon a form of government (presumably to restore the monarchy),[40] and then sign a treaty of peace with the national and lawful government.

At our vigilance league headquarters a German member of the league expressed his firm conviction that all local Bolshevik leaders of the revolted and most revolting rabble would be hanged to a man with the restoration of order (presumably, through German good offices). An arrival from Kiev after the German occupation[41] tells of the perfect order immediately established in the city. Stores, shops, cafes, restaurants opened, plenty of candies, wine, beer, and all sorts of merchandise were available, and German policemen were at every street crossing.

A gentleman who arrived from Kiev a few days ago and who had left it before the German occupation told me about his experiences in that city. He and two other gentlemen were lying over at a station about fifty miles this side of Kiev when it was besieged by the Bolshevik army, waiting for a chance to get in. When the city was taken by the Bolsheviks, all three had to face a Bolshevik officer, a little Jew, armed to the teeth, who after examining their papers impressed them into his service as sanitary assistants. In this capacity they received an automobile and easily got to Kiev, where they were at once set to work removing dead bodies. Some fifty of these were removed by them, chiefly from Palace Square. All the men seemed to have been killed with expanding bullets. One had his skull crushed in with the butt of a musket. Some bodies were removed by the victims' relatives.

The gentleman mentioned the methods of extortion practiced by the Bolsheviks on their business victims. In Moscow, for instance,

39. The last Duma elected in Russia (in 1912), and prorogued by the tsarist government.

40. People wanted an end to incipient civil war and a guarantee that the right to express a dissenting voice would be honored. Restoration of the monarchy, however, was a dead issue except in the most conservative circles.

41. The Germans occupied Kiev on March 3 and pressed toward Poltava, Kharkov, and Odessa. Their rapid advance toward Petrograd was halted only when Lenin convinced the Central Committee majority to accept Germany's new, harsher peace terms. As per the terms of the Brest-Litovsk Treaty ratified at the Fourth Congress of Soviets on March 15, Soviet Russia lost its western borderlands and in effect was reduced to the size of the state's seventeenth-century boundaries.

no checks are allowed above three hundred rubles (or two thousand rubles for factories and similar establishments) at a time. But the Bolshevik auditor at the Treasury Bank would sanction checks for 12 percent of that amount if it were paid him as a douceur. Many individuals and corporations submit to this extortion in order to save at least a portion of their property.

During my beat, between 2 and 4 A.M., much rifle and machine-gun shooting was heard in the direction of the railway station and the Volga. Passersby reported Moscow Street closed to traffic. About 3 A.M. eight machine guns were taken from there to the Military Section. Four cabmen were ordered about the same time from the corner of Aleksandrov and Nemetskaia streets to Moscow Street and went there under the escort of two armed troopers—to transport the victims of the shooting.

An attempt was made to rob Professor Birukov's apartment last night. The robbery was averted only by the servant's coolness and refusal to admit the suspicious characters who tried to force their way into the lodging.

After fifty Red troopers had been stationed in the yard of the building where Professor Pavlov occupies an apartment, a shoe-store was completely denuded of its contents, and another store across the street was robbed under the same circumstances.

March 12, 1918. By Professor Zabolotnov's[42] order there are no lectures today on account of the anniversary of the Russian Revolution.[43] At this writing (12:15 P.M.) numerous processions—artillery, cavalry, infantry, armed Red Guardsmen and citizens, men and women—are filing past our house, with red banners and revolutionary songs.

Moscow papers appeared yesterday and today to announce the supremely disgraceful Bolshevik peace with Germany.[44]

42. P. P. Zabolotnov, member of the faculty of medicine, 1910–26. As rector of Saratov University (January 25, 1914, to May 7, 1918), Zabolotnov was chosen as a delegate to the Moscow State Conference that met in August 1917.

43. An estimated 10,000 workers and soldiers took part in a public rally.

44. Despite strong opposition within the Bolshevik party as well as outside of it, Lenin, arguing that Russia's current situation demanded signing of the peace, convinced the party to ratify it. Its acceptance forced a break between the Bolsheviks and Left SRs, who resigned from the Soviet government. The Saratov Left SRs, however, denounced the actions of their Moscow comrades and continued to work within the local Soviet.

3 P.M. Just as I returned to my boarding house and entered my room, I heard several revolver shots from the corner of Volsk and Nemetskaia streets. Small boys, men, women, and soldiers with and without muskets began to run in the opposite direction. After a few musket shots, at 3:08 two cannon reports were heard. The crowd ran toward Aleksandrov at a lively pace. A little riderless pony trotted in a leisurely way past our house. People crowded near yard gates and at house doors, with their faces turned toward Volsk. Quite a number of Red soldiers appeared, stood on sidewalks, watched the housetops, and gesticulated. At 3:15 the street was entirely empty. The Jewish students' cafe opposite our house had its entrance barred, and stationed a man at the door who admitted patrons.

By and by the street revived. A red flag was carried by a soldier past our house—apparently a trophy taken from an interrupted procession. Later on two more red flags passed the same way, and at about 3:30 P.M. a mixed procession of musketed soldiers and Red Guardsmen marched down with red banners. The Jewish cafe reopened its doors. A party of armed soldiers passed toward the Linden Park. An army officer, accompanied by two guards, walked by with a couple of confiscated dilapidated swords.

3:55 P.M. Everything seems to be quiet on our street. Four persons are said to have been killed during today's fusillade.

March 13, 1918. 9:30 P.M. The Bacteriological Station janitor told me this morning that eight persons had been killed in yesterday's affray;[45] that a shot had been fired from the Astoria; that soldiers had wanted to enter the Astoria and kill all the guests; that *frontoviki* had opened fire on a Bolshevik procession from the post office building and three or four other buildings with machine guns and hand grenades. A gentleman running at double quick from a dangerous neighborhood told Mr. Luchinkin that about two hundred persons had been killed. Mr. Chegodaev thinks it's more like fifty. His boy of twelve happened to be on Nemetskaia Street just at the right time. He saw the general rush from the place whence the bullets came galore and hid behind an iron lantern base, which was struck by many a bullet; he saw people throw away their revolvers and was very much tempted to pick up one that lay not far from

45. An unsuccessful armed demonstration, resulting in shooting, took place near the Hotel Aurora and Covered Market.

him, but did not dare stretch his arm on account of a rain of bullets. He finally managed to get home without a scratch. The boy saw, too, a man rush from the Astoria and kill a man, and be killed in his turn in an attempt to escape.

The secretary of the Bolshevik Executive Committee, Tsyrkin,[46] was killed by a Red Army man who took him for an undesirable "bourgeois" on account of the trim, fashionable suit he wore.

March 18, 1918. 10:15 P.M. Tsyrkin's funeral took place this morning. Last night the most harrowing reports of the irate "comrades'" intentions were circulating, which many believed. Owing to these reports, many residents of the central part of the city migrated uptown for the night—to the outskirts of the city—in order to escape the threatened wholesale murder of the well-to-do people. But the Bolsheviks seem to have acknowledged their own fault in Tsyrkin's death. Nobody doubts now that he was killed by a Red soldier who shot him in the temple with a "Take this, you ——— Jew," while Tsyrkin was doing his level best to prevent a panic, and that the trouble arose from an accidental shot fired by a horseman who on his part, too, tried to quiet the crowd. The story of a shot fired from the Astoria has no foundation whatsoever.

Tsyrkin is well spoken of by Professor Veretennikov[47]—as the only person with whom one could deal and come to an understanding—a person representing the moderate and the better balanced element in the high-handed Bolshevik administration.

No prayers for the government were offered by the clergy at this morning's service in the New Cathedral.

March 22, 1918. Professors' salaries, due on the 20th of the month, have not yet been paid for March.

Returning from the university at 3 P.M., I saw an automobile full of soldiers madly hurrying toward the railroad station. Two or three minutes later a trooper passed me galloping as madly in the same

46. David Tsyrkin, editor of *Krasnaia gazeta,* which superseded the Bolshevik's *Sotsial-Demokrat* in early 1918. Tsyrkin may well have been killed in this manner. Other sources note that someone fired at the demonstration from the hotel or from a private home, causing the Red Guard to panic and to shoot indiscriminately. In response, the Provincial Executive Committee took measures to strengthen discipline and organization within the Red Guard and Red Army. It also issued new rules for conducting searches and the right to bear arms.

47. V. I. Veretennikov, member of the university's history faculty, 1917–22.

Saratov Railroad Station, 1918

direction. At 5 P.M. I was told on good authority (Dr. Bonovich's son) that a German consul had already been appointed for Saratov and that one thousand German soldiers had already come as far as Balashov to protect him.[48]

Again, too busy to get dinner.

March 31, 1918. Lieber, a Bund orator,[49] spoke last week at the railway station on the tyrannical Bolshevik rule before an audience of some eight thousand railroad employees. The crowd's attention was intense. Antonov and Vasil'ev tried to defend the Bolshevik policy, but were hissed away. Another attempt was made by Vasil'ev to defend the Bolsheviks at the Conservatory of Music after Lieber's lecture. But again the crowd would not let him speak.

Last week the Press Commissar, Alekseev, while trying to confiscate a printing office that was disobedient and unfriendly to the Bolsheviks' printing office, was shot dead by the proprietor, Mr. Ra-

48. A widespread, but unfounded rumor.

49. The General Jewish Workers' Union in Lithuania, Poland, and Russia, popularly known as the Bund, created in 1897. By 1917 the party's program was basically that of the Mensheviks. In 1917 strong internationalist feelings were popular among the organization's members, as were unification sentiments. The organization had enjoyed popularity among Saratov railroad workers.

binovich, who managed to escape with his life.[50] But his son, a student, was arrested, taken to the Military Section, and foully murdered there (several bayonet wounds were found in his back and a wound from a ball that had entered his left flank just above the hip and came out through the right shoulder). After the young Rabinovich's death his case was tried, and the dead man was found guilty.

Alekseev's funeral was to take place this morning with much display and many threats to the opponents of Bolshevik rule. He was to be interred on Theater Square with three other Bolsheviks killed since March 12 under various circumstances. The ground on Theater Square was already prepared yesterday, grave dug, etc., when suddenly the holes in the ground were leveled and all preparations discontinued. The railroad men are said to have protested against a public funeral and other Bolshevik plans—to have protested so vigorously, in fact, that Vasil'ev, to whom an appropriate message was transmitted by phone, is said to have fainted with the receiver in his hand. It is rumored that at the place where the ground had been broken for the Bolshevik graves a sign was found bearing the words: "No dumping here."

The railwaymen are said to have in their possession eighteen thousand muskets and plenty of ammunition.

Alekseev is said to have been a mere boy of nineteen and a former employee of Rabinovich Sr. On the eventful day he vigorously shook his revolver before Rabinovich's nose, shook it so much that the latter snatched it away from him and shot him.

April 1, 1918. No lectures at the university, no lessons in the upper classes of high schools today—a day of mourning in connection with the lawless execution of Rabinovich Jr. As far as I know, no days of mourning had ever been appointed in connection with as foul assassinations of Russian students.

April 3, 1918. At about 6 P.M. the dead body of a young smooth-faced highwayman was brought to the gate of the Aleksander Hospital in a roomy farm wagon. It turned out that about nine o'clock this morning six highwaymen attacked farmers on their way home from Saratov and robbed them of one thousand rubles. The farmers

50. Rabinovich did kill P. A. Alekseev. The former's son tried to prevent his father's arrest and in turn was sentenced to death and executed.

 immediately reported the fact to the Military Section. A mounted posse was given to the victims. While the posse hid in ambush, the farmers went ahead, were again attacked and signaled to the posse by shouting. The highwaymen at first opened fire, but soon took to their heels across the Volga on ice. The posse of thirteen men fired about forty rounds each, and downed three bandits. One bandit made good his escape, the fate of two others I could not ascertain. The crowd around the wagon expressed no pity for the dead man. "Wanted to get rich quick . . . a good warning to others."

The robbery took place within ten miles of Saratov. A citizen who left the crowd at the same time with me, a common, middle-aged man, expressed his dissatisfaction with the present "government" that is unable to put an end to the robberies and murders, that does not care an iota for public safety and looks only after itself, living in a kind of little fortress, with cannon and machine guns in the backyard ("haven't you seen them? . . . The yard is full of them").

April 7, 1918. I was told last night that the Cossacks are advancing on Saratov from Novouzensk[51]—that they are expected here by the 10th of the month, and that no tickets are sold farther than Ershov.

Mr. Imenitov told of an incident that took place at the Astoria on April 3. Two drunken individuals in military garb were trying to extort forty rubles from the hotel manager. A member of the Saratov Executive Committee passing by happened to take interest in the conversation. The drunkards claimed to be Bolshevik commissars from Uvek[52] and proved this statement by their documents. In spite of their official position, the besotted drunkards were searched, were relieved of the five revolvers which they had license to carry, and were placed under arrest. "Antonov and Vasil'ev will certainly see to our immediate release," they claimed.

That same night they had managed (before their arrest) to obtain one hundred rubles from the manager of the Rossiia, and the week before twenty rubles from the manager of the Astoria.

At about 11 P.M., when I was on my beat, a searching party of

51. A district center in Samara province, founded in the eighteenth century. After the revolution it was incorporated into Saratov oblast (province). The town had a major railroad station on the Krasnyi Kut–Aleksandrov Gai branch line.

52. A settlement (and rail station) on the Volga River, located six miles south of Saratov.

seven or eight entered the Tamara Castle Cafe and remained there till after midnight. My well-informed companion whispered to me that a search was an easy way to get a good supper free, wine and all.

April 9, 1918. This morning I noticed big red seals on some of the jewelry stores on Nemetskaia Street. This evening the matter was explained to me. Last Sunday evening some twenty jewelers were invited to the provincial auditor's office to discuss certain professional questions. The meeting was presided over by a Bolshevik commissar who behaved in a curious and rather inexplicable way, constantly leaving the room and returning. About 8 P.M. an old uptown watchmaker decided to go home and left the assemblage, but returned in a few minutes to announce that an armed guard had forbidden him to leave the building. It did not take much time after that to find that the meeting was a mere trap for the assembled jewelers, who were declared under arrest by two unceremonious individuals brandishing army revolvers. Then the jewelers were taken one by one to their stores, saw them searched, and all gold and silver were confiscated, without any receipt having been given them. Since there were not enough soldiers for the search, some of the jewelers were paroled and later searched at leisure, i.e., some two hours after their release. These, as a matter of fact, had no valuables in their possession, and would even decline to make heart-to-heart confessions to the searching parties.

The railroad workers are said to have passed a resolution not to give a single man for the Bolshevik Red Army.[53]

It is vaguely rumored that Trotsky-Bronstein and even Lenin himself are in Saratov, Moscow being unsafe for them.[54]

April 11, 1918. 10:40 P.M. My landlady and her children (with their

53. Such reluctance to fight and to deepen incipient civil war was not unusual at this time. Local workers also denounced a measure calling for Red Guard training for all workers. Workers failed to understand why the burden of serving in the Red Guard had not fallen on the bourgeoisie! Soviet leaders had to hold rallies at enterprises that were considered bastions of Bolshevik strength—the railroad yards, Zhest, Sotrudnik, and Gantke plants—to explain the dangers of arming the class enemy.

54. Somewhat doubtful, although Trotsky may well have passed through. Rumors of this sort tended to spread whenever a ranking authority visited from the capital.

toys and schoolbooks) have disappeared from the house. The flat is left in charge of the landlady's younger sister. The recent Bolshevik threat of repression in connection with the refusal of the Saratov businessmen to pay an outrageous "indemnity" to the Bolsheviks seems not to remain without effect on the "enemies of the people."[55]

April 12, 1918. Lenin is said to have spent two days in Saratov, without appearing anywhere. Removal of the central Bolshevik government to Saratov is expected. Residents of the better houses in the block, where local Bolshevik central offices are situated, are being turned out of their flats, their furniture and other possessions thrown out to the street by soldiers. The sentiment against Bolshevik rule is fed by these wanton proceedings. The Bolshevik Red Army decree has been laid aside in view of labor's unanimous opposition to it. It was said last night that Germany is going to disown its treaty of peace with the present "Russian" government, to set up a permanent and responsible government, and to make a treaty with it.

Bread can be bought only at about three rubles a pound, and of poor quality, owing to the Bolshevik policy of monopolies and Bolshevik inability to cope with the situation. The policy of reaping where one sows is beginning not to bear fruit.

April 13, 1918. As I was returning home from the university this afternoon, two Red Army men, mere boys, armed with muskets, crossed Nemetskaia Street at the corner of Volsk and made an army officer remove the cockade from his cap. Another Red Army man shouted to the former two from our side of the street: "Boys, don't make him take it off." But the officer meekly submitted to the insolent demand and cast away the offending article of his attire, which was immediately picked up by a small boy. Two quick uppercuts on the chin would have done for the would-be soldiers had the officer been a man.

55. Owing to the collapse of the economy and tax system, local administrations faced enormous financial shortages in 1918. Often local soviets levied indemnities on the bourgeoisie to make up for the unavailability of tax funds. In late December the Saratov Soviet, following the lead of the government in experimenting with what Lenin called "a Red Guard offensive against capital," had levied a 10-million-ruble indemnity on local industrialists and took thirty hostages. As late as April 9 they were still being held until payment was made.

April 14, 1918. Called on a Swedish consular inspector at the Rossiia
this morning. He has been in Russia for about six months, and is still unable to understand how things can be allowed to go the way they are going. He was kept three weeks under arrest in Kamyshin,[56] and his funds—320,000 rubles—were taken away from him but, after a diplomatic remonstrance, returned. Last night he left his shoes outside the door to have them polished, according to the time-honored Russian custom. This morning he, quite out of keeping with the custom, failed to find them in their place. Neither could anybody tell him what had become of them, and he had to send his secretary, a German, in quest of a storekeeper that would be willing to let him have a pair of shoes on Sunday.

April 23, 1918. Six burglars and robbers are said to have been shot at the prison without trial, in accordance with a secret order to dispense with formalities when a crime is self-evident.[57]

April 27, 1918. Lynch law has become quite fashionable in Russian villages. I have been told of a recent case when a man was sentenced to death by peasants for adultery, was killed and thrown into a grave, while the woman who betrayed her husband was put on top of her paramour and buried alive.

The faculty of Saratov University have sent a delegate to the Bolshevik Department of Education in Moscow with a protest against violations of university autonomy by the local Bolshevik rulers.

May 1, 1918. Today's celebration had an almost exclusively military and official character. The civilian population took no part in the ceremonies for the day, much as they had been advertised by the Bolshevik authorities. A worker said to me this morning: "Let them blow their sirens all they want: they won't see any of us in their processions!"

It is said that last year the whole population of the city had turned out on the first of May, that the parade had lasted over three hours and had been about five miles long.

56. Founded in 1667, Kamyshin became a district center in 1797. By 1917 it had a reputation for being a merchant's town, known for its sawmills and flour mills. It is now located in Volgograd oblast.

57. Although this event occurred, Lebedev, head of the local judicial organs, had no idea of who issued such an order or why. It should be recalled that criminal elements from other cities had flooded Saratov at this time.

May 4, 1918. At the vigilance league headquarters Mr. Mittel'man told us tonight about having been compelled to pay an "indemnity" of five thousand rubles to our Bolshevik conquerors. Four or five armed men drove up in an auto to his store and peremptorily ordered him either to pay the assessed sum or to go to jail with them. The attempt to bargain with them failed, and the money was paid, "in good money," too, since they would not accept any government stock whatever. Later in the evening a company of seven or eight Jewish businessmen settled themselves at the green table and gambled until 4 A.M., poor Mr. Mittel'man being one of them.

May 10, 1918. Yesterday afternoon I was told that three German delegates had come to Saratov and proposed to our satraps to move out of the city. Antonov is said to have resigned his position as member of the Executive Council, or to have even been arrested. This afternoon I heard of an order received by the president (Bolshevik) of the City Bank of Saratov to evacuate this institution immediately (apparently to Perm).[58]

May 15, 1918. It was stated last night that Tsaritsyn had been occupied by the Germans;[59] that the day before yesterday one of the steamer lines would not sell tickets to Tsaritsyn; that four hundred Anarchists had arrived from Odessa with bombs and other arms and occupied two buildings; that the Bolsheviks are quietly preparing for flight.[60] This morning machine guns are said to have been placed at Hotel Europa, to cover the Hotel Rossiia where some 150 Anarchists are lodging. The Anarchists came to the Rossiia last

58. Some extraordinary rumors once again. (Perm is a commercial center and important port on the Kama River and the administrative center of Perm province.)

59. The Tsaritsyn Bolshevik S. K. Minin also noted that such rumors circulated. The Germans had not occupied Tsaritsyn; however, there were grounds to fear that they were pressing toward the Volga. Approximately thirty miles separated Tsaritsyn from the Don "counterrevolution," and it was unclear where the Don forces and those of the Germans began and ended.

60. On the evening of May 14–15 the local Cheka disarmed an estimated two hundred Anarchist terrorists ensconsed in the Hotel Rossiia, who had arrived in town a few days before. In connection with their arrival, rumors spread of the imminent collapse of Soviet power, and armed attacks against citizens increased. A decision was then taken to create—to replace the militia—a department of revolutionary defense under the Cheka.

night or early this morning, causing other guests to leave the hotel, and had bombs in their belts. "Something's wrong with our Soviet again," my friend the coachman said to me about ten o'clock this morning: "Nobody is allowed to pass by Soviet headquarters on Konstantinov Street, and an armed patrol is barring the way on Ilin." "A decisive battle with the Anarchists is expected today," said Mr. Knaube this morning, meeting me on the street: "I have closed my store for the day."

But female bread vendors do not worry about the situation and carry on their trade in front of the Rossiia and the Europa.

7 P.M. During the arrest of the Anarchists this morning at the Rossiia two Anarchists and a certain Genkin, a commissar and a rather unbalanced agitator, were killed. At 11 P.M. two cartloads of muskets, sabers, and bombs were brought to the barracks in front of the university library.[61]

May 16, 1918. 10:15 P.M. I was giving an English lesson to Professor Tsytovich[62] and just asked him how old his daughter was when a cannon shot was heard, then another, and another. "What's up? Where are they firing?" we asked each other. As much shooting had taken place near Professor Yudin's[63] residence last year, my pupil telephoned to him, but received no satisfaction. While I was pressing for an answer to my question, a knock came at the door: my perturbed pupil's daughter came in to tell that both she and her mother were back from their walk, and were all right. Having extracted the important information as to the age of the professor's daughter (given as nine since he knew numerals from one to twelve), I went on with the lesson. Soon four more cannon shots shook the air, coming in rapid succession. By 9:30 P.M. we finished our lesson and started on an exploring expedition. But in the lower hall we ran into a crowd of ladies, one of whom explained that part of the Bolshevik army fully equipped for an expedition against the

61. The leading troika of the local Cheka (M. Deich, M. Vengerov, and Ivan Genkin) disarmed the terrorists. In the process, Genkin was wounded in the head. He recovered and later was expelled from the party (January 1919) for bribe-taking and swindling.

62. M. F. Tsytovich, professor of medicine, Saratov University, 1914–30. He later became a corresponding member of the Soviet Academy of Sciences.

63. K. A. Yudin, a member of the faculty of medicine who taught at Saratov University, 1912–30.

 Ural Cossacks all of a sudden refused to go and demanded that the Bolsheviks surrender their authority to someone or other and that a Constituent Assembly be given a chance to decide on the form of government for Russia. Local railroad employees and other workers insisted on the removal of all Jews from the local Bolshevik administration. The mutineers were said to have besieged the headquarters of the local Executive Committee, to be patrolling and guarding the railroad station and steamboat landings in order not to let any of the Bolshevik leaders escape or remove from Saratov any national funds.

May 17, 1918. 11:51 A.M. When I opened my eyes at 5:30 this morning I heard three cannon shots quickly following each other. Our street was empty as usual at this hour of the day. Half an hour later the milkman, the floorwalker, the newsboy, and the housewife appeared, then the *dvornik* [yardman—Ed.] with his birch broom. At 7:30 I heard four more volleys and, looking through the window, I saw the familiar little cloudlet of smoke from a shrapnel that must have burst pretty high in the clear air, somewhere at the crossing of Kazachia [Cossack] and Aleksandrov streets. More cannon, rifle, revolver, and machine-gun shots came; the traffic on our street ebbed and flowed with the cessation and renewal of the fire. At about 9 A.M. I went to the Bacteriological Station to feed Boss, who certainly could not be left to starve on account of somebody's fool civil war. Nemetskaia, Aleksandrov, and other streets did not look depopulated. People stood on street corners listening to artillery and other fire coming from Ilin Square, supposedly directed against the hated Soviet Executive building on Konstantinov Street. At the corner of Aleksandrov and Malaia [Little—Ed.] Sergeev there stood an armored car with two machine guns, with big white crosses drawn in chalk on its sides. At the Bacteriological Station I found out that the anti-Soviet artillery was stationed in Ilin Square. From the station the commands to gunners could be distinctly heard. At about 10 A.M. an automobile was heard near the station, and machine-gun fire directed apparently at the Ilin Square batteries. The latter seemed to have replied in kind, and the automobile disappeared. The inhabitants of a corner house at once began to flee to safer quarters, but soon changed their minds. Only at 11:30 A.M. I started on my way home. There was a crowd around the armored car on the corner of Aleksandrovskaia and Malaia Sergeev streets.

Questions were asked of the comrade who poked his head out of one of the turrets. He assured us that the machine was disabled, and that another car was expected any moment that would take his to the repair shop. He showed us, too, a special brass-tipped bullet that could pierce his car's armor.

There was a large crowd on the corner of Aleksandrov and Konstantinov streets. As I came near, I saw that a gentleman was being searched by a ragged and dirty-looking armed comrade. I, too, was ordered to stop and was searched for weapons by another ragamuffin. When I caught up with the searched man, "D——d sons of b——s," he ejaculated with zest. "Here they have been wasting ammunition all night long, and now are bargaining for terms. There is no doubt that the Bolsheviks will pay what is asked of them, and the matter will be settled. . . . What is it all about? . . . Why, part of the Red Army that was about to be sent against the Cossacks demanded three months pay in advance at the rate of 150 rubles a month, and proper insurance for their families. The Bolshevik authorities refused to consider the second part of the question, and consented to pay the soldiers as soon as they had reached their destination. But the warriors insisted on being paid before embarking on their dangerous expedition, and refused to leave Saratov. 'Then we will disarm and punish you,' threatened the Bolshevik leaders. 'Try it,' replied the soldiers. . . . And they are trying it."[64]

64. An uprising broke out in Saratov on May 16 among artillerymen from the Third Battery and more than 600 Red Army soldiers, who, in getting ready to depart for the front, announced that they would do so only if they received two months' pay in advance, better equipment, and additional training. The earlier departure for the Ural front of its most reliable forces made the Saratov Soviet particularly vulnerable. When the artillerymen refused to remove their artillery from Ilin Square, negotiations with the Soviet failed. The insurrectionists, led by N. Viktorov, a former officer, demanded reelection of the Military Department and the Soviet Executive Committee. That evening shooting broke out between the two sides. The Soviet was able to muster only 150 to 200 internationalists, Hungarians, and Czechoslovaks to defend it. On the morning of May 17 the insurrectionists shelled the Soviet building; by noon Viktorov announced they would bombard the city if their demands were not met. The seriously threatened Saratov Soviet cabled Moscow and the local district towns for help. Toward evening a Latvian battalion came to the rescue of the Soviet, which declared martial law in Saratov. On May 18 armed workers' detachments arrived from Atkarsk, Rtishchevo, and Kamyshin, and another thousand from the Ural front, to aid the Saratov Soviet. The Bolsheviks pinned the blame for this uprising on the SRs because that same day Right SRs had put out a

1 P.M. No firing. Traffic on our street is somewhat limited, and stores closed. [I delete a section of the diary in which Babine provides a blow-by-blow account of how many cannon, revolver, and musket shots he heard between 2:38 P.M. and 6:21 P.M.—Ed.]

At 9 P.M. our janitor was warned that a battle might take place on our street and that our house might be fired upon. My landlady went with her children to an upper-floor apartment for safety. I went to bed in my own room.

No streetcars were running today.

May 18, 1918. Waking up at night, I heard two musket shots. All was quiet in the morning, and at 7:30 I went to see Boss. People went about their business as usual, no soldiers were to be seen in the streets. No streetcars were running. I was sitting on a log in the yard of the Bacteriological Station and watching Boss, when a fusillade of musketry was heard from Konstantinov Street at 8 A.M. At 8:16 two cannon boomed from Ilin Square. Two minutes later a machine gun gave a short bark. At 8:18 a musket rang in the distance, at 8:42, another. On my way home I purchased a supply of smoked beef and butter—I had to live on bread and butter and cocoa during the last two days, all restaurants having been closed—and was about to go after some eggs, when firing began on our street. Pencil in hand, I noted the progress of it, reading Sienkiewicz's novel[65] the while. [I delete another detailed listing of what shots Babine

---

single issue of a newspaper, *Golos trudovogo naroda* (Voice of the Working People), which appealed to the Red Army staff to arrest the Executive Committee and hold new elections to the Soviet. (Mensheviks, SRs, and Anarchists had done well in elections to the Soviet in April, but were not allowed into the Executive Committee because they did not support Soviet power without stipulations. Only the Left SRs had joined the Soviet Executive Committee. They also denounced the "traitorous acts" of the Right SRs.) The Soviet liquidated the uprising on May 19, but only after thirty people had been killed and more than that wounded. A local investigatory committee was formed immediately to study why the uprising had taken place; N. I. Podvoiskii, a leading Bolshevik chairing the higher military inspection, arrived from Moscow to take part in the committee's work.

65. Henryk Sienkiewicz (1846–1916), Polish author who was awarded the Nobel Prize for literature in 1905. Babine may well have been reading Sienkiewicz's *Quo Vadis*, which depicts the early Christians' relationship with Nero, or *Whirlpools*, which is set against the background of the Revolution of 1905–7. Russian-language editions of his works appeared almost simultaneously with their publication in Polish.

heard and what he saw from his window between 9:26 A.M. and 8:25 P.M.—Ed.]

It being too dark for making notes now, with no light in the house, I put down my pencil and go to bed. The noise of the battle is dying down in the distance.

May 19, 1918. At 6:30 in the morning I went to the Bacteriological Station to see Boss. There were very few people in the streets and almost no soldiers. Numerous bullet scratches on house walls, plaster and brick dust, and shattered windows bore witness to yesterday's battle. The roadway in front of the Bacteriological Station was considerably scratched by bullets. The west-end windows of the main building were all broken, as well as the windows of a minor building facing the street.

But the anti-Bolshevik revolt has been suppressed. Streetcars are running. Houses are being searched for firearms. Martial law has been proclaimed. Armed mounted soldiers, infantry, and armored cars parade the streets and stop and search whomever they please.

3:45 P.M. A shrapnel head called at Professor Birukov's house quite unexpectedly at about nine o'clock yesterday morning, entering through the upper part of a southside window. The poor professor wants to leave the city as soon as possible.

May 20, 1918. "Are you a Menshevik or a Socialist Revolutionary?" Mr. Chegodaev asked me this morning, taking a seat near my desk. "They" are hunting them down, arresting and slaughtering them wholesale. . . . Two hundred fifty persons are said to have been shot just beyond the railway station. They put five or six prisoners against something or other and were about to shoot them when an old woman protested: "Aren't you ashamed to do this in the presence of mere children?" Upon this the prisoners were conducted somewhere else and executed. Do you know the Peasant Bank building? It is said that the floors are covered thick with the bodies of the Soviet's opponents shot there. . . . Six hundred men are under arrest, and awaiting their sentence. . . . An order has been received from Bronstein [Trotsky—Ed.] to show no mercy whatever.[66]

66. At a meeting of the Soviet on May 30 a certain Pashchenko from the investigatory commission denied that anyone had been shot, and he dismissed the sustained rumors that thousands had been arrested. According to statistics

 May 21, 1918. The report that 250 persons have been executed in connection with the recent uprising against the Bolshevik Soviet is being confirmed. The suppression of the revolt was facilitated by the fact that many of the insurgent soldiers were made dead drunk by a treacherous body which offered to relieve them temporarily of their labors, and furnished the liquor.

Professor Arnol'dov cannot find his son, a high school upperclassman.

Streets are cleared of the public by mounted patrols and armored cars at 9 P.M. It is understood that this measure enables the Bolshevik authorities quietly to dispose of the corpses accumulated in the cellars of the administration building.

May 25, 1918. Mr. Chegodaev was at my desk again today. "Last night I attended a meeting of the local Bolshevik Executive Committee for the first time. I'll tell you, a nervous person or lady might get a fainting fit hearing what was said, and seeing how it was accepted by the audience, seeing the audience itself. . . . Antonov is a big man, broad shouldered, with a face that reminds you of pictures of Christ, and sporting rather long hair. He is a good, impressive speaker, and has his audience under good control. He has merely to raise his finger to stop any noise, and with perfect ease puts an end to overheated encounters, and the moderates' passions. . . . Last night he advocated shooting on the spot every Menshevik and every moderate Socialist Revolutionary[67] they might catch on account of their sympathy with the recent uprising against Bolshevik domination. . . . Vasil'ev is a smallish man, with the face of a monkey, who rushes to and fro on the platform, and gesticulates like a madman. 'What have you accomplished, gentlemen compromisers? . . . You have betrayed the revolution. . . . We shot one hundred of you yesterday, we have shot one hundred today, and we will shoot another hundred tomorrow. . . . You have sold the

---

released later by the commission, 592 people had been arrested in connection with the uprising. Of the 592 arrested, 487 were released, 43 were banished from the province, and 62 receiving a guilty verdict were handed over to the Revolutionary Tribunal. It is impossible to say how many of them may have been shot.

67. Although Antonov did not publicly articulate such sentiments, he did issue a call to arms. He and other Bolshevik leaders expressed anger at the role of the SRs during the uprising (the Mensheviks had not taken part in it, nor had they defended the Soviet).

V. P. Antonov (Saratovskii) addressing a crowd on Revolutionary Square, 1918

Ukraine to Skoropadskii[68] and to German tyranny. . . . The blood of Skoropadskii's victims is on your hands. . . .' The audience roared and applauded wildly. I never in my life saw such a collection of criminal and desperado types as that audience was—and I am sure you never saw anything like it either."

May 26, 1918. At 2:15 this A.M., on my way home from my weekly vigilance league vigil, I met one of my neighbors. "I am just returning from a little party given by a friend of mine who lives in Antonov's house. I was the last to leave and, as we stood chatting in the hall, Antonov appeared and said solemnly: 'Gentlemen, do you know that this is a momentous night? Tomorrow we bury the victims of the recent counterrevolutionary riot, and searches are taking place all over the city. . . . I, therefore, advise you to go home and be prepared.'" "What kind of man is Antonov?" I asked. "He is a rather sleepy looking fellow in a white underwear suit, whose slumbers we evidently disturbed by our talk."

May 27, 1918. "My nephew was arrested, too, but was released by

68. P. P. Skoropadskii (1873–1945), leader of the Ukrainian nationalist movement during the Civil War, elected hetman of the Ukraine after the German occupation in April 1918. A German puppet, he fled to Germany at the end of the year when the occupation collapsed.

 order of the Supreme Military Commission that had come here from Moscow. . . .[69] The commission did not approve of the summary executions perpetrated by local authorities. . . . The latter had men shot on mere spies' reports. . . . About three hundred persons have been shot this way in the Executive Building and in other places. The corpses have been taken to and dumped somewhere beyond the city limits at night when martial law is in force."[70]

An old woman came to a friend of mine and called his attention to the fact that two corpses were lying in the city dumping grounds, one of them attired in a student's uniform.

May 29, 1918. Tsaritsyn is said to have been taken by the Germans; a battle to be in progress at Rtishchevo[71] between the Soviet and the Czechoslovak troops;[72] no tickets to be had at the railroad station.

June 1, 1918. "I just came back from the railroad station after posting an important letter, and was about to open the door, when out walked Professor T. and his wife, who had been calling in my absence. While we stood chatting in front of an open door, two soldiers quite unexpectedly entered the hall, called us in, declared that they had come by the order of the Military Section to search the premises, and at my request produced a search warrant on which my name was not mentioned. The man would not state what they were looking for. As there are four different families living in my flat, I proposed that each should go to his room. But the searching party would not agree to that, since things might be concealed in one room while they were searching another, and had us all

69. The reference here is to Podvoiskii's arrival on May 20. See note 64.

70. As noted, sixty-two people were handed over to the Revolutionary Tribunal. Some may well have been shot, but Babine's report is another rumor.

71. A railroad center in Serdobsk uezd, Saratov province, founded in the 1870s. Local workers had supported Soviet power early in 1917.

72. On May 25, Czechoslovakian troops seized Rtishchevo, Serdobsk, and Penza. Their uprising helped set off full-scale civil war, temporarily making possible the overthrow of Soviet power in Siberia and in the Middle Volga and Urals regions. The Czechs, prisoners of war and deserters from the Austro-Hungarian army, had joined the Russian army in the hope of winning Allied support for the creation of an independent Czechoslovakia after the war. They were in the process of crossing the country to the Far East in order to be sent to fight in France when they quarreled with Soviet authorities. Shooting their way across Siberia, they aided the Whites whenever possible. Their initial success highlighted the weaknesses of the new regime.

cooped up in my study. Threatening me with a revolver and a hand grenade, they made me open my desk, in which they found some twelve hundred rubles in cash—all our combined possessions—which they were bent on pocketing immediately. But I protested, and the searching party discussed the matter among themselves, in Lettish[73]—and seemed to be willing to leave me half of my money. But in the midst of our parley another party of well-armed Letts appeared who cowed the first (quite drunken) pair, found their warrant illegal, explained that no warrant was legal unless it contained the name of the party to be searched, adjudged me all my money, and invited both me and my earlier guests to the Military Section, where the fact of the illegal search was put on record. . . . The second armed force came in response to a call from some of our neighbors, who had refused to admit the imposters before their visit to me and who had had to stand some revolver shooting. . . . I was unable to call for help, since in addition to the two men operating on me and my family a third man stood guard in the hall and a fourth one in the hall downstairs, while the back door was also guarded. There were altogether about twelve men, of whom only two were taken to the Military Section, the rest having quietly and quickly disappeared." (Professor Stadnitskii.)[74]

June 2, 1918. No Moscow papers this morning.

June 10, 1918. There have been no steamers from Nizhnii [Novgorod] since last Monday. The reason is not known. But it is rumored that the Czechoslovaks have something to do with it. They are said to have sunk a steamer carrying Red Army men, and detained the rest of the Volga fleet at Syzran.[75]

June 11, 1918. The number of corpses brought to the university morgue was actually fifty-two. On another occasion Deutsch,[76]

73. Latvian workers who had been evacuated to Saratov during the war were one of the main sources of Bolshevik power. The Latvians' affinity for Bolshevism is well chronicled. See Andrew Ezergailis, *The Latvian Impact on the Bolshevik Revolution: The First Phase, September 1917 to April 1918* (Boulder, Colo., 1983).

74. N. G. Stadnitskii, a member of the medical faculty who taught at Saratov University, 1909–30.

75. A district center in Simbirsk province founded in 1683, located on the right bank of the Volga River.

76. Probably Maks Abelevich Deich, a Bundist who joined the Bolshevik

 president of some revolutionary body or other, brought a prisoner to the university, shot him, and had him taken to the morgue by the university attendants.

June 15, 1918. Germans are reported to have taken Balashov, and the Slovaks to be contemplating a descent on Pokrovsk, just across the Volga from us—whence they may bombard Saratov.

One Medovyi, treasurer of some Bolshevik organization, is said to have absconded with one million rubles in his possession. Bolshevik leaders executed in Samara are said to have had large sums of money concealed on their persons, some of them as much as 200,000 rubles.[77]

Count Mirbach,[78] German representative in Moscow, according

---

party in 1918. Of working-class origin, Deich had fled to America to escape a lengthy prison sentence for heading armed detachments in Dvinsk, Kovno, Grodno, and Belostok. (While in Detroit he met Emma Goldman.) In 1918 he played an active role in the local Cheka and also in suppressing the May 1918 uprising.

77. Owing to the uprising of the Czechoslovakian troops, an SR-dominated "Government of the Committee of Members of the Constituent Assembly" (Komuch) seized power in neighboring Samara on June 8, advancing the slogans "United Independent Free Russia!" and "All Power to the Constituent Assembly!" Relying on military force to stay in power, the Samara government put down Bolshevik uprisings in neighboring towns and, in capturing Kazan on August 6, uncovered large gold reserves from the tsarist government, which were put at the disposal of Admiral A. V. Kolchak. The government succumbed to Bolshevik forces on October 6, in part because it failed to arouse any popular enthusiasm, failed to win over the workers, failed to mobilize the middle classes and army officers, and ignored the peasants. As a participant in the government put it, "The Government was Socialist Revolutionary, unconciliatory even with the Kadets, and the armed force, in its majority, consisted of right-wing elements, hostile to the Socialist Revolutionaries." While in power, though, the Samara government hammered out an agreement with a rival government in Omsk to establish a national anti-Bolshevik government in Ufa. Conflict between socialists and liberals immediately surfaced as well in the Ufa government, which soon had to flee to Omsk; in November the socialists were ousted from it (with the support of the Allies) and Admiral Kolchak was named supreme ruler.

78. Wilhelm Mirbach, German diplomat who participated in the peace negotiations leading to the Brest-Litovsk Peace. In April 1918 he took up the post of German ambassador in Moscow. At the Fifth All-Russian Congress of Soviets the powerful Left SR caucus registered its lack of confidence in the government and attacked a Bolshevik decree establishing "committees of the village poor" (*kombedy*) (see note 94 below). A Left SR (Ia. G. Bliumkin) murdered Mirbach in Moscow on July 6, hoping to provoke a war with Germany. The assassination

to a railroad telegram, has left Moscow in protest against breaches of the Brest Treaty by the central Bolshevik administration.

The Pokrovsk Bolshevik Soviet is said to have received an ultimatum from Samara to surrender its authority within three days to a member-elect of the Constituent Assembly and to a member of the Imperial Duma residing in town. A like ultimatum is said to have been sent to the Saratov Soviet, too.

June 16, 1918. Went to the Volga boat landing this afternoon and saw two riverboats anchored in midstream with two launches sticking to their sides: the boats were being searched for provisions that are now a contraband at the sweet will of the searchers.

June 18, 1918. No ferry boats have been running to Pokrovsk during the last four days: the town is said to have surrendered to the Slovaks.

The Saratov Soviet has received an ultimatum to surrender within six days, tomorrow being the last day. A split is said to exist among the members of the Soviet. Vasil'ev advocates surrender, while Antonov would not mind having the city laid waste by the "enemy's" fire. All last night and today the Military Section, somewhere from its headquarters on Konstantinov Street, has been moving furniture of all kinds, and even palm trees, transporting them by motor vans and other conveyances to an unknown spot.[79]

---

marked the outbreak of a Left SR revolt against Soviet power, which the Bolsheviks were able to suppress within a day, and triggered Left SR uprisings in several provincial cities. The Saratov Left SR organization, an important source of Soviet power locally, actually condemned its party's attempt to provoke a war with Germany and remained in the provincial executive committee until December.

79. Babine again falls victim to fetching rumors, but Saratov was indeed in danger. Following a series of Bolshevik military successes in the spring, the tide began to turn in favor of the Whites. For one thing, the Czech uprising and establishment of the Komuch in Samara had struck close to home. Moreover, General Krasnov had liberated the Don region in May and, claiming Tsaritsyn and Kamyshin, pressed toward Saratov. On July 1, White forces seized Volsk and killed the local Bolshevik commissar; on July 15 they captured Khvalynsk. On June 11 Saratov's Special Army (*Osobaia*) was transformed into the Fourth Red Army on the new eastern front. In view of the growing military threat to Soviet power in Saratov and the mass formation of Soviet units, a special party organ was formed (the *Voennyi raikom*). Meetings were held at factories and in Red Army units to mobilize mass support. The Soviet stepped up measures to defend the city, while party organs expelled unreliable party members.

 No trains are leaving Saratov: the railroad workers seem to be preparing for a strike.

June 19, 1918. At 8 P.M. yesterday all entrances to "Lipki" (the Linden Park) were closed and everybody in the park—men, women, and children—detained almost till midnight and searched by the police. Many revolvers are said to have been found, and five hundred persons arrested. The park is closed today.

As I was walking Boss on the Volga beach, a boy called my attention to a gunboat at one of the landings. "There are cannon on it and machine guns all around. . . . Every tug carries a machine gun. . . . 'They' are going to fight the Slovaks who have taken Pokrovsk. . . . The Slovaks have given our Soviet several days, then gave twenty hours more."

June 20, 1918. Vasil'ev is said to have telegraphed to Antonov from Moscow to surrender without fighting since Moscow and Petrograd have surrendered, but Antonov refused. The Slovaks are reported not to intend to bombard Saratov. The Bolshevik leaders, taught by the example of Samara, where leaders had been cooped up in a grain elevator and six of them executed, have taken up residence in different sections of Saratov, some of them in the Military Suburb. A regular anti-Bolshevik and anti-German army is said to be in the process of organizing in Samara, and some twelve thousand men have enlisted to date.

No newspapers have been received from Moscow during the last two days.

June 24, 1918. Pointing to my stout dog whip, quoth an inquisitive citizen: "For whom is this? If for the 'comrades,' then it is not quite long and stout enough."

June 27, 1918. At 5:17 P.M. I was at last on a train to Riazan.[80] The train was very crowded, and it took me some time to secure a seat in the passageway. At Atkarsk and Rtishchevo bread peddlers appeared, selling four- and five-pound loaves for 12–14 rubles, the same loaves that usually had sold for 20–25 kopecks. Many passengers took advantage of this: "A loaf this size costs no less than 50 rubles in Moscow," they explained. Our porters were especially

80. Administrative center of Riazan province, founded in 1796. Riazan is an old historic town, situated on the right bank of the Oka River.

busy. In their compartment they had a special closet filled with breadstuffs for Moscow.

June 28, 1918. When our train stopped at Kozlov at about 11 A.M., we saw Red Army men rushing back and forth along one of the trains that had come before us and ordering the passengers to get out of the cars with their baggage. After a while both the passengers and their baggage were allowed to return to the cars, and the train pulled out. In about two hours of impatient waiting three or four armed ragamuffins went through our train, ordering the people to give up their firearms and searching the passengers and their baggage. In less than an hour a youthful armed ruffian went through the cars, commanding everybody to get out and to carry his or her baggage "to Kozlov." Since the town was some four miles from the station and the day was very hot, and some passengers had too much baggage to take it anywhere in the absence of proper accommodations, they appealed to the "comrade's" good sense and suggested that there might be some mistake about the order as he had propounded it. He disappeared for a few minutes, to return with an announcement that the baggage was not to be taken to Kozlov. But in about two minutes another armed individual appeared who peremptorily repeated the demand to take the baggage to Kozlov. Having no intention to do so, I entrusted Boss to one of my neighbors and went to look for the almighty commissar himself, to whose sweet will the crazy order had been credited. After a long hunt I finally spotted him entering our car and hurried after him. A sentry at the door tried to stop me. But my chin quickly and firmly went up; without even opening my mouth I showed him with my eyes and with a majestic motion of my right hand with whom it was my pleasure to confer, and entered the car without opposition. To my surprise there were absolutely no passengers or baggage in it—except my own five pieces which were reposing on the racks. I showed the "comrade" my personal identification papers connecting me quite impressively with my university, and pulled a bunch of keys from my pocket. "I'll be pleased to open any or all of it," I suggested. "Which is your baggage?" he asked curtly, and when I pointed to the scandalous amount of worldly goods I carried with me in our democratic times he as curtly said with a quick glance at the racks: "Your baggage has been examined," and resumed his interrupted inspection through our train.

 I immediately joined Boss, and began to watch my neighbors' and everybody else's baggage pulled out of its containers and scattered in front of our now empty train. An ugly looking cur of a soldier, seeing me caressing Boss, wanted to have him shot on the spot: food should not be spent on a dog when so many people were starving. It took some effort to assure the scoundrel that I would hang my dog with my own hands after the hunting season was over. The compromise was accepted, and the noble animal to whom I owed so much was saved.

While I was pleading for Boss, I noticed one of my fellow passengers, an emaciated old peasant who had managed to get 100 lbs. of rye flour for his family, on his knees before a commissar: he was imploring the Bolshevik to let him keep his treasure and save his family from death by starvation. The poor man was not with us when the train was at last allowed to proceed. Along the tracks toward Kozlov we saw large crowds of tattered men and women going south on foot in quest of bread. At Riazhsk a large quantity of flour was loaded on the roof of our car, which was filled with bread hunters, like many a train we met.

The train reached Riazan at 7 P.M. Finding the cabs too expensive, I accepted the services of a drayman who took another passenger besides me to the boat landing along with our baggage.

At the landing I found a long ticket line, and secured a ticket and a stateroom only through an old-time employee and a fair tip. The fare proved to be extremely high in comparison with the good old times, and so were the meals aboard the steamer. The pleasure of traveling on nationalized craft costs money.

A rumor is current that the Slovaks have taken Penza and are moving westward, toward Moscow. No trains have run from Riazan to Penza for several days, and our steamboat was packed with ragged, dirty, and ill-smelling peasants.

On the river bank by the boat landing a middle-aged, weather-beaten, sandy-complexioned peasant was telling about his bread hunting experiences. "We got two carloads somewhere near Viatka. . . . At Simbirsk the Red Army men tried to confiscate our flour, but we—eighty of us, all told—pointed to our army muskets. . . . After that they entrenched themselves and opened fire on us with machine guns. But we got through all right."

June 29, 1918. No trains are running between Riazan and Penza, but our captain saw two locomotives this afternoon, each with a single car, going toward Penza.

June 30, 1918. Arrived in Elatma at 7 P.M. Father and everybody else are well. The town is in the hands of the Bolsheviks, with two ex-convict murderers at their head that had been amnestied by the Bolsheviks after their victory over Kerensky and his crew. Fences are covered with illiterate "decrees," one of which prohibits the circulation of all anti-Bolshevik Moscow papers. The latter, therefore, are not delivered to subscribers, but are collected at the post office. The wildest of rumors arise and find credence in consequence.

Our house, along with many others, was looted last March after an unsuccessful local upheaval against the Bolsheviks, looted by the victorious Bolshevik soldiers and by the rabble from nearby villages. A chest of mine was broken open, a large number of trinkets, valuable tools, and a quantity of miscellaneous ammunition and supplies were stolen. My trunk, too, disappeared from Mme. Popov's brick fireproof vault, and with it all my guns, my American flag, etc., etc.

July 6, 1918. A Lazarevo[81] peasant dealt his wife a nearly deadly blow with an ax for stealing five rubles from him. Since the man was not even prosecuted, another peasant, a young fellow, killed his wife. Not seeing the woman, his neighbors kept asking him about her sudden disappearance. The murderer, in the meantime, paying frequent visits to the woods where his victim had been buried, was observed by the village shepherd, and confessed. The body was exhumed and properly buried according to the Orthodox Church ritual, the murderer and his accomplices (his father and mother) having been compelled to act as pallbearers. After the funeral the murderer, with an ax attached to his neck, was led through his own and two neighboring villages, and then he as well as his father and mother were sent to Sassovo[82] "for execution." But in four days all of them returned home scot-free. The murderer immediately joined the Red Army and is now enjoying its protection.

July 9, 1918. Yesterday the local Bolshevik committee posted a warn-

81. Most likely a village in Riazan province.

82. A settlement in Riazan province, located on the Tsna River of the Oka River basin.

 ing to the effect that all attempts to overthrow the Bolshevik regime would be punished by death. This afternoon I called at the Bolshevik headquarters in order to get a permit to purchase a shotgun, but was told that Lepniov, *the* commissar, had gone to Alferievo[83] for the day to disarm the local population that had brought all sorts of firearms from the front. The Alferievo rabble was the fiercest at the plundering of Elatma last March, and it struck me as somewhat curious that the same supporters of the Bolsheviks had to be disarmed now. At about 8:30 P.M. I saw a sentinel posted in the middle of Ilin Square, and a minute or two later was very privately informed that Murom[84] was in the hands of the Slovaks, who had gone there by steamer from Nizhnii, and that something was coming to Elatma from Sassovo, too.

July 10, 1918. The town jail warden reported to our neighbor this morning that the Slovaks have taken Murom and were expected here last night.

July 12, 1918. A meeting of citizens for the purpose of apportioning the town meadowland, announced for twelve o'clock, had hardly time to come to order when a messenger appeared from the Bolshevik Committee ordering the citizens to disperse at once. The citizens' protest was met with a threat to use force.

Half an hour later a mounted messenger rode all over the town announcing a meeting at 2 P.M. But this one was again dispersed as soon as it met. When the people walked out into the street they saw one Melioranskii rush by, a revolver in hand, shouting to everybody to disperse, threatening to shoot—with some thirty armed Red soldiers at his back. The warriors all marched toward the marketplace.

It is rumored that the Murom loyalist troops, with six wagonloads of arms and ammunition and two machine guns, have betaken themselves to Rozhnov Bor, for which the Elatma Red Army has set out to meet them. Those who passed the committee headquarters this morning say that the sentries and others look as though they had passed one or more sleepless nights, constantly rushing in and out of town and displaying much nervous activity and uneasiness.

83. Probably Alferova, a village in the western part of Riazan province.
84. A district center in Vladimir province, located on the Oka River.

July 16, 1918. F. P. Baikov, of Pustin,[85] was arrested by Lepniov's order for beating in argument a Bolshevik agitator at a public lecture. "What the devil do you attend every meeting for? You must promise never to come to any. . . . Besides, you must always advocate that power must be in the hands of the peasant, even if he be a notorious thief." The committee wrote down a deposition stating the prisoner's guilt, which the prisoner refused to sign. Baikov remained in custody only one night: a committee of his fellow villagers demanded his liberation and threatened the Bolsheviks to cut Elatma off from the outside world in case of noncompliance. The demand was immediately granted.

Having selected a day when all the men had to be at the market in Elatma, Lepniov & Co. raided Pustin and confiscated four army muskets. As soon as the owners returned home and were apprised of the raid, they went to the committee headquarters and, threatening to blow up everybody with hand grenades, demanded that the arms be returned, which was meekly done. Baikov's house was searched for an automatic pistol, which was not found. Certain villagers are suspected of spying for the committee.

July 17, 1918. A Kasimov[86] commissar driving through the village of Dmitrievo was astonished to see the house and the lawn and all the buildings of a local landowner in all their pristine glory as though there had been no Bolshevik revolution at all. "Whose house is it?" the commissar wanted to know. "Our old master's," his peasant guides explained. "What?! Why didn't you turn him out?" "Why should we? He never did us any harm." "Get him out at once," the grand official commanded. But the peasants refused to do anything without a written order. So the commissar went to Kasimov and issued a formal order to dispossess the old proprietor. Before the order reached the village council, the landowner had swept the house of absolutely everything he had, and distributed all his belongings among his peasant neighbors. When the storm passed away, he got his goods back to the last trifle. "Not even a single empty shell got lost," he commented on the event, being an inveterate hunter.

85. I was unable to identify this place.

86. A landing on the Oka River founded in 1152, located 164 kilometers northeast of Riazan.

 July 18, 1918. The Bolshevik detachment sent to the hamlet of Gud against the Murom loyalist troops failed to meet the latter, but has returned to Elatma with loads of gramophones, bedsteads, pillows, mattresses, etc., etc.

July 21, 1918. Vologda is said to have been occupied by the allies,[87] Yaroslavl and Trinity Sergius[88] by loyalist troops. The cholera takes one thousand victims daily in St. Petersburg. A scow loaded with munitions was tugged down the river past Elatma the other day, and had a gunpowder explosion that required some repairs.

From Vyksa[89] there is said to have come a demand for explanation of the causes which had led to the assassination of a forester by the Elatma Red Army detachment during its recent expedition against the Murom loyalists. Should the explanation be unsatisfactory, Vyksa threatens to attack Elatma in force. Lepniov is said to have gone to Sassovo in this connection. The forester was held in high esteem by everybody.

July 22, 1918. Mrs. Avaev went to Moscow last Saturday in connection with the execution of her son, Giorgii, by the Bolsheviks, announced in *Izvestiia*[90] for July 13.

87. Owing to the threat of a German occupation of northwestern Russia, Allied ambassadors had fled Petrograd for Vologda at the end of February, while the Soviet government began transferring the capital to Moscow. On March 5 a contingent of British marines landed in Murmansk to protect the area (and Allied supplies) from the Finns, then under German influence. The Allied governments' representatives actually fled Vologda in late July, and it remained in Soviet hands. See George F. Kennan, *Soviet-American Relations, 1917–1920*, vol. 2, *The Decision to Intervene* (New York, 1967).

88. The ancient city of Yaroslavl, founded in 1010 by Prince Yaroslav the Wise, is located on the Volga River. It is a port and railroad center today. Trinity-Sergius Monastery, the foremost monastery in Russia and hitherto the residence of the patriarch of the Russian Orthodox church, is located in the city of Zagorsk some forty-four miles from Moscow. St. Sergius of Radonezh founded the monastery in the 1340s, which helped unify the Russian lands. The monastery withheld a long siege by the Poles in the early seventeenth century; its rumored seizure by loyalist troops in 1918 is thus highly symbolic. On July 21, 1918, Soviet troops actually occupied Yaroslavl, which earlier had been seized by a group of conspirators linked to Savinkov and purportedly in contact with the French ambassador.

89. A city in southwestern Nizhnii Novgorod oblast near the Oka River, south of Murom.

90. *Izvestiia* announced the execution of Avaev (Sidorov) along with nine other leaders of the Union for the Salvation of the Motherland and the Revo-

The Vyksa forester's house was looted after the murder and his money appropriated by the raiders. The well-known beautiful mare of his is being driven in Elatma by a Communist slut. The forester's wife has committed suicide by hanging herself (after her husband's assassination she asked to be killed, too, but was only dealt a heavy blow on the head and left in an unconscious condition). Two orphans have survived the forester and his wife.

The Bolshevik official organ for July 19 contains a report of the "execution" of Nicholas II at Ekaterinburg[91] in view of the approach of the Slovaks and of a plot to escape from his prison.

July 27, 1918. Simbirsk is said to have been taken by the Slovaks. The Elatma Soviet has been appealed to to send assistance, with rations. The town of Aleksandrov, too, is reported to be in the hands of an organization opposed to Bolshevik authority.

July 29, 1918. This morning I went to the Bolshevik headquarters and asked one of the clerks, Pototskii, if it was possible to examine the fowling pieces confiscated a few weeks ago in Alferievo. Comrade Pototskii knew nothing about those arms, and knowing about my connection with Saratov University where he had friends, introduced me to Comrade Gubyrin, who also had heard nothing about the matter but, as a secretary, promised to make an inquiry of Lepniov himself. Having waited for over an hour in the formerly luxurious, and very familiar to us, drawing room of a vanished friend of mine, a drawing room now turned into a filthy den by the rabble infesting it, I finally accosted Lepniov as he passed by and asked him if it were true that some fowling pieces had been confiscated in Alferievo, that one of them had been identified by Simbirtsev and returned to him, and that he, Lepniov, had promised to restore to any owner a gun if informed in whose hands it

---

lution. The newspaper reported that Avaev, former chief of the Elatma militia, had led the armed uprising against Soviet power in Elatma (see Babine's entry for June 30, 1918). Afterward he fled to Moscow, where he worked as a militiaman in the food supply organs until his arrest. See *Izvestiia*, no. 146 (410), July 13, 1918.

91. Today Sverdlovsk, a major industrial city on the eastern slopes of the central Urals. On July 12, 1918, the Ural Territorial (Oblast) Soviet resolved that the deposed tsar and his family should be executed to prevent them from falling into the hands of the White Army. The executions were carried out at midnight on July 16; on July 25 the city fell to the Czechs.

 could be found. Having come home to rest after last year's work at the university and having no gun, I hoped to be able to borrow one temporarily from the authorities and to return it before leaving town. That was my reason for asking to be permitted to look at the guns found in Alferievo. The terror of Elatma said very politely that only two guns had been found; that one of them belonged to Rozhdestvenskii, and the other taken by Tiutchev, who still had it and could show it to me and possibly sell it. Having thanked my informant, who must have been aware of my peasant connections, I went to Comrade Tiutchev's house. He showed me the gun very readily. It was a domestic-made piece in fair condition, with a handsome sling. But the name on the sling was not Comrade Tiutchev's. I found the price asked too high for my limited means, and went home empty-handed.

August 6, 1918. A few days ago Sennin, one of the local Communist leaders, went to the country to see his sweetheart, and returned to his own old home in Bolshoi Kusmor dead drunk with a crowd of friends. He drove the murdered forester's mare. The poor animal was completely rundown and unfed, so Sennin unharnessed some villagers' teams who were about to start on a day trip to their faraway meadowlands' haymaking. His guns were his authority for this imposition.

August 7, 1918. Twenty gallons of alcohol have been brought to the Bolshevik headquarters from Shatsk for the Red Army's consumption. The Bolshevik authorities are "requisitioning" cattle in the neighboring villages and slaughtering them for their own use and for sale in town at fixed rates.

August 12, 1918. Michael the Hunchback, of Ivanchino, has been whipped by the Red Army men, imprisoned, and heavily fined for selling a pood of rye flour to a citizen for 180 rubles instead of the Soviet price of 5 rubles 50 kopecks per pood. All the excess money has to be returned to the buyer. Commerce having been nationalized, it is impossible, owing to volunteer informers of the most despicable kind, to purchase anything in the way of victuals.

August 15, 1918. I was told this morning confidentially at the Bolshevik headquarters that Lepniov had gone to Sassovo on a spree.

August 17, 1918. Being unable to purchase a central fire shotgun, I went today to Bolshevik headquarters and applied to the Military

Commander, "Prince" L'vov, for a temporary loan of a confiscated piece from their store. The "prince" said that Aleshin would not consent to it. I turned to one of the clerks, who knew both me and my brother, and got a promise from him to see if anything could be done. I took a seat in what used to be Mme. Popov's beautiful drawing room, now converted into a stable and an office of the Military Staff, where kidding clerks disported themselves in a rough and ill-bred manner. Within half an hour my friend whispered to me that there was some hope. A little later he whispered again: "They will give it." At the end of their business day, when Lepniov had left for his dinner, I had an order in my hands signed by Aleshin, directing the military instructor Tsyrkin to issue me a fowling piece for temporary use. I immediately went to the Bolshevik club in search of Tsyrkin and, failing to find him there, went to the barracks nearby. There I found him seated at a table within a circle of Red Army men who were drawing their monthly pay. The air was full of obscene jests and curses fostered and encouraged by the democratic "military instructor," who was not aware of my presence. I stood watching the filthy scrub gang for a few minutes, and finding Comrade Tsyrkin too much absorbed in his duty and his wit, quietly slipped away to call on him some other day.

August 20, 1918. Wishing to obtain some alcohol for V. V. Kurchatov, of Unzha, to be used in preparation of a rheumatism ointment, I went this morning to Dr. Levashev for a prescription. He wrote it out, but said that there was no alcohol in town: he himself could not get any two days ago. I went nevertheless to our only drugstore to learn from the druggist's wife that they had not a drop of alcohol, that my prescription was not valid without a stamp of the Bolshevik town soviet on it, and that her husband had gone to that same soviet in quest of alcohol. I found the druggist at 12:15 P.M. at the soviet headquarters, waiting for the almighty chief commissar. The druggist explained to me how the drugstore had been left without alcohol: the liquid was issued without loss of time to noted inebriates on physicians' prescriptions that are usually presented at certain intervals by the same persons. The druggist thus finds himself unable to fill bona fide prescriptions. The alcohol is issued to him by the Bolsheviks, who recently let him have one single gallon (and a short one at that) while the rest of the thirty gallons intended for his drugstore was used up by the soviet commissars and their boon companions, the city physician Tikhomirov being one of the chief drunkards, who abuse their official access to the now scarce and precious liquid.

August 23, 1918. All stores were closed today by the Bolsheviks and sealed. All merchandise is to be confiscated, and in the future will be sold from a national store, one for the whole town.

August 25, 1918. Complaints are heard of difficulties in obtaining necessary articles at the national store, insufficiently manned and managed by a capricious and willful individual.

August 31, 1918. Having returned from a duck hunt, I was told of several arrests that had been made in town by the Bolsheviks and of an attempt on Lenin's life by a woman.[92]

September 1, 1918. The arrests are said to continue. Lepniov, asked about the meaning of the arrests, blurted out: "They do not depend on me." M. M. Avaev, V. A. Ivanov, Gusev, L. P. Umnov and his son, P. A. Sangin's two sons, and N. P. Zameshaev's son are among those arrested, as well as Prince Gagarin's two boys left in Elatma by their parents who have sought refuge in Moscow from local persecutors.

September 2, 1918. While sitting at my desk, I heard somebody scale the wall of our house with an evident attempt to peep inside. I quickly removed the fly netting from the window next to me in order to catch the intruder, and saw Prince Kildishev's[93] little messenger boy, barefoot as usual. "I was afraid of the dog in your yard," he explained, "and so tried to speak to you through the window. The prince is arrested and wants to see you at once, but he has not been taken to the prison, being sick abed. A soldier is sitting there with a gun."

92. On August 30, 1918, an SR named Fania Kaplan (Roid) shot Lenin. That same day a young officer killed M. S. Uritskii, head of the Petrograd Cheka. Although unrelated, the murder and the attempted murder prompted the Bolshevik government to condone mass terror as a political weapon. Some 512 notables of the tsarist regime were taken hostage and shot; the government decreed that members of counterrevolutionary organizations would also be subject to execution. In Saratov the Cheka shot twenty people accused of counterrevolution, including five former tsarist executioners and fourteen who had participated in the May uprising. Thirty-four more were executed in Volsk for their part in an anti-Bolshevik uprising.

93. I was unable to identify which member of this old princely family Babine assisted at this time.

I hurriedly finished the letter I was writing and went to see the prisoner. Not being sure that I myself would not be arrested, I penned a telegram to a professor friend of mine asking him to intercede in case of need, called on my brother Peter, and asked him to send the telegram over his name in case of my arrest. But dear Peter refused to do it for fear of being arrested for interfering with Bolshevik activities, and I hurried to my friend's side. On my way there, I stopped at the Bolshevik club and found out from an old acquaintance that the arrests had been made in accordance with orders received from the district Bolshevik committee, that the prisoners would not be kept in prison for any length of time, that a fresh telegram had confirmed the report about the attempt on Lenin's life.

At Prince Kildishev's I was told that seven Red Army men had appeared at about ten o'clock that morning to arrest him, their guns with fixed bayonets, making a very strong impression on the womenfolk. When the soldiers saw the aged member of the Duma in bed and were told about his helpless condition, the leader sat down at a table and scratched a note to that effect, with a recommendation to higher authorities to leave him under house arrest. At the same time they referred the matter to a Bolshevik inferior medical assistant (a "feldsher") who soon appeared, but to give the matter more weight, demanded that a physician be called. Drs. Tikhomirov and Levashov then visited the old man and gave certificates on the strength of which the prince was set at liberty. His guard, too, disappeared on Commandant L'vov's order. The soldiers acted all the time as though they had little sympathy with the arrest, but nevertheless searched the house and carried off the remnants of wine found in one of the closets.

The report of Ianin's arrest in Tambov has been confirmed. Melioranskii, the town hospital washerwoman's prodigal student son, has been appointed to the post vacated by Ianin.

September 3, 1918. On my way to a cobbler's I learned from Baroness von Tornau that eight of the arrested men, including Avaev, Ivanov, Gusev, and Zameshaev, had been taken at one o'clock in the morning to Tambov.

No visitors are admitted to the arrested men, and even food brought by their families and relatives is not passed to them.

In the evening I was told confidentially, on good authority, that the above eight men had been taken from the prison on town fire horses, that the drivers on their return had told their friends that the men had been taken to a ravine not far from town, and there shot and buried.

Last Saturday a party of soldiers came to F. G. Shelokhumov's house and took a set of drawing room furniture, two blankets from his bed, and two pillows. "We have use for them," the men explained gruffly. Trying to save one of her pillows, Mrs. Shelokhumov started to run away with it, but was caught by one of the soldiers. "If I had my revolver with me, I would shoot you on the spot," one of the men hissed.

September 4, 1918. An old grizzly peasant is sitting on the steps of our porch and complaining of the impositions that everybody has to suffer from the Bolsheviks. At a recent village meeting those assembled insisted that 50 lbs. of bread a month should be allotted to every person, and pointed to the fact that owing to the amount of work a peasant has to do he cannot subsist on one pound of bread a day. But a fellow from Lubovnikovo, Skotnikov, a member of the Poor Committee,[94] an idler and a loiterer, like all members of these committees, insisted that thirty pounds was enough and tore

94. In response to the hunger threatening the Soviet regime in the difficult summer of 1918, the government enacted a series of desperate measures to guarantee bread for the starving cities. On June 11, 1918, a decree established "committees of the village poor" (*kombedy*), to be organized by local soviets and placed under the supervision of the People's Committee of Supplies. The committees were to extract grain, improve distribution of grain and basic necessities, and promote the policies of the new government in the villages. As an incentive to enroll in the committees, poor rural elements were promised shares of whatever grain stores were uncovered. Designed to split the peasantry, the measure granted arbitrary powers to the committees, and this soon resulted in a power struggle between rural soviets and the *kombedy*. A decree of December 2, 1918, called for reelection of rural soviets and disbanding of the committees. As in some other provinces, however, it later proved difficult to disband the committees of the village poor which had tried, instead, to break up local village soviets.

Located in a grain-producing province, Saratov city was better supplied with food than towns in the central "consuming" provinces. However, as a rich agricultural province, Saratov was targeted for heavy grain contributions. At the end of September an estimated 3,000 workers from Moscow, Petrograd, Ivanovo-Voznesensk, Vitebsk, Kronstadt, and elsewhere descended upon the province, where they resorted to force whenever necessary to achieve their goals. More grain was requisitioned from Saratov than from any other province in 1918.

up the minutes of the meeting and the resolutions passed by some five hundred men present. Everybody wanted to see him killed or trampled to death. And though nobody as much as touched him, he reported eighteen men to the Bolsheviks, who are at present locked up in the Elatma jail. The old man himself barely escaped arrest for raising his voice against the imprisonment of innocent men.

September 5, 1918. Petr Avaev has gone "after mushrooms"—apparently to avoid his brother's fate—the mushrooms representing this time St. Petersburg, as a harbor of refuge from our local murderers.

V. A. Ivanov's wife and three other ladies have searched the premises of the rumored execution, but found no traces whatever of the interment of their loved ones. Mrs. Ivanov has called on Lepniov several times, but always received the same answer—that her husband had been sent away. It is supposed now that the bodies had been thrown into the Oka.[95]

Another version of the affair is circulating now. When the prisoners were being led near a piece of woods, four of the younger ones tried to escape. Three of them were successful in their attempt—their names are given—but one was wounded, caught, and shot on the spot. The rest are said to have been taken to the Melenkii jail. While firing at the runaways, the guards shot one of their number through the stomach. He died at the hospital, and was buried today with military honors.

A member of the Bolshevik staff, Volkov, stated in my presence this afternoon that nine persons had been sent, after an investigation, to Tambov. But he evaded giving any particulars or throwing any light on current rumors as to their fate.

September 6, 1918. On returning home from a call yesterday at 1 P.M., I found Prince Kildishev's little barefooted page waiting for me. "The prince would like to see you at once. . . . They will have to vacate their house after all." I fed and walked Boss, and went to the prince's. The family was busy packing. The old man was quite crestfallen and grumbled most of the time, but the old princess was the usual model of self-control, and busy, while her sweet daughter even smiled faintly at the unexpected and inexorable turn of affairs. I lent a hand and did not return home until after 9 P.M., when more

95. A right tributary of the Volga.

 than half of the prince's belongings had been moved to a neighbor's stable and to a friend's who took in the family for the time being.

This morning I was again at my task by six o'clock, and did not leave it until I became useless. There was nothing left in the house by 4 P.M.

The district notary's clerk, a strong Bolshevik, claims to have spent the night before last at Lepniov's house and to have split his sides with laughter, with his host, over the rumor regarding the shooting of the prisoners. At the same time Lepniov is said to be very depressed over something, presumably the shooting affair.

The place of the execution has been shifted by rumor to the south of town.

September 7, 1918. A Bolshevik employee told me this afternoon that the victims had been executed just below the prison wall and that three of them had managed to escape, owing to darkness. One of the soldiers taking part in the execution had the stock of his gun broken and covered with blood. It is said that V. A. Ivanov had completely broken down and fallen to the ground in a fainting fit. He was killed on the ground, and his body terribly mutilated.

A prominent member of the local Bolshevik administration is credited with stating that the Bolshevik administration of Nizhnii Novgorod had moved to Pavlovo—up the Oka out of reach of the Slovaks.

Izvestiia for September 4 contains an official appeal for a wholesale extermination of all opponents of the Bolsheviks.[96]

September 8, 1918. V. A. Ivanov is said to have piteously pleaded with his executioners for mercy: "I have a small boy to raise." But pity he was granted none. Avaev is said to have been struck in the mouth with a bayonet. The squad did not fire the first volley willingly. There happened to be some confusion among the men. Taking advantage of this, the younger prisoners broke away, and three of them made good their escape. One young man, wounded in the leg, had pluck enough to run back to the city in a circuitous way—having been raised in the country and knowing every inch of it—to allay his father's fears before finally taking to the woods.

96. *Izvestiia* called for the arrest of all Right SRs, for the seizure of hostages from the bourgeoisie and former tsarist officers, and for the execution of these groups should they resist arrest. *Izvestiia* no. 190 (454), September 4, 1918.

Mrs. Ivanov has begged for her husband's body, but was repulsed by Lepniov.

September 9, 1918. Today I heard a new ditty:

Nikolai byl durachok—
Pri nem khleb byl piatachok
Teper' u nas respublika
Khleb stal tri rublika

Nicholas was a simpleton—
In his time bread cost five kopecks.
Now that we have a republic
Bread is three rubles a pound.

September 10, 1918. The execution took place on the other side of the Ivanchino gulch, just by the grove. Ivanov was the first to fall after the volley. Kalugin and two other young men fell, too, though unhurt, and, taking advantage of a thick fog and darkness, crawled away. Avaev also went down unhurt, and feigned death. Finding only six bodies instead of nine, the soldiers fruitlessly searched the woods. Then a hole was dug in the bottom of the ravine, and the dead bodies were cast into it. Avaev was the fifth man thrown in. He happened to fall on his back. His little bundle (the victims were ordered to take their things along with them as though they were to be taken to Tambov) was thrown in after him, and fell on his stomach. An involuntary movement on the part of the dead man made the executioners suspect the truth. At Lepniov's order the man was struck with bayonets in the stomach and chest, and then, after a vain attempt to ward off the blow, in the mouth.

The following persons have been "taken to Tambov": Kalugin, Ivanov, Sviatov, Zabozlev, Zameshaev, Gusev, Korobkin, Avaev, and Zvonkov.

Zvonkov was executed under peculiar circumstances, having been used as a substitute for Divishev. The latter immediately after his arrest sent word to his mother in Kasimov. She came to Elatma without delay, called on Aleshin, reminded him of the kindness with which her late husband always treated him while he was in their service (as a stable boy), and begged our grand ex-murderer and ex-convict to save her son. Being a heavy drinker, like everybody in power, Aleshin promised to spare the young man—for a gallon of pure alcohol. In spite of all scarcity of this important article, the old lady presented it to the satrap. On the morning of the execution, when the prisoners were taken from the death cell, Aleshin took the young Divishev by the arm, pushed him back into the cell and said: "This one is mine," refusing at the same time to surrender him after having locked the cell door and put the key into his pocket. But after the death sentence had been pronounced by the secret Bolshevik tribunal, a telegram was sent to Moscow advising whom it may concern that nine persons were to die for their enmity to the Soviets. Aleshin's interference unexpectedly vitiated this official report, as only eight persons remained at the powers' disposal. So, on their way to the execution ground, the murder gang stopped at Zvonkov's home, took him out of his bed, and shot him to make up the nine.

The place of interment, kept secret by the authorities, has after all been found by a forever inquisitive boy and made known to all interested. The small boy was the first to probe the unfamiliar fresh mound with a stick, to put the stick to his nose and make a face at the odor of the decomposing bodies lying not far from the surface.

September 12, 1918. Lepniov was arrested today at the Bolshevik clubhouse while he was eating his soup. He had his revolver on him, and a number of spare cartridges, and a hand grenade in his pockets. An eyewitness reports having seen him carrying a parasha[97] to his solitary cell in our city jail. Aleshin tried to evade arrest, but was eventually caught and locked up. The arrests were made by order of a special commission that had come from Tambov to investigate our tyrant's activities. With the commission came one Burevoi, a former member of the Bolshevik administration in Elatma, who had dared to disagree with Ianin, was imprisoned, and nearly starved to death by Ianin, but who finally succeeded in exposing this and other worthies.

September 14, 1918. [Here Babine provides more rumors about the executions—Ed.]

September 19, 1918. Lepniov and Aleshin were taken to Tambov today in irons and under a special trusty guard. The order to deport them was issued by the prosecuting attorney, Starchenko, a brilliant young man, graduate of the Lazarev Institute of Oriental Languages in Moscow and a former dragoman to the Russian legation in Persia. He is said to feel his present position under the Bolsheviks

97. A bucket used as a toilet in prisons.

and even his life unsafe. I have met him many times socially and failed to discern any traces of Bolshevik sympathies in him. The Tambov military commissar, Shidarev, after having investigated the murder of the Vyksa forester, is said to have expressed himself in favor of immediate execution both of Lepniov and Aleshin, but was dissuaded by Starchenko, who knew well enough that the Bolshevik garrison of Elatma could not be depended upon, and might revolt.

September 20, 1918. The bodies of the men murdered on September 2 were exhumed today.

September 21, 1918. This morning the funeral of the victims took place. The morning was rainy, but there was a goodly crowd at the old All Saints' Church and at the cemetery. The rumors as to the identity of the victims were correct. There were buried Avaev and Ivanov, my old schoolmates, Korobkin, Svietlov, Zameshaev, and Zvonkov. They were all good, influential citizens, selected to die during a drunken orgy in a brothel by our present ex-murderer rulers, Lepniov and Aleshin, after an order from Moscow, as a warning to the dangerous bourgeoisie in connection with the attempt on Lenin's precious life.

September 22, 1918. Sunday. With a permit of the local Bolshevik authorities to go to Moscow and Saratov, I left this afternoon on the Grandpa Krylov. By the same steamer went Princess Tamara Kildishev with her daughter, Baroness Von Tornau, and her little grandson, Mitya, with Petrograd as their final destination.

September 23, 1918. We reached Murom quite comfortably at 5 A.M. A drayman charged us thirty rubles to take our baggage to the station, instead of the customary fifty kopecks or a ruble. There we found an immense crowd and a long line at the ticket office. I immediately looked up my favorite old porter on whom I always depended for securing a ticket and a good seat. To my great disappointment, I was told that under the new democratic regime porters were no longer permitted to buy tickets for passengers, and that my good man could no longer be of service to me. The princess was brokenhearted in the face of the immense crowd ahead of us and of the slim chance of getting a ticket. Only a very few minutes before the train time my old porter succeeded in taking me to the administration office, where I explained my predicament, and without much effort got an order to the ticket agent. I bought second-class tickets for everybody, the first class being reserved exclusively for the new Bolshevik aristocracy, but on the platform we were refused admission to our car and were mockingly directed to our last chance, a freight car already full of passengers. Since there was no time to lose, our porter threw our belongings into it, and I hurriedly helped the baroness and her little son into it. The train already began to move slowly, while the diminutive old princess gazed helplessly at the creaking car starting up. There was only one thing left to do, and I ventured it. I picked up the princess like a baby—she did not weigh much over 100 lbs.—put her on the car floor where the rest of her family were already sitting, and swung myself after her. An amused smile from the blushing nobility and a look of decided approbation from the ignoble vulgar were my reward for saving the situation.

And there we sat on our baggage, with dirty peasants and factory hands, and Red Army men around us. Our appearance in the car at once hushed the conversation that was in progress when we first approached it. Although my titled friends were models of modesty in looks (and reality), they looked too trim to be trusted without having been sized up. My remarks to my friends in the vivid and to-the-point vernacular of our village folk put an end to the general restraint, and the conversation resumed its natural course. It was riveted exclusively to the Bolshevik despotism, cruelty, restrictions on commerce, and the constantly growing scarcity of food supplies. Not a voice was heard in favor of the Bolshevik policy of general restriction, oppression, with starvation as their result.

It was a beautiful sunny day. The country we went through was picturesque with its panorama of forest, stream, and broad unfenced fields sometimes stretching for miles along and away from the track. Mitya slept soundly with his head in his mother's lap till we came to Kovrov and had to change cars. Here we were unexpectedly joined by a countryman of ours, and started together to look for accommodations on the new train to Moscow. While the rest of the company went to the second-class cars, I ran toward the international sleeper which I espied in the distance. Quite fortunately I found two vacant compartments, engaged them, and again played a guardian angel for my friends by securing a through compartment to Petrograd for them.

At Kovrov I parted with Princess Kildishev and her family. I arrived in Moscow at 1 A.M. Knowing how hard it would be to secure hotel accommodations, I was only too glad to accept my new friend's, Mr. Shemiakin's, invitation to go to his hotel, the Moscow, kept by an old acquaintance of his and always open to him. It was not easy to get even to the hotel door. Owing to the late hour we had to wait for some time before a cab was in sight. For a trip of a few blocks we were asked twenty-five rubles, or a pound of bread, the latter being preferred. With some hesitation we agreed on the bread, and within five minutes were in front of our hotel. A sleepy porter flatly refused to admit us—the hotel was full. However, having rubbed his eyes open at Mr. Shemiakin's suggestion, he recognized him and let us in.

September 24, 1918. In the morning I went to the International Sleeping Car Office, but was refused a ticket to Saratov without a special pass from the Moscow Workers' Bureau, a body that had sprung up under the free democratic regime. Trying to get around this I went to the Riazan depot with a letter to Mr. Borodin, the stationmaster, but found that Mr. Borodin had died eight months ago. However, his successor promised to help me.

In the evening I went to hear "The Tsar's Bride" by Rimsky-Korsakov at the Bolshoi Theater.

September 25, 1918. At 12:15 P.M. I was at the Education Commissar's office in the old Lyceum building, and with some difficulty and red tape found the person charged with issuing permits to leave Moscow. It was a rather imperious and curt old Jewess dealing out her orders to her subordinates in a rough tone and extending her manner to other persons. I was ordered to write out a formal application, given a scrap of paper, and told to sit where I pleased. But at 4 P.M. I was given the necessary permit, signed by Pokrovskii and duly stamped, with a paper to the Soviet of Workers' Deputies that was to issue final permission to leave the city.

September 26, 1918. At 9:45 A.M. I found at the entrance of Basmannaia 2 a crowd of some four hundred persons lined up and waiting to be admitted. With my special permit in hand I was admitted at once. At 10 A.M. I had my "pass" and at 10:45 a second-class ticket in the international sleeper to Saratov. Saw "The King of the Jews" in the evening, at Nezlobin's [the New Imperial Theater—Ed.]. The play by the royal author was well received.

September 27, 1918. Instead of four, there were nine persons crammed in our compartment. Among these there was a Tatar merchant, a lively old fellow partial to young colt flesh, an old Jew from Astrakhan, and two screechy Jewesses. The last two at first spoke in broken Russian, but soon comfortably settled into their mother gibberish. No food could be obtained at the way stations formerly well supplied, and I had to depend exclusively on the small store of boiled eggs I had with me. The train was searched four times before we reached Saratov. Counterrevolutionaries, weapons, bombs, and anti-Soviet literature were said to be chief objects of the searching parties.

September 29, 1918. Sunday. The train reached Saratov only at 5 A.M., eighteen hours behind time, owing to a large number of freight cars filled with "sackmen"[98] that had been attached to it in Moscow and remained with it until we reached Rtishchevo.

October 1, 1918. Have temporarily settled at a friend's, am sleeping, with him, in his combined study bedroom on a comfortable sofa. I have been unable to find a room as yet. Am dining at a cooperative restaurant fairly inexpensive and neatly managed by intelligent women. Bread and tea, with occasional egg and cheese serve as breakfast and supper.

October 2, 1918. One hundred thirty-five conservatives are being kept on a Volga barge as hostages. They were arrested after the attempt on Lenin's life, in connection with which some twenty persons have been shot in Saratov without even a semblance of a trial.[99]

98. Or "bagmen" (*mesochniki*). Much of the provisioning of towns went on at this time outside the state supplies system. The bagmen trundled objects to trade for food. Although the government disapproved of the practice and occasionally cracked down on the violators, it turned a deaf ear to the practice, which was so necessary to prevent wholesale starvation.

99. By the end of October local Soviet authorities had taken forty hostages in Saratov and sixty-seven in Tsaritsyn. As an interesting aside, it should be noted that a week earlier the Executive Committee, rejecting Trotsky's wishes, refused to place Saratov under martial law. While visiting Saratov, Trotsky clashed with Antonov and Vasil'ev, purportedly not only because of the local leaders' opposition to the powers of military authorities outside their jurisdiction, but also because Trotsky was displeased with the reception he had received. Moreover, local leaders refused to release the hostages mentioned above, despite Trotsky's insistence that they do so. When Trotsky overruled the Executive Committee and introduced martial law anyway, local leaders appealed to Lenin (who sided against Trotsky); moreover, the Soviet announced that it was not subordinate

Since the beginning of Bolshevik rule, about 350 corpses have been brought to the university morgue. Cases are reported when the would-be lifeless forms revived, asked for water, were reported to the powers, and killed for good by Red Army men.

October 6, 1918. Sunday. "I had some interesting experiences while you were on your vacation. . . . I spent a month in jail," said V. I. Petrovskii,[100] settling at my table in a restaurant. "You remember the newspaper report of a trial at which one Sliozberg had stated that the Bolshevik public attorney, Tsyrkin, at one time had been engaged in illicit alcohol traffic and had even been accused of theft. Sliozberg was indicted, referred to me as one of his informers, and I was arrested, tried, and sentenced to three months of imprisonment for libel, though my statements had been supported by a number of witnesses. The tribunal that sentenced me even tried to deprive me of the right of appeal to a higher court, and I was shut up. Nevertheless appeal I did, and the sentence was set aside."

October 13, 1918. At the Second High School for Men the work has not begun yet. All last week was devoted to consultations between teachers and pupils, which developed into political meetings. "It's downright demoralizing," a teacher friend of mine remarked many a time on his return from such consultations. At the First High School for Men the teacher of German, a Jewess, explained to her pupils the importance of the study of languages in general and the German language in particular, the latter being especially important for the study of "The International." In the history class it was proposed to study biographies of celebrities, and first of all of Lenin and Trotsky.

October 14, 1918. For the sake of consistency in their fight against the church, the Bolshevik authorities ordered this morning all markets and stores open—the day being one of the most popular Orthodox Church holidays.[101] The employees of the railway station

---

to the local Revolutionary Council. Trotsky's patronage of T. Khvesin of the Fourth Army resulted in yet another dispute with local leaders and his accusing them of "localism" (*mestnichestvo*).

100. Perhaps Babine is referring to V. V. Petrovskii, a soil scientist who taught in Saratov.

101. It is not clear to which holiday Babine is referring. I suspect that the local church still followed the Old Style calendar and that the holiday was the Feast of the Protection of Our Most Holy Lady Theotokos and Ever Virgin Mary.

 failed to report to duty this morning, with few exceptions, and disregarded the customary siren. The soldiers tried to reinforce the siren with shooting in the air, but only drove the few that had turned up away to their homes. At the university the lectures are to take place as usual: the learned teachers have not the stamina of the common folk.

October 15, 1918. A young woman felt jubilant yesterday because during the day she had obtained meat, jam, and salt by having stood all day in three successive lines.

My hosts are spending most of their time hunting for provisions, in bread, meat, and other provision lines, and cooking and washing dishes. Their work—teaching and hospital duties—at present is a mere side issue with them. I have to go to the bakery shop each morning for my three-quarters of a pound of black rye bread, and to waste there three to four hours in the line for bread.

October 17, 1918. Some five hundred persons are said to have been arrested recently in Saratov for supposed anti-Bolshevik activity.[102]

In front of a mobilization broadside a citizen remarked this morning: "They are going to mobilize three million men against the Allies. Surely, these millions will shed many a bitter tear."

October 18, 1918. The local official organ contains an order to those evicted from their lodgings on twenty-four hours' notice not to trouble the authorities with petitions for leniency, but immediately to move to the outskirts of the city, where basements stand ready to receive the evicted bourgeoisie.

October 19, 1918. Professor Pavlov's charming daughter was buried yesterday. She was killed in a tram accident when the brakes had refused to work on a steep grade and the car, leaving the track, stood on its head. It is said that after the nationalization of the streetcar company last year, three-quarters of all cars got entirely out of repair and that the running ones are mostly unsafe.

October 20, 1918. Sunday. This morning I came across a squad of Austrians[103] dressed in Russian army greatcoats, but armed with

102. I was unable to verify this report. Undoubtedly some arrests were made, but Babine's figures seem exaggerated.

103. Most likely former prisoners of war from the Austro-Hungarian army, and probably Hungarians. The latter formed local revolutionary committees

Austrian muskets. They were moving toward the railway station to embark for the front.

It is rumored that Tsaritsyn has been taken by the Cossacks.[104]

October 21, 1918. In order to save wood we have abandoned the use of our regular kitchen oven and cook our food, almost exclusively potato soup and grits, in our big brick Dutch heating stoves, not at all built for that purpose. Our entire evenings are spent at this task, and we have no time to think about books or to prepare thoroughly for our lectures and lessons. Both our, and everybody else's, pervading problem is to keep alive and to outlast the Bolsheviks.

October 22, 1918. My friend Boris Aleksandrovich Shakhmatov, formerly the head of the National Horse Breeding Department, has fallen victim to our local Bolshevik tsars. He was arrested as a hostage after the attempt on Lenin's life and, as a wealthy landowner, was immediately sentenced to death. A charming man personally who had never done anybody harm, he had many friends to intercede for him in Moscow. The peasantry of his own county and of three neighboring counties sought his immediate liberation. A telegraph order finally came from Moscow to release the prisoner. But the local rabble held back the telegram, had the old gentle-

---

that supported Soviet power. Some of the Hungarians took local wives and stayed in Russia rather than return to Hungary because they were attracted to the possibility of acquiring land.

104. Of extreme strategic significance, Tsaritsyn had been the object of P. N. Krasnov's efforts since summer. On September 22 Krasnov launched a second major assault against this "Red Verdun," and by mid-October the Don Army reached the outskirts of town; however, by October 25 the siege was lifted. (Tsaritsyn finally fell to P. N. Wrangel's forces in the summer of 1919, but by then its strategic significance had been diminished.) The siege of Tsaritsyn occupies a prominent place in the historical (and polemical) literature because of the intense feud between Stalin and Trotsky that broke out in part over the defense of Tsaritsyn. Stalin had been sent there in early June to arrange for the transfer of grain from the northern Caucasus to hungry Moscow. Circumstances forced him to stay in town and involve himself in the conduct of the Civil War. Blaming (Trotsky's) military specialists for the breakdown in transferring grain, Stalin asked for special military powers in order to restore rail transport between the Volga and North Caucasus. It was at this point that local leaders refused to submit themselves to the authority of the commander of the southern front (Sytin), a former tsarist officer. Subject to falsification during the Stalin years, much of what has been written about the episode is jaundiced and must be used with extreme caution. In the second half of October, Stalin was recalled from Tsaritsyn.

 man shot at once, and explained the execution by a delay in the transmission of the telegram.

October 23, 1918. Four thousand wounded Red soldiers are said to have been brought to Saratov from Tsaritsyn. The question was posed of the expediency of converting two university buildings into hospitals.

While I was writing a letter at about two o'clock this afternoon, somebody pulled quite roughly at our front door, then knocked on it, then pulled again, then kicked it. My flurried landlady wanted to know who the uninvited visitor was. "Open!" was the imperious answer. "But to whom shall I open?" she wished to know. "We are from the Housing Section," a rough voice answered. The door having been opened, four unceremonious looking individuals walked in, and a ruffianly looking leader asked: "Who lives here?" "Mr. ———, a high school teacher; Mr. B., a university professor, and myself, Dr. ———." "How many rooms have you?" She showed the men our three small, bare rooms, after seeing which the visitors turned to the door without any further remarks. "There are three of us living here," explained the lady as the men crowded at the door. "Not many," quoth the ruffianly looking leader stepping out. The company went upstairs, then to other apartments in the house.

When the landlady came to, she wondered what the visit could have meant. After my friend's return from his school and their call on our upstairs neighbors, we decided that we would be evicted, since Trotsky and his staff are expected in Saratov[105] and one hundred lodgings have been ordered to be prepared for them.

October 25, 1918. One of the city hospitals received an order a few days ago to remove all icons from its wards. The order was read to the inmates, and the icons removed. A hospital maid expressed great satisfaction with the order: now she could fill her entire room with icons.

October 26, 1918. Passing two women on a street corner I overheard one of them say: ". . . and now He will turn His face away

105. Trotsky did visit Saratov at this time (see note 99 above). Ia. M. Sverdlov, president of the Soviet Executive Committee, also arrived in town (on October 18).

from us, and the earth will open and swallow us for all our indifference. . . ."

A lady physician from Astrakhan, my landlady's old friend, spoke this morning about the destruction and waste of human life wrought last winter in Astrakhan.[106] Last August there was another revolt against Bolshevik power there. A small body of newly drafted men overpowered the local garrison, took possession of arms and supplies, drove the garrison out of town, and occupied the "fortress." The population was jubilant over the prospect of living without the tried and trying Bolshevik rule. Processions took place celebrating the happy event. The workers sided with the insurgents. So did the sailors from the port of Astrakhan. But the joy lasted only three days. One night the sailors arrested the insurgent leaders and had them shot, and disarmed such of the insurgents as had not managed to escape. Then a reign of terror followed. A great many army officers were taken into custody, and later executed.

In connection with the attempt on Lenin's life a large number of persons were wantonly shot, and many were detained on a prison barge on the Volga. It is said that from the latter there is no return.

One of the prisoners, named Kalmykov, was placed in a hospital for treatment. One day two Red Army men entered the hospital, looking for a place for a comrade of theirs. They contrived to dress up Kalmykov and to let him out of his confinement. When the report of his escape reached the Bolshevik authorities, an order was issued to execute all those who had been arrested at the same time as Kalmykov, and immediately to report the execution of the order.

Last July a lady went from Tsaritsyn to the village of Aksai with a military train. Constant and aimless machine-gun fire was kept up during the trip, and the prairie plowed up with bullets first on one side of the track, then on the other. She mentioned cases when plain country folk had been wounded by stray bullets. Farmers are everywhere terrorized and impoverished by endless confiscations of property and supplies—the famous (and infamous)—"requisitions." Aksai was held for one day by the Cossacks: these paid cash for everything they took, and made a favorable impression on the peasantry.[107] The countryside is thoroughly drained of

106. A Cossack uprising against Soviet power had broken out in Astrakhan on January 11–12, 1918, as a result of which part of the city had been destroyed.
107. Complaints against the Cossacks also were expressed.

 foodstuffs. In olden times the prairie at this time of the year used to be covered with endless grain stacks: one sees hardly any of them now. And nobody knows where all this wealth has gone.

Travelers' baggage is constantly searched. In the lady's presence an invalid old man was robbed of his medical thermometer. "We need it ourselves," quoth the searcher.

October 27, 1918. Sunday. Mr. Bogomolets,[108] secretary of the university faculty, was released last Friday from his confinement on the prison barge with fifty-eight others; twenty-eight persons were sent from the barge to the city jail. The barge was dispensed with because the sentries had found it too cold at this time of year.

October 30, 1918. The janitor informed me this afternoon that university janitors were holding a meeting in my lecture room, but that another room would be vacated in ten minutes.

October 31, 1918. My landlady rushed in yesterday afternoon and announced that after the 1st of November coal oil would be issued by ticket, ¾ lb. per ticket a month. She immediately emptied her six demijohns into one immense glass jug and ran after the precious liquid. I followed her example, but after an hour's wandering returned home empty-handed. All stores were either closed or had no coal oil. My landlady found nothing either, but said there was a line in the yard of a house on Ilin Street. There I went with a couple of bottles and found a line of two hundred people. Darkness prevented most of us from getting anything. We were to come next morning, since there were two barrels left over. To make sure of our chances, we gave numbered slips of paper to the disappointed customers. At eight in the morning we were in the yard again, but found two lines there: one with last night's tickets and another one consisting of this morning's arrivals. By both there stood a tricky-looking Jew who refused to recognize last night's tickets. The Jew-tradesman supported him. A compromise was struck by which members of each line were served in turn, though the Jew favored his line, the ticketless one, and quite soon brought it to his own

108. A. A. Bogomolets, a member of the Saratov University faculty of medicine, 1911–25, later elected to the USSR Academy of Sciences. Bogomolets had been a staunch opponent of the autocracy and, more than most members of the Saratov University faculty, gradually came to accept the Bolshevik regime. His sympathy for the new order probably accounts for his release.

turn, and received 15 lbs. of kerosene while everybody else was getting only 10. More than 150 persons went home disappointed, I among them.

November 2, 1918. Last night I attended two inaugural lectures by the newly elected professors, Alekseev and Durnovo.[109] In their colorlessness, lack of organization, poverty of delivery, and general weakness and lack of interest, these two lectures surpassed everything I have so far heard in this university, though last year's inaugural outpourings had been poor enough. Had I not heard Durnovo's lifeless drag last night, I would not believe a lecture could be as poor as that. Even students looked annoyed and bored, and sighed with relief when the bell saved us and put an end to the general torment.

November 3, 1918. Sunday. German farmers[110] just arrived from the southern part of Saratov province report heavy fighting some fifty miles south of them. Ex-soldiers have been taken to the firing line literally from the plough. The Cossacks seem to have left Tsaritsyn to the east of them and to have advanced on Saratov.

November 5, 1918. Lenin is said to have arrived in Saratov today. It seems singular that he should have left Moscow for the first, and probably the only, anniversary of the installation of Bolshevik rule.

November 6, 1918. Today is a half-day holiday. All schools, stores, etc., closed at 12 P.M., and the city has been decorated with red flags (quite shabbily). The statue of Alexander II has been replaced by Chernyshevsky's bust, which is to be unveiled tomorrow.[111]

November 7, 1918. Today is the anniversary of the seizure of power

109. P. I. Alekseev, professor of law at Saratov University, 1918–30. N. N. Durnovo was a philologist who taught at the university, 1918–20.

110. Catherine the Great (1762–96) had subsidized the resettlement along the Volga of German colonists, most of whom settled in Kamyshin district. According to the 1897 census, Germans, residing mainly in Kamyshin district, composed 6.92 percent of the province's population. See Roger P. Bartlett, *Human Capital: The Settlement of Foreigners in Russia, 1762–1804* (Cambridge, England, 1979).

111. N. G. Chernyshevsky (1828–89). Radical social theorist whose ideas influenced generations of Russian revolutionaries, including Lenin. Chernyshevsky was born in Saratov province and undoubtedly for this reason was honored by Saratov Bolshevik authorities as early as 1918. Today Saratov University is named after him.

Mitrofan Market (Photo courtesy of the Hoover Institution)

Waiting in line for bread (Photo courtesy of the Hoover Institution)

Scene from the market (Photo courtesy of the Hoover Institution)

by the Bolsheviks. The system of bread, produce, and other lines is firmly established. The nation unproductively wastes an immense amount of time in obtaining the supplies that have been removed from the market merely to please the despotic rulers' socialist fancies. No butter, cheese, bacon, sausage, sugar, honey, meat, eggs, are to be had in the face of a great abundance of these items in the country.[112] People still have to get up at 3 A.M. in order to get near enough to the head of lines for kerosene, meat, linseed oil, and other items, and frequently go home empty-handed.

The utter disregard of the people's right to life, liberty, and property, the ease with which everybody endowed with intelligence and foolhardy enough to show the courage of his convictions is swept out of existence by order of a small but cleverly organized band of degenerates and by the hand of its pervert hirelings and blind tools, and the pitiless, bloody cruelty of the band begin more and more to convince the intelligent surviving unwilling thralls of the regime that all liberal declarations and slogans of the Bolsheviks are a humbug; that they are meant merely to befool the dark, uneducated masses, to deceive them by promises of liberty, equality, fraternity, and Communist material blessings without end, and thus to secure their physical aid in overthrowing a civilized and hence unfriendly regime; that the real object of the Communist party is to sweep

112. Earlier Babine had complained about the devastation in the countryside. In general, peasants simply refused to market their produce because they received nothing in return from the urban centers. Russia had broken apart into local economic units.

 out of its way everybody to whom the undeceived and awakened people might turn for guidance in their active protest against oppression, and thus to perpetuate its rule.

November 12, 1918. The monthly allowance of kerosene at present is 3 lbs. per person. As I need about 33, I went to the manager of our district store in order to get a larger allowance. A former government official, he criticized the order which limited students to 3 lbs. a month, criticized the red tape that ran riot under the new regime, and advised me to call on one Kondolaky, of the Central Bureau of Supplies. This I did, had my situation appreciated, but not remedied owing to an absence of orders to make exceptions for anybody. The most I was able to get was an order to let me have my allowance direct, without waiting endlessly for my turn.

November 13, 1918. Having obtained by chance the address of a peasant woman of whom millet could be purchased, I walked this morning a distance of about five miles to a certain village and found the old lady making bread. Her little granddaughter informed me of cases when people had been stopped, searched, and robbed of flour, milk, etc., on their way home. I felt rather uneasy, and the old lady did not reassure me in the least, but suggested taking only a small amount of grain. So I took 20 lbs. in my grip and, following her advice, stuck to the city cemetery wall as long and as far as I could, and then, selecting the less crowded streets, stole home. In the afternoon I repeated the operation, followed still a more deserted route, and again got home safely, once narrowly escaping the scrutinizing eye of a Red sentry.

November 18, 1918. Kamyshin is said to have been occupied by the Cossacks, who have taken Balashov, too, and are going to cut Saratov's communications with the rest of the world.[113] The Lettish troops have disappeared from Saratov and apparently have gone to the fighting line.

November 20, 1918. A large two-story log house on the next block is

113. November marked a turning point in the Civil War. Kolchak expelled the SRs from his government and the European war ended, a development that enabled the Allies to step up support for the Volunteer Army. As the front moved closer to Saratov at this time, a peasant uprising broke out in Saratov uezd. Peasants in the village of Alekseevka killed nineteen workers sent to requisition bread.

being torn down by the Bolshevik authorities, with its big barn and storehouse in the yard, for fuel. A sentry in full gear is standing by the ruin to keep citizens from helping themselves to this novel fuel of Soviet invention.

November 22, 1918. At the tea table of a socially humble friend's, with the samovar hospitably whispering and sizzling, I was introduced to a friend of the family, a Soviet official, pale from rheumatism, but good-looking and well built, apparently a mechanic by profession. When the conversation turned to the treatment of the bourgeoisie by the new regime, my new acquaintance spoke firmly in support of a statement of his: "I by no means regret shooting and killing my fourteen men, not in the least." My friend, giving him a quiet look, explained: "Of course, you only saw to their being executed," and nicely shifted the conversation to another topic. My friend is a perfectly respectable man, but his company—sumptuously treated considering the times—was a revelation to me.

November 24, 1918. Was fortunate enough to get the address of a peasant woman in Monastyrka[114] that sold me 10 lbs. of onions for only forty rubles. It was a three-mile long jubilation to carry them home on my back in a gunnysack, without risk of confiscation, onions being an article the Soviets have forgotten to nationalize.

November 25, 1918. The Allied powers are said to have presented an ultimatum to the Bolshevik misrulers in Moscow, demanding unconditional surrender. An order is said to have been received here from Moscow to disarm the Red Army. Some local companies have refused to part with their weapons, though willing to surrender.

November 26, 1918. Petrograd is said to have been occupied by the Allies—to everybody's secret joy.[115]

November 28, 1918. A sudden search of guests in one of the new socialist cafés produced an unexpected result. One customer had a large amount of small change that is so scarce nowadays; another had a large sum of money in Astrakhan and Samara local currencies.

114. A village on the northern outskirts of Saratov.
115. Although threatened, Petrograd did not fall.

November 29, 1918. The cesspool of our nationalized house situated in the center of our small courtyard has been full to overflowing and contaminating the air for over a week. All requests addressed to the authorities to empty it have so far proved ineffectual.

December 4, 1918. It is whispered that Saratov is being quietly evacuated; that trenches are being dug at Uvek, some six miles from the city. Antonov has been given some important post in Moscow, but his local coadjutors would not let him go, preferring to hang together rather than to hang separately.[116]

December 5, 1918. The store of eggs I had laid up before their sale was prohibited is exhausted, and no more are to be had. The official meat allowance is a ½ lb. a week per person of the "second category," i.e., the more favored one. Butter is sold as contraband, and is now offered at forty-five rubles a pound. No tea or sugar was issued last month. I have been reduced to an almost exclusively vegetarian diet. I have rye bread and butter (purchased through a friend's favor) and barley coffee (the genuine is not to be had in Saratov) for my breakfast; cabbage and potato (and at times—but seldom—rice) soup, a very, very diminutive piece of meat, a millet cake, rice and cabbage roll or rice "cutlets," and lentils (or thick millet broth) for my dinner, and millet broth warmed up in a frying pan (sometimes seasoned with sunflower oil and even with onions) and barley coffee for my supper, with hardly any variations from day to day. I take my dinner at a cooperative boarding room, extremely crowded, poorly and negligently organized, very filthily conducted (from a civilized standpoint), but located not very far from my lodging. Once or twice I was lucky enough to get a piece of liver—which I cooked on my faithful oil stove in plain flour gravy

116. Antonov and Vasil'ev had been called to new posts in Moscow, but not for the reason Babine gives. During the second half of 1918 a major feud erupted between local leaders such as Antonov and Vasil'ev and the so-called Dashkovites and other refugees from the Ukraine. In brief, the bone of contention was whether or not the provincial executive committee (*gubispolkom*) should be subordinated to the city executive committee (*gorispolkom*). After a provincial congress of soviets resolved that the city executive committee should be subordinated to the provincial executive committee (the Dashkovite position), Antonov, Vasil'ev, and Lebedev refused to work with the provincial committee and were recalled by the Central Committee. However, local supporters requested that they stay in Saratov until after elections to the Soviet were held in December. They actually stayed in town until early 1919.

or with slim remnants of bacon and bacon rind. I am obliged to hurry to my line for bread soon after 6 A.M. four times a week. But I get enough bread for my consumption only through the courtesy of friends who have no use for their black-bread tickets, having laid up a store of wheat flour some time ago. Not getting any sugar from the Soviet store, I have tried a substitute, the saccharine secretly sold at six rubles a gram. In November only 3 lbs. of coal oil were issued on every provision ticket. In December the quantity was raised to 10 lbs. for individual users, and for lamps. Oil stoves, on which so much cooking has to be done nowadays, have been left out of consideration.

Lodgers, tenants, people in general continue to be "condensed," i.e., packed like herrings in their lodgings. Professor Krylov[117] had fifteen workers lodged in his hall and his student son's room by order of the Housing Committee. Doctor Murashev had his nursery invaded by total strangers under orders from the same committee. Last week a young woman called at Professor Chuevskii's house with a paper from the Housing Committee, authorizing her to examine the lodging. Having done so, she departed, and within an hour she returned, went to the professor's study, put the small bundle she had brought along with her on a sofa, declared that she took her lodging there, and produced a paper from the Housing Committee authorizing her to take possession of the room. She is employed in one of the Bolshevik bureaus, and stays away most of the time, but returns "home" at about 8 P.M. and leaves the professor without any place for his work. An appeal to one Genkin,[118] who is in charge of the condensation work, so far has given no result. A question is now raised of putting somebody—a Bolshevik worker—in Professor Chuevskii's study, i.e., of having the house invaded by total strangers in spite of the owner's courteous (and powerless) opposition.

December 6, 1918. A businessman who had just arrived from Astrakhan and lodged at his sister's was arrested. Three hours later the sister's apartment was searched for money and valuables: sofas, mattresses, pillows were torn open, backs of pictures torn off, men and women ordered to undress to the skin and their clothes exam-

117. D. O. Krylov, a member of the university's faculty of medicine, 1913–25.
118. Babine may be referring here to I. B. Genkin. See note 61.

 ined, women were ordered to undo their hair, etc., etc. Nothing whatever was found: hardly anything could have been better than a three hours' warning.

The Second High School principal has been evicted on twenty-four hours' notice. With his family of six he was occupying four tiny rooms. The authorities have given him lodging consisting of a single living room and a kitchen.

December 7, 1918. Voronezh is reported to have been occupied by the French, St. Petersburg by the English.[119]

December 8, 1918. Sunday. A Bolshevik official has been injected into Professor Granstrem's[120] flat without the professor's leave.

Lepaev, a dry goods dealer, is in jail for selling some of his winter goods without the Bolshevik authorities' permission.

December 10, 1918. Professor Chuevskii's apartment was searched yesterday on his disgruntled cook's complaint. Flour, cereals, butter, tea, and sugar were confiscated. The old professor did his best today to rescue his provisions. The military commandant is willing to admit that the family is entitled to some foodstuffs, and has ordered the confiscated articles returned. But the Soviet financial agent threw in his opposition, and out of mere spite handed the matter over to the auditing department. "Now you may go and try to get it out of them," wailed the old man.

December 11, 1918. The Bolshevik official lodged forcibly in Professor Granstrem's study had four cords of wood issued to him the other day, paying 180 rubles for it. To an ordinary mortal, the same quantity of wood would have cost about 700 rubles.

December 12, 1918. Our ultraconservative Professor Tsytovich[121] spoke diplomatically well about the leading Bolsheviks as men of action today. "They at least have done something. Under the existing conditions one cannot get along without murders if one wants to carry out his policy. And the Bolsheviks have been consistent and

119. Krasnov's forces entered Voronezh province during the summer. On October 6, 1919, the city fell to Denikin and was recaptured by the Red Cavalry commander, S. M. Budennyi, and his forces on October 24.

120. E. A. Granstrem taught in the university's faculty of medicine, 1916–26.

121. See note 62 to this chapter. The reader will encounter Tsytovich again in 1921. See note 15 to the July 10, 1921, entry.

firm in theirs. I have had occasion to deal with their bigwigs and found them intelligent and accommodating. Though I was evicted from my apartment this fall, I still have saved my furniture. . . . When in the process of the lodging condensation they were going to force some 'comrade' on me who had already received proper authorization papers, I called on Genkin, who, it is true, at first turned me out of his office, but later directed me to our local Housing Committee manager who called at my house the next morning at nine o'clock, examined the limited quarters I am occupying, and canceled his 'condensation' order. . . . Then, again, in the case of income tax. I never keep account of my income. For the purposes of income tax, I estimated it at 25,000 rubles a year. But the Bolshevik fiscal agents estimated it at 40,000 rubles and assessed me accordingly. Expecting no good to come out of a protest, I paid my 4,000. But later on, a new 'contribution' was assessed me, as to many others, amounting to 4,000 rubles. This I failed to pay, was fined 1,000 rubles, and had to pay 5,000 rubles in all. This time, in view of the demand to pay the sum within three days and of the danger of having all my property confiscated, I went to one of the bigwigs who scribbled on my notice to postpone the payment. . . . I have not heard a word about the matter since. . . . The new man who has taken Vasil'ev's place, Petr Nikolaevich Minchenko,[122] seems to be a decent chap. I had to operate on him the other day, and he is coming again tomorrow. The excellent tobacco I am smoking this minute comes from him. And I paid only the regular price of 50 rubles a pound, while very poor tobacco now costs 160 rubles a pound."

On the Volga barge the prisoners are said to have been examined with unusual brutality, whipped with an iron chain whenever their statements did not come up to the Bolshevik officers' expectations. One "bourgeois" got more than his fill of the chain and died. It turned out afterward that he had been insane.

December 14, 1918. "What sort of official is that man who just passed you with a red emblem on his sleeve? Is he a Red Cross man? He looks like a Jew, too," a soldier addressed me on a street this morning. "Yes, these Jews like money first-rate, and get all the

122. P. N. Minchenko, a Bolshevik party member who worked in the city's administration. Tsytovich is mistaken about his role.

 best-paid positions. I am going to the Prisoners' War Bureau, having just returned from Germany and am looking for my family. . . . I found my mother-in-law yesterday and learned from her that my wife and four children are in Novouzensk, where life is tolerably cheap. . . . I was confined in a camp in Mecklenburg, near Denmark. There were English, French, and Belgian prisoners in the same camp. . . . Everything that has been published in newspapers about the cruel treatment is true . . . the fare was exceedingly poor, and if we managed to live through it all it was due only to the English and other prisoners who always received plenty of provisions from home and let us have their rations. . . . The English had so much and, toward the end, when English prisoners had been released, many of their parcels were left over and the German authorities had to ask the English government for directions as to how to dispose of them. 'Let the Russians have it all,' was the reply. There were seventeen hundred of us in our group when we got entrained, and each one got a parcel with the most exquisite things in it—canned meat, chocolate, tobacco. You could not get the likes of it in Russia for any price. Our conditions had become especially hard after the traitorous peace: after it we received absolutely nothing from home."

December 18, 1918. Not having been prepared for the emergency of cooking my own food, I had no vessels for the kind of food that was accepted at our house under the new conditions, namely, pots to boil potatoes in, etc. It would have taken a fortune to buy them, and I only suffered in silence for the lack of them. Owing to my social position, there was no hope for me of buying the necessary wares at a Soviet store, to which not even every member of the privileged, the rabble, class had easy access. Yesterday, passing by one of these stores and wistfully glancing inside, I espied Mr. Maizul's sister-in-law, a sweet, modest girl of sixteen or seventeen, who is always seen and never heard, at the cash register. As soon as I got through with my lectures, I stopped at my Jewish friend's. This morning I was at the Soviet store, and gave the manager Mr. Maizul's greetings. "What is it you wish?" In less than five minutes I chose three cast-iron pots, weighing nine pounds and a half, saw them charged to a fictitious purchaser on the books, paid my 29 rubles and 66 kopecks, and went home absolutely happy. Had I met Mr. Maizul' on my way home, I am sure I would have hugged him.

December 19, 1918. Paid eighty rubles for five pounds of sunflower oil (for my grits) that under the bloody tsarist regime used to cost from five to seven kopecks a pound.

December 26, 1918. My regular English lesson with Professor Tsytovich was interrupted at about 6:30 P.M. by a stranger's voice in the dining room wanting to know where the professor lived and how many rooms he occupied. The professor hurriedly stepped out and in a minute or two brought in an unshaven individual in an army cloth "poddevka,"[123] with a woolen helmet and a cheap fur cap on his head. "Who is this?" he pointed to me. The professor explained. "You know who I am and what I am here for. . . . He," nodding toward me, "may act as a witness: it will be unnecessary for me to call in a policeman." [Babine provides a detailed but uninteresting description of the search process—Ed.]

A quarter of an hour later the professor, with a bundle under his arm, after kissing his wife and daughter, left for the Cheka.[124] I took a cup of tea with the rest of the family, went home, and promptly jotted down my experience as a witness to the most dreaded of Bolshevik institutions.

December 27, 1918. Professor Tsytovich was released immediately upon his appearance before the Cheka members, who did not even examine him. He was allowed to keep his shotgun. My impression was all the time that the search was made in order formally to pacify somebody's spite against the man, without any intention of doing him harm.

December 28, 1918. In the line for bread this morning, between six and seven o'clock, the common men and women bitterly complained of the waste of time in all sorts of "lines," severely criticized

123. Men's light, tight-fitting coat.

124. The All-Russian Extraordinary Commission for Combating Counterrevolution and Sabotage (Cheka). It was the first Soviet secret police, founded in December 1917 under the leadership of Feliks Dzerzhinskii, as an agency to investigate opposition to the Soviet regime. During the Civil War its operations expanded to include punitive measures. On February 14, 1918, the Saratov Soviet had created a special department to combat counterrevolution; in May it was transformed into the local provincial Cheka, which opened branches at the district level. See George Leggett, *The Cheka: Lenin's Political Police (The All-Russian Extraordinary Commission for Combating Counter-Revolution and Sabotage), December 1917 to February 1922* (Oxford, 1981).

 the economic policy of the Bolsheviks, and pointed to the disappearance of meat from Soviet stores. "Only the Jews have all the meat they want," was the general refrain. A young worker said: "We have twelve or fifteen of them in our office. When we began to blame them for the present state of affairs, they said: 'Remember 1905–1906.[125] You dipped your fingers in our blood then. Now we are washing our hands in yours.'" The worker was from the Soviet Supply Department. A woman seconded him. She had heard a Jew boast: "We have put you into a bag: soon we will tie the bag."

December 29, 1918. Sunday. Last year the bourgeois tenants were driven out of the large two-story brick apartment house across the street from us, and the building was used as a barracks for "the pride and glory of the revolution." Soldiers began gradually to dismantle it of metal work and of everything else of value. The building had to be abandoned when cold weather came, and now only a ghastly ruin of a dilapidated brickwork remains: doors, window frames, windowsills, and everything else that could be used for firewood was carried off by neighbors—the normal, accustomed supply of cheap wood no longer coming in rafts from the far north, since the forests there had been declared the property of the Soviets, and since nobody wants to work for the Soviets.

125. During the Revolution of 1905–7 conservative elements in Saratov unleashed a bloody pogrom against the city's Jewish population and against the socialist intelligentsia.

1919

The fate of Soviet Russia was decided in 1919. The ever-shifting eastern front remained a major center of military operations. The war advanced on Saratov, which had not only strategic significance, but economic and logistical importance as well, for it had become a major source of scarce bread for the hungry cities of central Russia in 1918. As Admiral A. V. Kolchak approached Kazan and Samara and General A. I. Denikin seized the Donbas and Tsaritsyn, the Poles moved into Lithuania and Belorussia, and General N. N. Yudenich's forces marched on Petrograd. Tsaritsyn, Balashov, and Kamyshin all fell to the Whites that summer, and Saratov itself was on the verge of surrender. Desertions from the Red Army reached alarming proportions. The prominent Bolshevik leaders M. I. Kalinin, V. M. Molotov, L. Kamenev, and A. V. Lunacharsky, as well as local-born men of influence such as V. P. Antonov, who had been recalled by the center earlier, returned to Saratov to bolster the defense of the city. Saratov had been turned into an armed camp.

As the city's Communist rulers became more isolated from the population in 1919, civilian life and administration became militarized. Continual mobilizations further depleted and changed the membership and leadership of the local Communist party and Komsomol organizations; by summer power was concentrated in the hands of a Revolutionary Committee, headed by V. A. Radus-Zenkovich, which had few ties with the district towns in the province. Relations with the peasantry became exacerbated as food requisitions, which the regime deemed essential in order to survive, were carried out more by force than by persuasion, driving many peasants to fall under the influence of bandit leaders. This unfortunate and desperate policy, along with the fact that military operations had greatly reduced the total amount of territory sown, brought on the early stages of what was to become by the end of 1921 a tragedy of harrowing proportions.

Military operations and chaos had disrupted normal life to such an extent that Saratov no longer comes alive on the pages of Babine's diary. Compulsion had replaced market forces, leaving the city without food, fuel, or supplies of any kind. The children's homes were packed with diseased, hungry, and often violent waifs. Refugees continued to stream into the city from the front as townspeople took to the countryside in search of food. The heavy concentration of unbathed soldiers proved fertile breeding ground for epidemic diseases. Corruption, with its long tradition in Russian history, now thrived in conditions of civil war. Human degradation gave rise to preposterous rumors. A telling sign of the times is an article carried in local papers, denying that the wife of the Communist boss in Atkarsk had given birth to the Antichrist, "horns and all."

Babine's entries now concentrate almost exclusively on reports of military operations and on acquiring food, prices for which, according to some sources, had shot up over 900 percent since 1914. Middle-class Saratovites now found that keeping themselves clothed and fed consumed the bulk of their energies. Babine himself left Saratov for the surrounding countryside as the Whites approached, in the hope that he could do better fending for himself rather than relying on an uncertain lilliputian ration that would condemn him to starvation. The reader can also observe how much Babine's political beliefs had hardened: the experience of 1919 convinced him that Russia was incapable of saving itself.

January 6, 1919. A frozen dead horse has been lying for the last three days on the sidewalk in front of the Mitrofan Market, just back of some provision stands. Nobody seems to care about removing the carcass, and the only attention it gets is from hungry dogs painfully sharpening their teeth on the stone-hard meat.

January 12, 1919. Bought two hares yesterday morning at the market, frozen stiff. The two weighed twenty-five pounds and cost me one hundred rubles. By this morning they have sufficiently thawed off to be dressed. To perform the operation, I suspended them from the crossbeam of our closet door by the hind legs, comfortably seated myself in a chair in front of them and, armed with my sharp hunting knife, emptied their insides into a large basin below. I saved the skins for an old lady doctor who intends to have them tanned and later used for a costume. After dressing and unfrocking them I cut up the meat into one-day portions, stuffed it into my precious iron pots, and boiled it on my brazier for about three hours—three hours of constant attention and application of no end of firewood and charcoal. When ready, I put the pots with their contents outdoors to freeze and thus to preserve it as long as it would last.

January 23, 1919. A rumor has landed a large amount of war matériel in southern Russia—heavy artillery, 120 carloads of muskets, a large number of tanks, and 80 "blinding machines."

January 23, 1919. A rumor has landed a large amount of war material in southern Russia—heavy artillery, 120 carloads of muskets, a large number of tanks, and 80 "blinding machines."

There is no meat in the city. Only the Red Army is favored with it, as with everything else that common mortals of all conditions only sigh for. Butter is 50 rubles a pound, flour 5.75 rubles a pood, a chicken can be had only for 80–100 rubles, a goose for 160, a rabbit for 40–60 rubles, a pound of millet for 5–6 rubles. Nobody even thinks of rice nowadays. Even lentils have disappeared this month. It is said that a large quantity of herring, potatoes, and cabbage has spoiled in government storehouses owing to official ignorance and neglect. Kerosene is not to be had in sufficient quantity in a regular manner, i.e., through government stores, and must be purchased from speculators at a high premium. In the line for bread, both common men and women proletarians are protesting against the intolerable and wanton oppression, but cannot mend matters, and pray to heaven for the Allies.

January 25, 1919. The Ural Red Army is said to have revolted, and the Bolshevik rulers to be despondent over the outlook in general. Stavropol is reported to be in the hands of the Allies.[2]

January 26, 1919. Sunday. Am living like a king. When ready for

1. Again, it must be stressed that the Saratov region became a central battleground of the Civil War in 1919, as the ring around the Bolshevik-held area of Russia was almost completely closed. By March, Kolchak's forces had seized a number of Volga-area cities and were marching on Kazan and Samara, while Denikin held part of the Donbas region and was pressing on toward Tsaritsyn. The Soviet government now conscripted the bourgeoisie to complete such tasks as digging trenches, removing snow, chopping firewood, etc. When the Soviet tried to mobilize local prostitutes to dig trenches in July, however, sailors and Red Army men came to their rescue and got into fisticuffs with local police.

2. The Red Army had engaged the Volunteer forces in a decisive battle for the possession of Stavropol on October 23, 1918. After twenty-eight days of combat the city fell to the Whites.

 my dinner, I boil a handful of millet in a pan on my brazier, split off a chunk of frozen hare meat with a hatchet, or a chisel, or a hunting knife, jelly and all, throw it into the boiling pan, and in fifteen minutes have a panful of delicious, nourishing soup that, with black rye bread, keeps me in good humor until I am ready for the next daily dose of the same medicine.

Trotsky is said to have arrived in Saratov.[3]

January 28, 1919. . . . and to have gone to Pokrovsk, across the Volga.

January 29, 1919. 7:30 A.M. The line for bread claims that the reported capture of Uralsk by the Red Army is a canard; that no less than eight Red regiments have gone over to the Cossacks and, naturally, entered their capital; that four Red Army commissars have been killed by soldiers that have mutinied; that to the south of Orenburg[4] six Red regiments have been trapped into wolf pits; that the insurgent troops have occupied the railroad from Uralsk to Ershov.

January 30, 1919. A punitive expedition sent to Uralsk has simply vanished. Nobody knows what has become of it.

January 31, 1919. The Bolshevik central organization has received an official report of the capture of Uralsk by the White Army, which had lured the Reds into battle.

February 9, 1919. Sunday. A Red Army instructor who had smuggled some butter from his native village and sold it to my landlady was led into a talk on military matters. "After all it is curious that having fought Dutchmen for four years we should hobnob with them and wage war against our own people. . . . Soldiers are not in love with Trotsky. . . . Peasants hate him. . . . A peasant has to pay 3,000 rubles for a horse now—a common work horse, and not less than 7,000 rubles for a good one."

February 11, 1919. The flat occupied by Mrs. Kirikov, widow of

3. Trotsky may well have been in Saratov. According to the organ of the Balashov Executive Committee, he had addressed the Balashov Communists on January 14.

4. City on the Ural River, founded in 1735. It served as the main fortress on the Orenburg Military Frontier and was an important center of trade with Central Asia.

Professor Kirikov,[5] was searched recently for jewelry and other valuables. Since part of her furniture is stored in the old university building, the searching party ransacked the latter, too, devoting a whole day to the job and discovering next to nothing. But the day after the search a member of the searching party, a sailor, called on Mrs. K. "We found a piece of broadcloth in your possession yesterday. . . . You may as well let me have it." The poor woman was so frightened that she immediately brought out the required article, and even offered the guest one of her late husband's cigarettes, which the visitor lighted before departing with his booty.

February 12, 1919. I have been told of another search party that "confiscated" everything it could lay its hands on: a wooden snow shovel, a samovar, a hammer, old nails, a piece of cord, etc., etc., leaving the owner in pitiable condition.

February 14, 1919. A terrible epidemic of typhus raging in Tsaritsyn, the local Bolshevik authorities decided to ship ten thousand patients to Saratov, which is better situated with respect to food supplies. Since the Povorino line is partly occupied by the Cossacks, the first transports were dispatched by camel trains to Vladimirovka, on the Astrakhan line, and thence by train to Saratov.

February 18, 1919. At a card party one professor is said to have won recently 3,000 rubles, another 400 rubles.

Some professors are still taking their wonted dram before dinner, diluting pure alcohol with boiled water and adding a bit of sugar to the mixture.

February 25, 1919. No spectacles or eyeglasses are to be had in Saratov.

My hair tonic having given out several days ago and the steady black rye bread and nasty Soviet barley coffee diet proving monotonous and unpalatable, I allowed myself the luxury of pork this morning, having bought three pounds of it for sixty rubles.

February 26, 1919. Reverend Benning, pastor of the Lutheran church of Saratov, has been imprisoned for his refusal to pay a "contribution" of fifty thousand rubles imposed on him by the Bolshevik authorities on the strength of his having formerly handled

5. N. N. Kirikov, professor of medicine at Saratov University, 1911–15.

 large sums of money in connection with his work on behalf of certain war prisoners' relief organizations.

March 4, 1919. Last Sunday afternoon the city's chief criminal attorney was shot by a gang of criminals at the very gate of the prison.[6] Four of the gang were shot by the guards, while the fifth escaped. The murdered man was famous for his competence in tracking down evildoers and was their constant bugbear. It is said that some time ago Antonov had paid him a personal visit and given him carte blanche to deal with the criminal element in the city.[7] "In this case I shall have to imprison at once one-third of the local Bolshevik Executive Committee," the man is said to have suggested. But to this measure Antonov would not give his approval.

March 6, 1919. The price of rye has been raised at government bakeries from 72 to 96 kopecks a pound.

March 8, 1919. The lodgings of one Davydov, on Ilin Street, were searched last night. About 6 cwts. [hundredweight—Ed.] of wheat flour, 1 cwt. of kerosene, some moonshine vodka, and 8,000 rubles in "Nicholas" currency[8] were found and confiscated.

March 9, 1919. Sunday. Passenger traffic between Saratov and Moscow has been discontinued owing to lack of fuel. Only Bolshevik officials will be carried by rail. For common mortals, stage lines are going to be organized.

March 10, 1919. Spent two hours hunting all over the Upper Market for a tablespoon, but found none. Did the same a few days ago in search of some silk buttons for my cutaway, and with the same result.

March 11, 1919. The price of bread has been raised by our Bolshevik authorities to 1.28 rubles a pound—for "Famine Week,"[9] it is said.

6. I was unable to verify this report.

7. Antonov remained in Saratov until the spring of 1919, after he had been recalled to Moscow for reassignment.

8. Currency issued by the former tsarist authorities.

9. Local authorities often resorted to such campaigns to supply grain for the center, enroll new members into the party (party week), clean the city, mobilize forces against illiteracy or epidemic diseases, etc. The food supply situation in Saratov had become particularly grim at this time. In late May rations were reduced to one-half pound of bread per day (three-quarters pound for workers). By May 10 rations were further reduced to one-quarter pound per day.

March 12, 1919. A holiday has been ordered for today to commemorate the overthrow of the monarchy. The experience of the last two years has incontestably proved that politically Russia has been all this time in the clutches of the stiffest and the most brutal monarchy imaginable.

Street robberies, burglaries, and murders are beginning again after a goodly interval of quiet.

March 14, 1919. Today, for the first time since January, I received at our regional store a quarter pound of common laundry soap. The soap is to be had only through speculators, at thirty rubles a pound.

March 15, 1919. It is rumored that the Astrakhan garrison has again revolted against the Bolsheviks and surrendered the city to the English and to Russian loyalist troops that had come from the Caucasus along the Caspian. The Bolsheviks are said to have been besieged in the city Kremlin.[10]

March 16, 1919. Sunday. Ufa is said to have been taken by Kolchak.[11] The Whites seem to be moving toward the Volga.

March 17, 1919. An emissary of Denikin[12] is said to be hiding in Saratov. He assures us that all statements concerning the Allies' indifference to Russia's fate is mere rot; that the Allies will not abandon Russia; that people have no reason for despondency.

10. An anti-Bolshevik uprising did break out in Astrakhan in the spring of 1919. Backed by moderate socialist elements, workers demanded increased bread rations and restoration of free trade. Unrest also erupted in the countryside. Although British forces were located in south Russia, they were not in Astrakhan (they did, however, bombard the city in June). Sent to Astrakhan as a representative of the central authorities, S. M. Kirov successfully suppressed the rebellion. It was here in Astrakhan that he feuded with Trotsky and became part of the cohort that included Stalin and G. K. Ordzhonikidze. See John Biggart, "The Astrakhan Rebellion: An Episode in the Career of Sergey Mironovich Kirov," *Slavonic and East European Review* 54, no. 2 (April 1976): 231–47.

11. A. V. Kolchak (1873–1920), one of the major leaders of the White forces, established the so-called White Directorate, which "governed" Siberia, the Ural region, and the Soviet Far East from November 1918 until January 1920. On March 13, Kolchak's army launched an attack against the Volga, capturing Ufa. In late April he was stopped before reaching the Volga, as a result of defeats in the Buzuluk and Buguruslan regions. On June 9 Red troops retook Ufa, and Kolchak's retreat continued.

12. A. I. Denikin (1872–1947), one of the founders of the so-called Volunteer Army and its commander from October 8, 1918. The Volunteer Army was the chief anti-Bolshevik force in South Russia from the fall of 1918.

 March 18, 1919. Another holiday has been ordered for today, in commemoration of the Paris Commune.[13] While troops were forming on Mitrofan Square for the parade, the bells of St. Mitrofan's Church slowly tolled funeral changes—appreciated, of course, by the Russian rank and file, but not by the non-Christian commanders.

Owing to a very limited kerosene allowance for this month, I have had to resort to the use of charcoal for cooking my dinner and coffee and to devise a special caldron in shape of a double-bottom bucket, with drafts and a tight cover for smothering the fire, which works very satisfactorily and economically.

No firewood is being allowed to private individuals any longer by the Bolshevik authorities. Dreading a winter without any firewood in the future, some people are making plans for moving from Saratov altogether—unless the Allies come and save Russia. Everybody is sure that Russia is entirely incapable of saving herself.

March 20, 1919. Professor Tsytovich has to make his own bed and to wax the floors in the three rooms that his family occupies in Professor Yudin's flat. Professor Yudin was sweeping the floors in his part of the flat this morning, three rooms, a hall, and a small corridor. I spent about five hours today cooking my spare meals.

March 22, 1919. It is rumored that Samara is in Kolchak's hands;[14] that all available troops have been dispatched from Saratov to Samara; that quarters have been prepared here for the Bolshevik Executive Committee of Samara.

March 23, 1919. Sunday. The hand of the clock has been moved forward an hour by order of the Moscow authorities throughout the Bolshevik Empire. Even sluggards have to get up and go to bed quite early, at present two hours ahead of the normal, sun, time.

March 24, 1919. Kolchak is said to be intending to cut off the Uralsk Red Army from its base of supplies by a forced march from Samara. Somewhere in the Urals a deserters' army is said to be forming for

13. For a discussion of the powerful influence the image of the Paris Commune of 1871 had during the Russian Revolution, see Ronald G. Suny, *The Baku Commune, 1917–1918: Class and Nationality in the Russian Revolution* (Princeton, 1972), pp. 353–62.

14. On October 8 the Red Army had seized Samara.

an advance on Saratov. About twenty thousand deserters are said to have collected at Pokrovsk, just across the Volga.

April 6, 1919. A number of searches and arrests are said to have taken place last night here. Several Bolshevik commissars have been arrested, all in connection with "St. Petersburg and Moscow events"[15] hinted at in Moscow papers but unknown to the public.

April 10, 1919. The bread allowance has been reduced from 1 lb. and ¾ lb. to ¾ and ⅓ for the first two categories of Soviet citizens respectively. I have only ½ lb. a day, and am compelled to buy enough for my sustenance at an extortionate price from a Jewish bread profiteer.

April 11, 1919. Lights were put out at one of the theaters, and a proclamation from Kolchak was scattered among the public.

April 12, 1919. The bootleg meat—the only kind to be had—being beyond my means and my university work not connecting me with any laboratory whose alcohol I could trade to peasants for provisions, I took advantage of today's bright, clear morning to buy some eggs. These are now brought from the country by the wagonload and are reasonable in price. Stopping at one of the wagons, I began to "candle" the eggs against the sun, while the peasant owner of the eggs assured me that they were all alike and fresh and I was wasting my time. When I had chosen my lot and laid aside a few, he called to a peasant woman that was watching me with a smile through the operation. The look she gave after examining the two piles was certainly complimentary to a mere townsman.

April 17, 1919. Kolchak is said to be within twenty miles of Samara. There is no general account of military operations in today's local paper.

April 19, 1919. "Samara has been taken by Kolchak." The general is said to be marching on Kazan, Simbirsk, and Uralsk besides. His vanguard is armed exclusively with "hand machine guns." The rear is led by clergy in full robes, with white standards inscribed: "For the salvation of Russia." This rear is uniformed in black with white crosses on the breast: the Red Army never attempts to strike a blow at it, but falls on its knees and surrenders. It is stated by some,

15. It is unclear what events Babine is referring to here.

 even by eyewitnesses, that there is no eastern front: so complete is the demoralization of the Red Army which has neither the wish nor stomach to meet the loyalist Siberian troops.[16]

April 28, 1919. Monday. The bread allowance has again been reduced—to ½ lb. for the first category and ⅜ lb. for the second, and the price of bread raised.

I have been compelled to become my own laundryman.

April 29, 1919. Cossack scouts are said to have appeared not far from Saratov, on the opposite side of the Volga. One thousand men have been sent on motor trucks to meet them.

12:30 P.M. "Novouzensk has been taken" (by the Whites).[17]

"A few days ago sentries at the Bolshevik monument on Theater Square heard cries and groans, as of one weeping, from the little chapel nearby. They threw down their muskets and ran to the Bolshevik authorities to report the fact. Two Bolsheviks were sent to investigate the matter. When they entered the chapel, they saw tears running from the eyes of the wooden icon of Our Lady. One of the emissaries dropped on the floor in a dead faint; the other ran away in terror." Incessant services have been held for the ebbing and flowing crowds of worshippers. I was unable to elbow my way into the chapel this afternoon.

6 P.M. "Urbach has been taken."

16. The spring of 1919 was a major turning point in the Civil War. The Don and Volunteer armies united under Denikin (Krasnov had retired) and in April moved against Tsaritsyn again, this time to link up with Kolchak's eastern front, which approached Saratov. Saratov was transformed into a military base. On April 19 the Saratov Komsomol Organization mobilized all members and sympathizers to battle against Kolchak. That same day the Pokrovsk Bolshevik Organization mobilized its members as well. Not surprisingly, desertion was an enormous problem facing the Red Army and Soviet authorities. Threats of concentration camps, confiscation of property, and execution were used to convince peasants to serve, but often to no avail. Desertions increased when the Red Army was losing ground. They were to become particularly acute that summer in the Balashov region, which fell twice to Denikin. Denikin also seized Kamyshin, located about forty miles from Saratov. According to Soviet statistics, there were 2.8 million deserters from the Red Army in 1919 and 1920. One and a half million of them turned themselves in, in response to promises of amnesty. The rest were captured in raids. Babine's description of the collapse of the Red Army, however, is colored by wishful thinking on his part.

17. Novouzensk did fall to the Whites, but was recaptured by the Red Army at the end of May.

May 4, 1919. Sunday. A general muster of citizens from eighteen to forty-five years of age was called yesterday, to report at 6 A.M. this morning at one of the Volga wharfs, thence to be taken to an unknown place to dig trenches. The *ex tempore* sappers are to bring along bread and water for one day. The present bread allowance is from ¼ to ¾ lb. a day. Last Sunday government employees were mustered the same way. They were taken to Pokrovsk, thence marched fifteen miles into the country, and after completing their tasks under supervision of special taskmasters were marched back to Pokrovsk, returning home at 4 and 5 A.M. Monday.

A party of Cossack scouts is said to have raided Ershov, slaughtered Bolshevik officials in the village, and disappeared into the steppes.

May 5, 1919. The bread ration having been reduced to ¼ lb. per diem, I decided to institute a bread hunt yesterday and went with Professor Tsytovich, his wife, and a lady friend of theirs to the village of Muravievka, about four miles from Saratov. On our way we were joined by Mr. Trutnev, a student of Saratov University, who on his part intended to try for sweet milk in the same place. But in Muravievka my student friend and myself found neither milk nor bread, and went to Rokotovka, another village not far distant. Inquiring at every house, we passed nearly half of the village, finding neither of the products in which we were interested. At the new house of a casual acquaintance of mine, Mr. I. I. Alekseev (or Vorobiev), whom I had met on a woodcock hunt last spring, we were invited to tea, after which we began our labors with renewed vigor, but met with the same luck. We were told many a time that milk had been taken earlier in the morning by other visitors from the city; that as to bread there was hardly any hope of finding any, since the villagers had to buy grain and flour for their own consumption. Some of the villagers rather pointedly referred to the condition into which the country had been thrown by the present government. Entering one of the board-fenced yards and following to the house door a middle-aged man, apparently the head of the family, I saw Mr. T. listen to a refusal administered by a buxom young woman rather neatly dressed and groomed for a village girl. "*Is* there any milk?" asked the man quietly and firmly. "Go and ask your mother." The mother appeared from an inner room, glanced at us with a shy smile, and explained to her lord and master that somebody had promised to bring soap in exchange for milk that same evening. But at her husband's bidding she went to the cellar. "Why only one pot? Bring another so they might have one apiece." And another pot of rich milk came from the cellar and was emptied into our demijohn. Without too strong an entreaty on my part, the host bade the lady to give me a loaf of bread, and when she brought a stale loaf from the closet, he insisted on her giving me a fresh one. I was so touched by his attention that I wished to make him a present of some tobacco (a scarce article in the country)—which he, though not a smoker himself, courteously accepted in order to present it to a friend of his—but gave me some country pastry in return. We flew home delighted, I especially, being rid of the prospect of living without bread for part of the week.

May 6, 1919. Took my turn today at washing the floors in my room and in the kitchen.

May 12, 1919. Last Saturday by 4 P.M. I came to Professor Tsytovich's house in order to join him in a bustard hunt out in the country. But the family sat to dinner only about 4:30. Though I declined the invitation to join the family in their meal, having had an ample dinner at home, I was finally compelled to give in: Professor Yudin had produced a moderate jar of fresh caviar which I had to taste. The caviar naturally had to be washed down with something, so a moderate quantity of alcohol was diluted and a wine glass placed even before me. The mixture was very strong, and I sipped it only slowly, never intending to keep my host's pace. The first installment of the mixture having rapidly disappeared, another dose was prepared. Professor Yudin's eyes became livid, and his speech and behavior began to show the effect of alcohol on him in spite of the rather small quantity swallowed. In reply to Mrs. Tsytovich's remark that of late Mr. Yudin began to show the effect of this poison altogether too quickly—an observation supported by her husband—Mr. Yudin spoke of a change in mutual relations that had taken place since the Tsytovichs moved to his house. He spoke of it in a tone of contrition, but explained it, with tears in his eyes, by certain family reverses that he had not mentioned to anybody. "Oh, 'tis only because you are a gossip and are terribly suspicious withal," quoth Tsytovich good-naturedly, filling another glass. When Professor Yudin stepped out to refill the bottle for the third time, Mrs. Tsytovich whispered to us: "She has refused him. . . ." My glass remaining full, Mr. Yudin insisted that I should finish it, and when I still lingered, he had it passed to him and drank it himself. Then he offered a glass to Miss Tsytovich, who drank it with her father's leave (and two more when he was not looking—out of girlish mischief). Mr. Yudin's movements, and tongue, became very languid, and the kind Mrs. Tsytovich as well as her husband entreated him to take a nap before he began to receive his patients. But he stoutly refused to heed their advice, and soon after 5 P.M. we heard him talking rather raucously to his patients in the next room (his office). In a while the maid appeared and told Mrs. Tsytovich and myself that the professor had put something in a female patient's eye that made this organ swell frightfully—to the patient's consternation, followed by a flood of tears and a piteous appeal to the professor.

At about 6 P.M. we were ready to start on our trip. Professor Yudin came to the yard and begged us to take another drink before leaving the house, but prevailed only on our driver.

By midnight, after a tedious journey in a rickety wagon dragged by a tired horse, we reached Gladkovka, some eighteen miles from Saratov, and put up at Fedor Egorov Grachov's house. Our host reported that the other friends of Professor Tsytovich were fast asleep after a big spree the previous night when two thousand rubles' worth of moonshine vodka was drunk by the company. However, he soon went out, waked up and brought to the house Osip Ivanovich, Nikolai Ivanovich, and a few others who did honor to a bottle of our vodka, to the samovar, and to a very good supper.

We slept on the floor, with black cockroaches disporting themselves freely over our tired frames, and after an early and hearty breakfast (washed down with vodka) our company, enriched by the accession of Makar Ivanovich Rogozhin, a veteran hunter of great experience, drove off in a spring wagon, six guns strong, hungry for bustard meat. The day was cold and windy, and we sighted only one bird, who chose to leave us in the cold. We returned to the village empty-handed, dined at Nikolai Ivanovich's, took a fresh team, Mr. Tsytovich and Rogozhin going in a cart by themselves, and started in quest of bustard once more. We came across three of them this time—but they, too, got away safely. Mr. Tsytovich shot a teal on a pond, and that was all the party got for its pains. After a supper at Grachov's and new libations (Rogozhin was so affected that he had to lie down on the floor) we left Gladkovka.

 Following Rogozhin's advice, we kept one shotgun ready when we approached the Saratov woods, but passed it unchallenged. On the outskirts of the city, and again in the city, we were stopped thrice by Soviet police who wanted to know whether we were smuggling in any provisions. I was in my bed only at 2 A.M., and slept till noon. My booty from the trip was a loaf of fresh bread, a pleasant addition to the daily Bolshevik rations.

May 15, 1919. Comforting rumors are circulating in the city. The Bolshevik Fifth Army has laid down arms. The Sixth Army is totally destroyed. One hundred thousand men of the Red Army have been taken by Kolchak at Buguruslan and Bugulma. Kolchak has crossed the Mother Volga somewhere. Novouzensk has been taken by the Cossacks. The Bolshevik fleet on the Caspian has been totally annihilated by the English. Denikin has sent a part of his force to Uralsk by the Caspian and the Urals, while moving at the same time on Povorino. The Astrakhan fortifications have been leveled to the ground. Sailors, the mainstay—and a bloody one—of the Bolshevik authority in Astrakhan, are fleeing the city.[18]

May 16, 1919. For two days there have been no reports of military operations on the Red fronts. Today's report is evasive and does not satisfy the public that is anxiously waiting for the Bolshevik bubble to burst.

May 17, 1919. In order to purchase some paper shells and other supplies, I had to get a written permit from the head of our county police, who happened to be quick and ready (owing to a note from a friend). But at the nationalized store I found only the shells I wanted (allowed to take only one hundred, and those only because I use a somewhat odd size and high-priced ones) and a bag of cork wads. No powder or shot were to be had, and no primers except the hard Berdan ones.

May 22, 1919. Petrograd is said to have been occupied by the Allies with four army corps.[19] Local papers are reticent about it. An arrival

18. Babine is wrong here. The Red Army actually stopped Kolchak's offensive before it reached the Volga.

19. This report is not true. However, at this time Denikin launched an offensive against Soviet troops on the southeastern front. Pushing outward from the east, north, and west, he concentrated his efforts on reaching Moscow.

from Moscow is quoted as saying that four days ago no passes were granted from Moscow to St. Petersburg.

A private from one of the companies stationed near Uralsk has cheerfully reported that out of two companies only twelve men were left after an engagement with the Cossacks.

Nikolaevsk is said to have been taken by the Cossacks and all Bolsheviks there slaughtered to a man.

There is no money at the government treasury branch, and government employees were not paid on the 15th of the month.

The gold and silver coin shipped from here to Moscow was not allowed to reach its destination: at Kozlov workers detached the specie car from the train and hid its contents somewhere. The special train guards have returned to Saratov, and have been arrested.

"The telephone of the chief war censor was particularly busy all day yesterday and last night. So was the war censor. 'It would be a good idea to lay up a store of supplies and provisions. . . . We may soon have to spend a couple of weeks in our cellars.' "

May 26, 1919. Lubokonskii,[20] a noted Chekist, arrived in Saratov from Moscow last Thursday, and spent the night at Professor Tsytovich's old house in preference to a room prepared for him at Hotel Europa. Since several attempts have been made on his life, he travels with two special detectives in constant attendance. Lubokonskii reported a battle in progress within ten versts of St. Petersburg. According to him, if things should go the way they are going, the liquidation of Bolshevism in Russia may be a question of only a few days. He denied that the Allies had occupied St. Petersburg. On Friday he left for Astrakhan by boat.

May 27, 1919. Have received my salary for the first half of this month today.

Kolchak's position is said to remain firm and unshaken, in spite of all the reports of the official press to the contrary.

May 31, 1919. Desertions from the army are a cause of much concern to the Bolshevik government. Severe penalties for deserting and for harboring deserters do not cure the evil. In the woods surrounding Saratov the deserters are said to have built dugouts in which they

20. I was unable to identify Lubokonskii. Babine may be referring to P. I. Lukomskii (1892–1935), a political officer in the Red Army.

 hide in daytime, coming to neighboring villages after provisions at night. Many deserters live quite openly in their villages, hiding only on the arrival of outsiders.[21]

A member of the local Bolshevik Executive Committee has shown a wireless message to a civilian friend of his stating that St. Petersburg was taken by the Allies on the 26th of this month. "Why don't you make this public?" the civilian asked. The answer was: "We will take the city back in a couple of weeks and then publish all about it."

June 6, 1919. Army desertions do not cease in spite of all government measures against them. A Central Market night watchman tells about a large number of deserters being taken to the execution ground every night "in black carriages." A lady friend of mine was nearly caught recently in a "drive" at the Linden Park directed against deserters. Another lady asked her husband to go to the market and buy some buttons for her. The man did not get home till 9 P.M.; he was caught in a "drive" (which embraced the whole market) and missed his lunch and dinner.

June 10, 1919. Astrakhan is said to have surrendered to the English four days ago.

June 12, 1919. My supply of charcoal running short, I went at 6 A.M., after my daily dose of Sandow,[22] a bath, and a light breakfast, to the woods about six miles from the city, and at twelve o'clock returned home with a bundle of twigs which have made good firewood and may last two or three days.

Electric trolleys have stopped owing to lack of fuel, both hard and liquid.

No war news in today's local paper.

June 19, 1919. "Yesterday at noon came the last telegraph message from Tsaritsyn: 'Send no more messages here. We are abandoning everything.'"

21. *Izvestiia Saratovskogo Soveta* supports these claims. Desertions from the Red Army appear to have peaked at this time. And no wonder. The 35,000 soldiers in the local garrison lacked equipment and boots.

22. Babine was exercising. E. Sandow was a German doctor whose principles of physical exercises using weights became popular early in the twentieth century.

"Tomorrow's local paper will announce the surrender of Tsaritsyn to the Whites."

June 20, 1919. The announcement has come out in an obscure form.[23]

June 26, 1919. Our Lettish neighbor, Mrs. Putz, returned from Novgorod yesterday. The "enemy" is within twenty miles of the city. The Bolsheviks have sent their families away from the city and are ready to flee at a moment's notice. At Chudovo she was told by several passengers from St. Petersburg that part of the city was occupied by the "enemy"; that a great explosion of artillery stores had taken place.[24] "I believe, and so everybody says, that everyone will be White soon. . . . My husband has been sent to the front in my absence—I have no idea to which one. Some say to Rtishchevo to quell a riot of the Greens. . . . [25] But then others say that the troops dispatched to punish the mutineers have joined the latter—my husband, too, perhaps. In this case I may soon see him."

July 1, 1919. My bread allowance has again been reduced to ⅜ lb. a day of rye bread (from ½ lb.). It is rumored that Rtishchevo has been occupied by an organized body of deserters from the Red Army.

July 3, 1919. The Green Army (the deserters) has destroyed the track near Atkarsk, and no trains have been dispatched westward. In Saratov the Greens have "stolen" nine cannon from the batteries

23. The local *Izvestiia* did announce Tsaritsyn's surrender (but not in an obscure form) on June 20. Many Western secondary sources erroneously date Tsaritsyn's fall to June 30, July 1, and even July 2.

24. May through June 1919 was a trying period for the Red authorities of Petrograd who had to defend the city. Although I was unable to confirm Babine's report, the city was under siege at this time and trouble broke out in several large factories.

25. It is true that large bands of armed Greens gathered in Rtishchevo and Arkadak at this time. The Greens were peasant insurgents opposed to Bolshevik practices. Occasional local outbursts grew into major insurrections in some of the black-earth provinces, the Volga basin, North Caucasus, and Siberia in 1920–21. The Green uprising about which the most is known is the rising in Tambov led by a former SR, A. S. Antonov. The Green program called for reconvening the Constituent Assembly, reestablishment of all civil liberties, full socialization of the land, and restoration of a mixed economy. See O. Radkey, *The Unknown Civil War in South Russia: A Study of the Green Movement in the Tambov Region, 1920–21* (Stanford, 1976).

outside the city. This may explain the proclamation of martial law, with its strictest prohibition to citizens to appear in the streets between 11 P.M. and 6 A.M., the authorities making use of the interval in order to remove from the city all grain, sugar, dried fruit, and other material the character of which the night watchman of my acquaintance could not determine.[26] Some government offices, too, are said to be evacuating Saratov.

According to the report of some six hundred wounded brought in last Saturday, Balakovo has been occupied by five hundred Cossacks with two cannon.

A railroad comptroller who just arrived from Astrakhan reports that the city has been bombarded by British airplanes and that many government buildings and some private residences have been destroyed. An ultimatum has been sent to the Bolshevik authorities to surrender the city next Saturday under threat of destruction by hundreds of flying machines in case of noncompliance. The Astrakhan government bank has been moved to Saratov.

The leading Bolsheviks are said to be leaving Saratov. The Jews are moving to villages near the city, which is considered significant.

July 4, 1919. About four thousand searches and arrests were made last night—of army men, lawyers, priests, merchants, and others prominent under the old regime and suspicious to the present band of ex-criminals in the face of the approaching enemy.[27] The working classes of Saratov are said to be in favor of surrendering the city without resistance, while the ardent Communists insist on defending it to the last, though the means of defense are limited, if not problematic. The Greens are beginning to attack, and to destroy,

26. As the Ural and southern fronts closed in on Saratov and Tsaritsyn fell, Saratov was declared to be under siege and all power was concentrated in the hands of a Military Revolutionary Committee. In July and August the Red Army was on the run all along the front; more than at any other time, perhaps, a White victory seemed likely.

27. In view of the deteriorating military situation, arrests were made at this time, but it is unlikely that they were of the magnitude suggested by Babine. The local Cheka had uncovered a plot headed by a former tsarist police agent, Korshen. Local anti-Bolshevik elements had managed to link up with similar-minded groups in Moscow and Samara and plan an uprising that was to coincide with Denikin's maneuvers and with the Green uprisings. On July 19 the Cheka shot eight of the most active members of this "counterrevolutionary" group.

representatives of Bolshevik authority in villages within ten miles of Saratov, and even less. Even the local Bolshevik paper frankly acknowledges the Green danger.[28]

In the meantime the university lights of learning, taking advantage of the latest official salary scales, have swelled their salaries to enormous figures—8,000 rubles a month for the president, 7,000 rubles a month for the deans of faculties, etc. The auditing department, abashed by the figures, has refused to endorse the payroll, and university employees will have to wait for their semi-monthly June salaries until the matter is adjusted between the learned big sharks and the treasury watchdogs.

July 5, 1919. The Russian Orthodox Church bishop of Saratov is said to be among those arrested.[29]

The Lettish railroad regiment of "militia" has received orders to be ready for any emergency within the city—"to be ready to shoot."

The Bolsheviks are said to have telegraphed to Moscow for help, stating that they have in Saratov an army of thirty thousand men, all barefoot and unclad. The working classes, too, demand that no fighting be allowed in town which might endanger their dwellings.

A regiment of thirty-five hundred men has been sent to Uvek with only 500 muskets. Another regiment is about to be sent to the near front with only 45 muskets among them.

July 8, 1919. A "deserter" jumped out of the Military Tribunal building window yesterday, was shot at and missed several times by the guard, and finally killed by a policeman on Ilin Street.

Yesterday I washed my pongee coat. This morning I ironed it with my own hands—and not badly.

July 12, 1919. In order to avoid, at least for a while, the annoying struggle with lack of provisions and to escape from the unsanitary conditions of Saratov, I have moved to Muravievka and taken lodgings (in a haymow) with a peasant acquaintance of mine.

28. This is true.

29. I was unable to verify this report; however, on October 10 thirteen "counterrevolutionaries" were sentenced to death and shot. Among the victims was the former bishop of Saratov, Germogen (N. V. Kosolapov), an acquaintance of Rasputin's and an avowed leader of the local Black Hundreds. His involvement with right-wing groups and ties with Rasputin had scandalized Saratov society earlier. It may well have been that it was Germogen who was arrested as per Babine's account.

The fare is poor. My hosts are disgustingly untidy—but there is plenty of fresh air, a pond to swim in, a steep hill to climb for exercise, woods to tramp in—and a pleasant family nearby to call on.

July 14, 1919. Men, women, boys, and girls are crowding the village in quest of potatoes, milk, bread, eggs, carrots, and carrying their loads in gunnysacks on their shoulders back home. Many return home empty-handed and disappointed.

On my way, at the freight station, a train emptied a crowd of men, women, and children of both sexes under twelve carrying on their shoulders, in their hands, and on the peculiar Russian yokes, bundles of fuel gathered some ten miles away along the Volga banks, and sought after in expectation of the impending firewood famine. "I have laid up enough to last me through three months," a young woman bent under the weight of her heavily loaded yoke joyfully confided to me.

July 15, 1919. Have no bread whatsoever today—my hosts do not furnish it. The Soviet allowance of ¼ lb. for two days did not go further than this morning's breakfast. A neighbor has given me a small piece of bread for my supper.

The necessity of living from hand to mouth and depending on somebody's pleasure for your food gives one a rather curious sensation.

July 19, 1919. Reports of a heavy cannonade come from somewhere down the Volga. Denikin's army is said to be within thirty miles of Saratov.[30]

July 22, 1919. Soldiers, cannon, and ammunitions are being moved toward Uvek. Citizens are drafted to dig trenches around Saratov and to do all manual labor in erecting barbed wire lines, which

30. By the end of July it appeared as if Saratov would fall. All Communists were mobilized to defend the city; the Mensheviks now sided with the Reds against Denikin. Rumors spread throughout the city that Saratov was to be surrendered. Although the local press denied these reports, local party officials had to hold rallies at factories to convince workers otherwise. On July 21, M. I. Kalinin, president of the Soviet Central Executive Committee and a peasant by origin, arrived on the well-known "agit-train" called "October Revolution" to rally the local population.

now surround Saratov on all sides except the riverfront. Professor Tsytovich took advantage of the fact that much wood had been cut down in connection with these operations, and brought three or four wagonloads of it home for fuel.

July 24, 1919. A number of our neighbors come quite regularly to my landlady's every evening for milk. Usually the crowd assembles too early, sometimes before the cows get home; occasionally it will turn into an indignation meeting—a mild one, to be sure—if the news from the outside world or the acts of our much cursed government justify it. Although everybody is cautious, hardly anybody ever has a good word for the Communists. The few peasant Communists in the village—the dregs of the community—are both despised and hated by their neighbors, and justly feared as Soviet spies and informers.

July 25, 1919. Meeting a peasant in the woods, I gradually brought the conversation down to the present Russian situation. "Well," said the tattered, unwashed, and unkempt citizen of the new Russian republic, "No matter how poor a shepherd may be, the herd cannot get along without him."

July 26, 1919. A professor friend of mine came to my village quarters this morning and mysteriously asked me to follow him. We went to his summer cottage along a dense patch of brush, chatting about this and that. Within some hundred yards of the cottage my friend asked me to stop, to watch in all directions away from the brush, and to call if I saw anything out of the ordinary or a stranger approaching. Then he went to the cottage and, emerging from it with a bundle in one hand and a spade in the other, disappeared in the brush. Soon he joined me, spade in hand. "I've buried my silver," he explained.

July 27, 1919. Sunday. Wagon trains of Bolshevik refugees are seen from my hill "observatory" moving toward Saratov before Denikin's advancing forces. The refugees I have met are uncommunicative. The people here are far from friendly to them, since they represent the unpopular Soviet regime, and everybody thinks they got just what they deserved.

August 12, 1919. Somebody said yesterday that Denikin's Cossacks are looting villages and helping themselves to everything in the occupied territory they happen to take a fancy to.[31] The report has made quite an evident impression on my peasant hosts, who have accumulated quite a little money from their sales of milk and other supplies to the starving town people. This afternoon, returning from my tramp to Saratov, I saw the old lady sweeping the cellar floor with a birch broom. There was no doubt that the family had taken advantage of my absence and buried in their cellar under a pile of potatoes their worthless Soviet currency treasures.

August 15, 1919. A lady friend of mine got three weeks in jail for making her own soap, an article monopolized, but not supplied, by the Soviets and much missed by the people who under the old regime had become accustomed to buying it in the open market in any quantity and at a low price.

August 27, 1919. Not wishing to patronize the dirty Soviet barbershops and out of respect for the typhus raging all around, I have been clipping my hair myself with a 000 clip.[32] It takes over two hours, and two mirrors, to do the work right. Two years ago I would not have thought the trick possible.

August 28, 1919. A couple of bachelors have been poisoning cockroaches in their kitchen with arsenic. They threw the dead insects into the yard, upon which their neighbors' chickens died one after another. "Don't worry about our being suspected," quoth the younger of the two: "I've already thrown a quiet hint that our Jewish neighbors must have done it."

September 5, 1919. A paroled prisoner of war happened to come in quest of milk. My peasant landlord wanted to know what Denikin's political platform was. The soldier mentioned among other things "the one and indivisible Russia." "That is right," said my landlord, with an air of supreme satisfaction stroking his long gray beard: "What's mine is mine, and I ain't got to divide it with no riff-raff as they wants it done under this here Communism."

September 18, 1919. Went to the woods this A.M.; with the guard's leave sawed off five stumps with a small handsaw (a laborious operation)—but could only carry four, even those being too heavy

31. And this is one reason why peasants, despite Bolshevik abuses, did not rally behind the Whites as might have been expected.

32. Babine was giving himself a crew cut.

to lift on my shoulder. Finally, I tied them in bundles of two and carried them with the rope over my neck, supporting the loads with both hands. The rope cut my neck and shoulders very badly, and I could proceed only by easy stages—thus having secured some 80 lbs. of oak wood for my little burner, and made about ten miles to do it.

[Babine returned to Saratov for the start of the school year.—Ed.]

October 10, 1919. Got up at 5 A.M., had my cold sponge bath and black bread and coffee substitute for breakfast, and went shooting. Missed two woodcock and brought home one, returning by noon; cooked it for my dinner; lectured at the university in the afternoon; sawed up and split wood for my brazier in the evening; and went to bed by 8 P.M., there being no coal oil to light my lamp with.

October 18, 1919. An army officer who managed to slip in here ascribes Denikin's failure to lack of organization, to inadequate associates in command of the army, to absence of a fighting military spirit among officers, to the dissoluteness and inebriety of the latter, and to the entire absence of reserves that might relieve the worn-out and discomfited ranks in case of occasional defeats. "Denikin is a fine man, but a poor organizer and no disciplinarian."[33]

October 20, 1919. Pencils cost 40 rubles each at the Student Co-op. Today's prices: eggs—16 rubles each, butter—350 to 375 rubles a pound, millet—25 rubles a pound, rye flour—40 rubles a pound, milk—220 rubles a gallon.

December 7, 1919. Going to the university this morning, I noticed a very curiously attired figure ahead of me. In a brown Kalmyk pattern fur cap on his head, a short light-brown coat, and a dark skirt protruding from under the coat, the figure looked like a Chinese. I caught up with him in a hurry, and recognized one of our professors reduced to, or pretending, extreme destitution and wearing an old-fashioned raincoat under a heavily padded, but short sack. Two years ago a man would have been ashamed to appear in the street in so unconventional and shabby a garb.

December 8, 1919. Water pipes having frozen in our unheated kitchen, I had to buy two water pails to carry and to keep water

33. Most historians would agree with this assessment.

in. At the suggestion of an experienced friend, I went to the manager of the household supply section of the United Consumers' Association, but was turned down on the grounds that all pails and washbasins had been assigned to various professional unions. I found myself compelled to bow to my union that I had previously ignored, and armed with a paper from it returned to the Consumers' Association, where an order was issued to me on a Soviet store. At the store I was told that no washbasins were to be had. I therefore returned to the Consumers' Association once more and asked to have a teakettle instead of the washbasin. To get this substitution, I was obliged to apply to the head manager, whom I found fairly intelligent and tractable. At the store I received two iron horse pails for 60 rubles each and a tin coffeepot for 25 rubles. The regular profiteer market price of the pails is 450 rubles apiece.

December 9, 1919. Encouraged by yesterday's success, I went to my union once more. The president, an old man, apparently a worker, scanned my shabby overcoat over his dilapidated spectacles, reinforced with coarse red thread, and with great sympathy in his voice ordered the secretary to endorse my application in full. "God help you to get at least one-third of what you ask for," said he, as he signed it. The manager of the Consumers' Association scaled my list considerably; but still I brought home a tin frying pan (25 rubles), a tin oil can (20 rubles), an iron dipper (18 rubles), and a whetstone (1 ruble 80 kopecks). It took me two mornings to get these things, and plenty of walking.

December 27, 1919. Salted cucumbers are sold at 10 rubles apiece on the market. For this month I, and the rest of the citizens, have received 10 rubles and 12 kopecks worth of provisions from our Soviet store to live on.

1920

Although from a military perspective the tide of events had shifted in favor of the Bolsheviks by 1920, keeping oneself fed, and poorly at that, remained a Sisyphean labor. In the words of contemporary documents, the "economic front" had become every bit as important as the political one; the regime believed forced mobilization of civilians to perform sorely needed tasks remained the only way to avert total economic collapse. From Babine's diary we learn of the growing effects on the city and its population of neglect, physical poverty, and exhaustion. Babine himself succumbed to malaria in August. To put things in better perspective, we might note one local source according to which there had been a 4 to 5 percent discrepancy between workers' wages and expenses in 1914. By 1920 there was a 150 percent discrepancy, and food costs now consumed 75 percent rather than 44 percent of a worker's budget. Sale of one's clothing, it was estimated, made up a substantial percentage of local income as late as 1922. No such study is available on the impact of economic ruin on the middle class. However, from Babine's diary we learn that university professors were grubbing for food like everyone else, and were doing a brisk business in the sale of spirits. The bright side was that they had more things to hawk on the black market than the poor.

The domestic politics of Soviet Russia at the time attracted the interest of foreign observers, sympathetic and hostile alike. Fortuitously, a much acclaimed British Labour party delegation to Soviet Russia in mid-1920 was permitted to include Saratov among the cities it visited. The delegation members' published accounts of their experiences in Red Russia provide brief reactions to Saratov, which complement Babine's observations. Despite the terrible conditions in Saratov, it struck the visitors as a cleaner and better organized town than other Volga cities. Even though Saratov had been turned into a Potemkin's village for the delegation, the great scarcity of food and the tenuous foundations on which Soviet power rested did not escape all members of the group.

As the White armies withdrew from the immediate environs, a new threat challenged local Communist leaders: Anarchist and Menshevik agitators now had little trouble convincing people that Russia was not yet ready for socialism. A good barometer of the proletariat's mood is the behavior of workers at the Zhest factory, a Bolshevik stronghold, who refused to take part in a volunteer workday (subbotnik) *scheduled in honor of May Day, the workers' traditional holiday. The revolution made on behalf of workers had caused civil war and had impoverished the entire country. The popularity of Soviet power by the end of the year must have sunk to its lowest level.*

January 5, 1920. Got up at 3:45 A.M. and immediately started for the bread store. I went to three, to make sure of it, but even at that early hour was 97th, 64th, and 133d in the lines for bread already formed. At 5:30 I returned home, cooked my coffee on my faithful tripod, drank it, and went to the Mulberry Street store. On my way there, I met *our* bread sleigh, followed it, helped unload it (a great and much coveted privilege accorded through the favor of the driver), received my bread second, and was home at 6:45 A.M. On the strength of a new regulation,[1] I received 4 ½ lbs. of bread for six days at once.

January 31, 1920. This morning the crowd at the marketplace, some three thousand persons of all ages and both sexes, was surrounded by soldiers and driven to the railway station, thence to be taken a few miles from the city to shovel snow from railroad tracks.[2] The procession formed a line about two miles long.

February 3, 1920. Went to buy a date stamp at the Soviet store. A girl clerk entered my request on a big sheet of specially ruled cardboard and made three copies of an order to pay the cashier. At the cashier's, six copies of papers were made out and taken to be OK'd by somebody, and only then my money receipted (115 Soviet rubles). With my slip duly stamped, I returned to the first girl, who now wanted a written application for the date stamp. With some

1. Rations were increased as the front receded from Saratov.

2. Militarylike mobilizations of civilians to perform such tasks had been in practice now for roughly a year. See note 1 to the entries for 1919.

difficulty, I persuaded her to wave the point and let me have the article wanted. It was fortunate that I was purchasing it for the student library now in my charge.

February 4, 1920. Wanting about five pounds of wire nails for the new shelving I am going to put in the student library of which I have taken charge (the office carries an extra ration with it), I decided to attend to this business myself, hoping to overawe Soviet officials in my capacity as librarian. Calling at the Sovnarhoz (State Supply Department), I was directed to the Metal Section across the street, fourth floor. There my application was scrutinized and endorsed by two men. A young lady made out an order to the Bookkeeping Section. There I was given a slip of paper with a number on it and with an invitation to call in an hour or so. When I called at the expiration of that hour, my paper was not yet ready—it was to be ready "in ten minutes." I decided to wait and to worry some speed out of the Soviet officials by my unyielding presence. The plan worked: I firmly watched the clock. A boy was sent after my papers, but reported that the "president" was too busy, and that nobody else would sign them. Then the chief went himself, returned with the papers, and passed them to a girl who made out a receipt in three copies. One of these was given to me—to be presented to the cashier of the institution—"second door to the right." Having paid 28 rubles ($14) for five pounds of wire nails, I returned with my receipt to the bookkeeper. After carefully examining the cashier's signature, the bookkeeper returned the receipt to me, adding to it three copies of an order to a central Soviet hardware store to issue the nails to me. I had to walk two miles to the banks of the Volga where the store was, since streetcars have not been running for over a year.[3]

February 20, 1920. During the last two weeks the temperature in my room never went above thirty-five degrees Fahrenheit. Today it is thirty-three degrees. This phenomenon is common everywhere. An assistant of mine usually has thirty degrees Fahrenheit in his room. To keep warm at night, one of my neighbors piles on himself four blankets, a quilted overcoat, and a fur coat. I cannot take more than half of this dose—which is all I have, anyway.

3. Streetcars had not been running, owing to a lack of fuel in Saratov, and to a lesser extent to the disrepair and neglect of equipment.

 February 21, 1920. Just in front of the university this morning, in a heavy blizzard, I met a teacher of German descent of the "People's University" hurrying home and wearing a coarse gray army private's greatcoat, as a clever adaptation to the "democratic" circumstances and tastes of his flock—as he understands it.

February 22, 1920. Constant standing in bread and other lines has resulted in my clothes being so filled with lice that I have to take off my undershirt every night and institute a thorough hunt before going to bed, without being able to exterminate them entirely.

March 1, 1920. Trotsky is said to have arrived in Saratov with his Chinese bodyguard. Lenin is said to have gone to Samara. The flight of both from Moscow is interpreted as the result of a rumored workers' uprising in Moscow and the slaughter wrought among them. The Bolshevik administration is said to have been slaughtered to a man in Astrakhan by the marines who have revolted.[4]

One hundred sixty Anarchists were arrested last Sunday night in connection with their preparations for a revolt against the party in power.[5] Anarchists are said to be conducting energetic propaganda among the Red Army, their program including immediate cessation of war, disbanding of the army, restoration of private property, free commerce, [the slogan] "everybody his own master," and a constituent assembly.

March 28, 1920. Professor Lebedev[6] and his wife are doing their laundry in the kitchen this morning. They have managed to borrow a small wooden tub somewhere, and are heating the water on their little sheet-iron firebox.

4. These rumors are not true. In fact, early 1920 brought major victories to the Red Army, which occupied Tsaritsyn (January 3) and Rostov-on-the-Don (January 8). In mid-January the Allied Supreme War Council lifted its blockade; Kolchak was shot on February 7; and on February 19 the northern government in Arkhangelsk fell to the Bolsheviks.

5. The Saratov press confirms that Anarchist activities and popularity among workers picked up at this time. During recent elections to the Soviet carried out at the Star Factory, for instance, workers endorsed the Bolshevik mandate (a list of desiderata presented by electors to deputies) but elected Anarchists and nonparty deputies. Reports of Anarchist agitation continued through March, and in June a group of them was arrested on charges of counterrevolutionary activity. Although some Anarchists may well have been arrested in February, it is unlikely that 160 were.

6. A. D. Lebedev, an economist at Saratov University, 1920–24.

March 30, 1920. In his Zlatoust speech[7] Trotsky denies the allegation that the Bolsheviks have introduced Egyptian slavery in Russia, and are repeating the pharaohs: the latter had merely carried out their whims, while the Bolsheviks are working for the good of the republic. But the time has passed when Russians could listen to such declarations without derision.

A box of matches costs 90 rubles, a pound of butter, 1,000 rubles, a dozen eggs, 1,000 rubles.

April 2, 1920. My application for 10 lbs. of coal oil was turned down by the Sovnarhoz[8] on the ground that days were long enough for study and literary work without using artificial light. I am compelled to purchase coal oil from a profiteer at 500 rubles a pound.

Butter is 2,000 rubles a pound, meat is 300 rubles, eggs 840 rubles a dozen.

April 6, 1920. Have paid 150 rubles for my hunting license. Under the bloody tsarist regime the fee used to be 50 kopecks a year valid all over Russia.

April 7, 1920. Quoth Professor Tsytovich: "I was made happy today by Mr. Travin, the new director of the Star Factory.[9] He had not a good word to say about Americans after twelve years' residence in the U.S. Americans are a dry, unfeeling nation. A Russian could not live there. It is good for an engineer to spend a couple of years in the U.S., but never to live there."

April 14, 1920. Returning home at about 9:30 P.M., I saw that my dark gray sackcoat was missing from its hook on the wall by my bed. A thief seems to have slipped in through the back door when Dr. Lebedev went to a neighbor's after water. With my present ridiculous income of about 10,000 rubles a month, I cannot think of duplicating a coat worth not less than 25,000 rubles. The doctor

7. Babine may be referring to Trotsky's report at the Ninth Party Congress (March 29–April 5), when he proposed to introduce military conscription and discipline with respect to the labor force in order to deal with pressing economic problems.

8. Acronym for *Sovet narodnogo khoziaistva*, or Council of the National Economy. In this case Babine is referring to the local regional economic management board, responsible for the Saratov economy.

9. The Star Factory had been evacuated to Saratov from Kharkov in March 1918.

 adamantly asserts the door was never open, though our landlady has seen it ajar.

April 22, 1920. My cobbler tells me that all shoemakers have been ordered to surrender their tools to the Soviets, to join their union, and to work in Soviet shops for a fixed salary—a salary entirely insufficient to support a family. My man speaks about this Soviet step with contempt and derision. Of course, he has a new supply of tools and material, and cut his Soviet shop hours to work at home as usual.

May 6, 1920. I was amused today to see tattered, dirty, and barefoot sentries in front of the Center Market Soviet warehouses. Even their bayoneted muskets looked neglected and dirty.

May 9, 1920. I started for the woods at 7:15 A.M., and went to a place I found a month ago while chasing woodcock. I sawed down four oak stumps with my pocket saw and brought them home on my shoulders, which are quite sore just now. Last Sunday I limited myself to three stumps and felt less uncomfortable as a consequence.

May 27, 1920. Last Saturday, May 22, I went with a company of mechanics from the university shop by steamer to Shakhmatovka[10] on a woodcutting expedition. There were thirty-three men in the party. The steamer left us on a barge, from which we went ashore in a skiff. A Soviet agent supplied us with rations for three days —four and a half pounds of sour rye bread and ridiculously small quantities of millet, potatoes, and salt. From our landing we were conducted afoot, lugging our impedimenta on our backs, to a ravine some two miles off where we encamped for the night. The place was full of small gullies, where we began to work the next day at daybreak, before we had our breakfast. A rainstorm cooled down our enthusiasm in the afternoon, and left us very wet and uncomfortable, as we were shelterless. However, our little party of five managed to put up about two cords [a cord is equivalent to 128 cubic feet—Ed.] of mixed wood that day. The next day it again rained in the afternoon, but again we had our two cords done, and had to move to a new place since there was no wood left where we were. We worked two days in the new place and cut about three

10. A small settlement along the Volga.

cords of heavy oak wood mixed with aspen and linden. At that we decided to stop and to go back home. Our nourishment was very insufficient. All we had was millet, rye bread, potatoes, and a little over a pound of meat during the entire four days: the meat we happened to get in a village nearby. Our biggest man had a headache one night after an afternoon of particularly strenuous work. Stopping our work at 3 P.M. yesterday, we walked to Shakhmatovka, bought three pots of milk for nine hundred rubles and drank it, rested for two hours in a straw stack by the village, walked seven miles to Neftianaia this morning (having crossed Burkin Barak[11] in the dark), and were in Saratov by noon.

May 30, 1920. Professor Aleksander Andreevich Tikhomirov,[12] a zoologist of note and a high-handed conservative official of the tsarist Ministry of Education, has been elected to the chair of zoology at Saratov University in spite of certain opposition. The ballot stood seventeen to twelve, with five abstentions. Professor Tikhomirov is represented as an extremely religious man and an opponent of the Darwinian theory. At present he lives in destitution at Trinity-Sergius Monastery. His election is looked upon as a sign of the times —of disappointment in the former quasi-progressive (anarchist) tendencies among the Russian "educated" classes.

June 9, 1920. My diet: black bread, butter, and Soviet coffee for breakfast (at 5:30 A.M.); potato or millet soup and some (very little) millet pudding or mashed potatoes for dinner (12:30 P.M.), and bread, butter, and Soviet coffee for supper. Sometimes I prepare a hasty Russian dish of mashed black bread seasoned with sunflower oil and diluted with water, when in too much of a hurry to boil water with my slow contraptions, or when returning home late at night.

June 10, 1920. When a British labor delegation came to Saratov,[13] the

11. I was able to verify the existence of this settlement in Saratov province but could not determine its exact location because several settlements clustered together have similar names today.

12. Taught at Saratov University, 1920–21.

13. The British Labour party delegation arrived on June 3. It included Bertrand Russell, who, owing to the illness of a colleague, stayed on board the Volga steamer and did not disembark at Saratov. One member of the delegation, Mrs. Philip Snowden, found Saratov "the finest city we saw on the Volga." See her *Through Bolshevik Russia* (London, 1920), p. 172.

 only English-speaking person that was allowed to meet them was the Cheka official interpreter, a Jewish woman, posing as an Englishwoman among the unenlightened. The day before the British came I was waked up about midnight by this woman and another Russian linguist of great local fame, with an official message for me to prepare there and then a translation of a sensational address to the guests and of an equally sensational editorial that were to appear on the following morning in local Soviet papers. Neither the "Englishwoman" nor the local polyglot ventured to tackle a matter of such great importance. I went to work dauntlessly, and knowing that I shall be unable to talk to any of the unusual guests, I did my best to hint to them through my vocabulary with what blackguards and choice scoundrels they were dealing.[14] For my pains, I was favored with a seat in one of the front rows at the public reception given to the delegation by our Soviet. Just before the address was read by a leading Communist of the local Soviet, my translation was distributed among the delegates, and I had the pleasure of seeing Mr. Williams[15] nudge his neighbor with a knowing look after he examined the paper. I had my reward. It was a wonder to me if the English speakers were aware of the travesties that were given to the public, as their speeches were translated by official Soviet interpreters.

June 11, 1920. The English guests are said to have refused to eat meat and fish offered to them in Saratov: they found out that both had been taken from hospital patients. Some people have insinuated that the English have no taste for camel meat.

June 13, 1920. When a woman refused this morning the low price

14. Babine was probably asked to do the translation because his written English was better than that of the Cheka interpreter or of the local linguist. I read Babine's translation and found that he indeed tried to hint to the British that Soviet power was not all that it was trumped up to be. I wonder, however, whether the British actually picked up on Babine's real intentions. They may simply have been amused by the ambiguous and contradictory prose.

15. Robert Williams, chairman of the Federation of Transport Workers. Marguerite E. Harrison, an American reporter for the *Baltimore Sun* and the Associated Press, took part in the British Labour delegation's Volga trip. She avoided the public functions in Saratov "and went out to talk with the people." From such encounters she learned of the great scarcity of food locally. See her *Marooned in Moscow: The Story of an American Woman Imprisoned in Russia* (London, 1921), p. 176.

offered for her goods (onions), a Red soldier declared he had the right to take anything he pleased, and compelled the woman to accept his terms. Bystanders watched the scene in mute amazement and powerless disgust.

June 15, 1920. It is stated on good authority that professors are doing brisk business in alcohol issued to them for scientific purposes: one part of it goes to the Soviet officials approving the applications for the stuff, the rest is exchanged for provisions, fuel, etc., peasants nowadays being extremely thirsty for things spiritous.

June 16, 1920. Energetic means are being taken to fight army desertions.[16] One of them is confiscation of the deserter's property. Cases have been reported when deserters were taken from home under heavy guard and their cattle driven after them—to go to Soviet authorities.

June 18, 1920. A lady is said to have flatly refused to be lodged by Soviet authorities in a room with a person having a nasty skin disease. The Soviet housing agent tried to induce her to change her mind by holding his revolver close to her forehead. But even this argument failed with the mere woman, and the house agent found himself all of a sudden hauled up before what is still called the "proper authorities."

June 19, 1920. The Soviets keep open only one meat store for the whole city of Saratov having about 400,000 inhabitants.[17] The lines for meat are endless, even though meat is issued only to the sick, on physicians' certificates, and, of course, to all the Communist elite.

June 20, 1920. The local Soviets have sanctioned this summer certain "labor bands" for agricultural purposes, which have turned out to be defenseless objects of Soviet exploitation. The "bands" are compelled to turn all their products over to the Soviets at a set price that is by far lower than the market prices. Special inspectors have been appointed to watch the bondsmen and to keep them from

16. See note 16 to the 1919 entries.

17. This is a swollen figure, for Saratov's population had steadily shrunk during the Civil War. According to *Materialy po statistike g. Saratova*, vyp. I (Saratov, 1921), the city's population in 1920 was 191,996. By 1921—before the famine—it had dropped to 187,964.

 trading with anybody. A "band" to which one of my friends belongs has been forced to plough a piece of land and to plant potatoes on it for a government-backed "commune" of riotous idlers, without any compensation whatever for their labor.

A spool of thread costs one thousand Soviet rubles.

June 24, 1920. Drunken officers of Denikin's army are said, in case of reverses, to have taken care only of their lewd women, and to have invariably left their troops to fend for themselves.

July 3, 1920. An unwed youngish woman doctor, in order to avoid a compulsory Soviet typhus mobilization, has decided to have a baby that is due within two months and is already much in evidence. Formerly it would have been considered a disgrace to shirk any kind of mobilization no matter how dangerous.

July 4, 1920. Stockings being very expensive, coeds, and elderly ladies, too, go slipshod. With much abbreviated skirts it makes a sight to which one has to get used.

July 8, 1920. Our house register having been lost, one of the tenants has been unable to get his bread tickets from his Soviet bureau and had to go without bread since the first of the month. (The issue of bread tickets has to be noted in house registers to prevent duplication and abuse.)

July 9, 1920. Beginning today the post office refuses to accept parcels with flour or grain. I am unable to send anything to my starving folks.

July 15, 1920. A St. Petersburg professor lectured today in a soiled soft shirt and very dilapidated shoes, like any of our provincial professors. Lack of soap and absence of laundries is felt everywhere, and professors do not make good washerwomen.

July 23, 1920. Have just returned from our wood-loading trip. Our agent was notified last week that our wood was on the riverbank and waiting for us. A friend called on me post haste last Sunday to announce the good news. So, twenty-nine of us went by steamer to Shakhmatovka again at 3 P.M. last Monday, leaving our work in town. The steamer left two hours behind time and landed us at Pudovkina, more than six miles below Shakhmatovka, a distance we had to cover on foot, loaded with our bedrolls and other baggage. When we came to our place, we found no wood and no barge to load it on. Our delegate went to see Tikhonov, the government agent, the same evening, and was promised the barge, the wood, and the rations the next day. We spent the night in a rye haystack near a village. The following morning we lay on the riverbank doing nothing—resting, swimming. By-and-by the barge was brought, placed in position with some difficulty, and a bridge was built to connect it with the bank. That was all we did on Tuesday. On Wednesday morning wood began to be dumped down the high and steep hill just above us, and to crash down in great style. The rations were announced to have arrived from Saratov by team (about twenty miles away) and fetched to our camp by a select party of six a distance of some two miles. The ration amounted to two pounds of bread apiece, two suspicious-looking salted herring, and a ridiculous amount of millet and salt (black and dirty, but strong) per day per man. On this diet we worked two days loading heavy oak logs. We were all worn out, sunburned, and thin by Thursday evening, when we went back to Pudovkina, caught a steamer (which was terribly overcrowded), slept on its indescribably dirty bare floor with others, and reached Saratov at nine this morning.

July 24, 1920. The 70 million poods of crude oil purchased by the Soviets in Baku have been paid for in grain at the rate of 3 poods of grain for a pood of oil. This explains the embarrassing and aggravating reduction of bread rations here from a pound a day to half a pound. One-fourth of a pound is promised on and after August 1.

August 1, 1920. A large portion of Saratov burned down yesterday[18] between 3:30 and 12 P.M. owing to a windstorm, official negligence, and absence of water. Most firemen were out of town—some cutting wood, others making hay, still others absent on leave. A little cluster of houses on Gimnazicheskaia has escaped the conflagration. A university janitor friend of mine had already carried his scanty belongings to the street, when his wife "took an icon and faced the fire and the wind. She barely reached their street corner, when the wind turned, and their little cottage was saved with a few others around it."

August 6, 1920. Wheat flour is 16,000 rubles a pood, eggs 700 rubles a dozen, fresh tomatoes 350, white bread 300 rubles a pound.

18. I was unable to determine how much of Saratov was actually lost.

August 8, 1920. The bread ration has been cut down to ¼ lb. per day per man.

August 15, 1920. Having a bad attack of malaria, I have been unable to get quinine anywhere and am obliged to resort to arsenic.

August 17, 1920. A large two-story brick house on our street corner, "nationalized," has been turned into barracks for transient troops and fresh draftees. The weather being warm, the soldiers, tattered and dirty, sleep right on the bare sidewalk, as they have been doing all summer. At times they are so thick that one has to go onto the road to pass the house. At meal hours I see them carrying their tin pails with steaming "soup" that looks like thick, unpalatable slop water.

August 20, 1920. A Saratov physician's daughter went to Samara to rescue her arrested fiancé. She was arrested immediately upon her arrival. Then her father went to her rescue. An army surgeon on whom he called said to him: "Don't ever go to the Cheka. If they happen not to take a fancy to your face, they will shoot you in no time." Through the intercession of influential friends, the physician effected the release of his daughter. She fell into his arms gasping: "Oh, father, I have been kept in an underground cell, knee deep in blood."

August 21, 1920. Have not yet received my salary for the second half of July and the first half of August: there is no money at the local treasury office.

August 25, 1920. Bread issued by Soviet stores contains chaff and has made me very sick.

September 1, 1920. Had my dinner at the regular student boarding house today. Soup and boiled beans were served. Both had a sharp stale taste. Students devoured their food with avidity. It was awful and disgusting.

The university has not issued my salary for a month and a half owing to the temporary insolvency of the government. People have to sell their belongings for what they can get to save themselves from starving.

September 16, 1920. No bread issued by the Soviets to citizens for the last two days. Patients in hospitals are said to be left without bread. I had to pay 2,300 rubles for a 4-lb. loaf. And all this in

Saratov, which used to ship immense quantities of grain to other parts of Russia and abroad under the "bloody tsarist regime."

September 17, 1920. It is rumored that about one million men were lost in the Warsaw operation.[19] One hundred fifty thousand cavalry perished under the grilling fire of the enemy, with men going mad under its effect. Baltic seamen are said to have charged Trotsky with useless waste of human life and to have summoned him to Petrograd for trial.

October 8, 1920. Salaries have not been paid since September 1. Bread is 300 rubles a pound, and one has to buy it, since the Soviet ration of 3/8 lb. a day cannot keep a man alive.

October 10, 1920. For the last two weeks I have been combining my woodcock shooting trips with fetching wood for my brazier. Today I brought one bird home (having cooked another and eaten it in the woods) and a long oak pole that will last me at least a week. It was quite a problem to take the log out of the woods without being caught by the guards.

October 26, 1920. When we cut wood last May, the Soviet stipulated that we would receive 7/12 of a "cube" apiece for every cube cut. Today we were given 1/3 "sazhen" (fathom) apiece, for which we have to pay, in addition to our work, 4,000 Soviet rubles. The official measurement used was found to be short at that: it measured only 1 arsheen 6 vershoks instead of 1 arsheen 8 vershoks.[20] "They will never miss a chance to cheat somebody," grumbled one of the victims of Soviet imposition.

October 27, 1920. My supply of woodcock has come to an end. To date, I had one every day for my dinner for about two months.

19. The military operation of Soviet troops against Warsaw, July 23 through August 25, during the Soviet-Polish War of 1920, which aroused a storm of national feeling stimulated by propaganda. The Soviet government struck against Warsaw in order to spread world revolution. (The atmosphere at the Congress of the Third International, which had gathered in Moscow in the summer of 1920, had been fanatical.) Babine's report, though, grossly exaggerates things. Only a fraction of that number of men was actually involved in the operation. That it was a disaster for the Red Army, however, there can be no doubt.

20. Cube = cubic meter; sazhen (fathom) = a measure of length equivalent to 2.13 meters; arshin = 28 inches or 71 centimeters; vershok = a measure of length equal to 4.4 centimeters or 1.75 inches.

 With bootleg meat at 400 to 600 rubles a pound, and with a very inadequate and irregular pay, I may turn a vegetarian.

November 24, 1920. Had to be my own cobbler this morning. It took me two hours to put a patch the size of a penny on my shoe in an inconvenient place.

November 27, 1920. A hen is said to have been found hanging on a public thoroughfare with a note tied to her neck saying: "Nobody is to blame for my death. I end my days being unable to fulfill my civic duty and to lay two eggs daily as required by the Soviet regime."

December 9, 1920. A friend of mine, returning home from a birthday party late at night, was stopped in a narrow lane by two armed men and relieved of his gold watch and chain and of two thousand rubles in cash. Very early the next morning he was at the local police station to report the fact and to see to it that necessary steps were taken to apprehend the robbers. My friend found himself almost at the end of a long line that had been formed before he got there —everybody with a complaint similar to his own. He waited patiently for his turn. When he came close enough to the table where the depositions were being taken down and saw the clerk that was taking them, he recognized him as the man that had robbed him a few hours before. Not choosing to face the human again, Mr. B. stepped out of the line and went home.

December 10, 1920. Soviet bread issued this week is hard, badly made, and full of chaff.

December 14, 1920. The following document has been received by our normal schools: "Private circular. To all sections, bureaus, unions, and student bodies it is proposed to keep track of anti-Soviet remarks and statements of professors in their lectures and to report the same to proper authorities—without taking any individual steps. Utmost secrecy imperative."

December 24, 1920. An excellent gunsmith friend of mine, having a wife and six children, constantly runs out of bread (not to speak of other things, such as meat or sugar, of which one does not even dream), the Soviet ration of ⅜ lb. a day being utterly insufficient. Last Sunday I gave him a large loaf of bread. Today he received half of one from a friend. There is no meat, no butter, no milk, no cereals, no coffee (not even Postum) in the house. The man's business and shop have been taken away from him, and he has been made a Soviet employee earning at present ten thousand Soviet rubles a month and a stingy ration, on which even one person cannot subsist.

December 29, 1920. An old drayman (68 years old) raised a pig and killed him just before Christmas. The fact was reported by a mean neighbor to Soviet authorities; the meat was "confiscated," and the drayman and his family of eleven left without meat for Christmas.

1921

At the national level the Soviet government realized that some respite from civil war was necessary, and in early 1921, following a spate of urban and rural uprisings, it introduced the New Economic Policy (NEP), that "pact with the devil," whose purpose was to restore the national economy. In Saratov, workers went out on strike in early 1921 to protest conditions, a development that led to the introduction of martial law in the city; moreover, banditry posed a serious threat to the authorities. Conditions in Saratov reveal how necessary the New Economic Policy was in order to reforge links with the people. This is not to suggest that Soviet power was on the verge of collapse. Despite the success of peasant insurgents in the Volga region and turmoil in the city, political power in 1921 remained firmly in the hands of the party administrators, who, according to their own evaluation, functioned well but "were divorced from the masses." As we shall see, however, the horrors of famine prevented the NEP from bringing relief to the battered population of Saratov as it did to the urban population of central Russia. The termination of civil war did not end the ordeal through which Saratov was living.

Famine had been foreseen already in January 1921, and it owed a great deal to the regime's futile, desperate policies of the past. By May famished Germans were flocking to Saratov and mortality levels from disease reached alarming proportions. Demobilization of the Red Army that summer increased unemployment and hunger. Reports in the local Communist paper suggest a fearful population preparing for another winter of want, a city "dirty beyond all imagination," widescale unemployment, and hordes of women driven to prostitution to stay alive.

While Soviet authorities blamed the famine on the ills it had inherited from the old regime and the devastation of war, the peasants pinned the blame on Bolshevik agrarian policies. Ironically, the very land that had been

Victims of famine (Photo courtesy of the Hoover Institution)

the object of such a violent and determined contest for so long, which had shaped the character of the revolution, was now lying idle. Large portions of it were, at least, and the size of the fallow lands increased with each year of civil war. The collapse of industrial production and prohibition of free trade contributed to the reduction in sown area: the peasant had little incentive to produce more than he could consume. The introduction of a tax in kind, more onerous than the money taxes that had been abolished, had placed on the peasant's shoulders a much resented burden. Peasant farming had become more primitive and the standard of living had declined precipitously, just as in the cities. It was a terrible time for climate to now take its toll, too.

Babine returned to Elatma in 1921, but this time we learn nothing about his family: hunger is the major focus of his observations, which depict a society in desperate search of something to eat. By the time of his return to Saratov famine was claiming victims, especially in the trans-Volga districts of Saratov and Samara provinces. In Novouzensk, for instance, 90 percent of the population was listed as starving by March 1, 1922.

It was against this background that the American Relief Administration (ARA) opened up operations in Saratov city and elsewhere in the province in October 1921. The rich documentation of the ARA branch office, found at the Hoover Archive, especially the lengthy report of John P. Gregg, who became district superintendent of the Saratov operations, provides information on conditions along the Volga, on relations between the ARA *workers and the Soviet authorities, and on political attitudes and conditions in general. The* ARA *records complement Babine's diary entries, and paint an all-too-familiar picture of puzzled Soviet authorities suspicious of the possible agenda hidden behind the generosity of their foreign benefactors. M. M. Litvinov in the Commissariat of Foreign Affairs, for one, feared that food was a political weapon. Such feelings help explain why local soviet executive committees made it difficult for the* ARA *staff to assess famine conditions and to obtain information on the size of seeded areas, crop output, level of taxation, etc. Soviet officials struck the American workers as being evasive and unwilling to take the initiative. And, even though the* ARA *would complain of local authorities' efforts to convince the starving peasants that America shipped food to avoid revolution at home(!), the peasants, as one report put it, were more likely to believe that the* ARA *people were "sent from God."*

The ARA *operation in Saratov province, in conjunction with other relief agencies, provided significant famine relief and also welcomed packages of shoes, linens, and medicines. Letters of appreciation and gratitude from the local population flooded the Saratov* ARA *office. Although the authorities claimed that* ARA *assistance "would never be forgotten," Soviet writing on famine relief, much of which is polemical, grossly distorts the reasons for and impact of these humanitarian efforts from abroad. The record needs to be set straight.*

January 4, 1921. A doctor who was a member of my special English class took pity on my worn-out leather shoes that are entirely out of season in this severe weather, and got me a pair of old felt boots reconditioned in a prison shop in his charge, for only ten thousand rubles. A friend in need whose deed I greatly appreciate.

January 15, 1921. Reports have been coming for some time that the Volga region, this granary of Russia, where farmers always had more grain than they would or cared to sell,[1] has been swept clean of its stores by the Soviets that need money to pay the Polish indem-

1. Although Saratov province is located in the eastern tip of the fertile black-earth zone, it suffered nineteen famine years between 1871 and 1925, two-thirds of which were caused by drought. For a discussion of the complexity of the demographic crisis experienced at this time, see S. G. Wheatcroft, "Famine and Epidemic Crises in Russia, 1918–1922: The Case of Saratov," *Annales de démographie historique* (1983), pp. 329–51.

 nity. A terrible famine is foreseen. The despoiled peasants begin to appear in cities, begging. In German settlements the Bolshevik robbers met with armed resistance, and mercilessly gunned down the "rebels."

February 3, 1921. Bread, salt (½ lb. for January), matches (one box for January), yeast (1/16 lb. for January) were issued free this afternoon at Soviet stores.

March 2, 1921. About a month ago the university faculty applied to the local Soviet authorities for the "academic ration"[2] granted by Moscow to 244 members of the teaching staff. After a month's tribulations the ration was at last issued, and yesterday the meat was distributed. When I came to the store, I saw that four professors (Frank, two Skvortsovs, and Il'inskii[3]) had brought back their portions stating that they had weighed them in one of the university laboratories and found them 2½ and 2¼ lbs. short of the 7 lbs. due them. Mr. Minzburg, in charge of the distribution, blandly asked the discontented teachers to examine his decimal scales, and this was immediately done. It was clear to all present that the scales had been doctored, at which nobody seemed surprised since Mr. Minzburg always had an unsavory reputation of supplying the slippery president of the university (Zernov)[4] and other leading manipulators with alcohol and kerosene from the university stock. The distribution of the ration was entrusted to him by Zernov without any authorization from the faculty, even under protest from it.

March 3, 1921. This afternoon the committee on Germano-Romanic studies discussed the question of promoting Mr. Dinges.[5] This was strongly pressed by the chairman. During the debate it leaked out

2. Beginning in 1919 the Soviet government started placing professors and distinguished scholars in rationing categories that were higher than those of other members of the bourgeoisie (and of some workers).

3. V. A. Skvortsov, a member of the faculty of medicine, 1912–22, and again in 1926–29; V. I. Skvortsov, also a member of the faculty of medicine, 1913–24; G. A. Il'inskii, member of the philology department, 1918–29 (later a corresponding member of the Soviet Academy of Sciences). S. L. Frank was no longer in Saratov at this time.

4. V. D. Zernov, distinguished professor of physics at Saratov University, 1909–23, and rector. It is unclear why Babine held him in such low esteem.

5. G. G. Dinges, member of the philology department, 1921–28.

that the same question was on the program of the faculty meeting for March 4, where it had no business being without a previous resolution from the committee. The chairman gave a lame explanation that made his unscrupulousness clear to all present. In order not to disappoint Mr. Dinges, the question was decided in his favor.

March 4, 1921. At the faculty meeting an objection was raised to the promotion on the grounds that Mr. Dinges had not yet passed his master's examination. But the Jewish and German clique of the faculty got its way and beat the native element.

Just as I was about to leave my lecture room late this afternoon, a student walked in and said that martial law had been proclaimed in Saratov in connection with a workers' strike of which the public knew nothing.[6] I had to cut my lecture short, as well as to cut another appointment, since streets were to be cleared by 10 P.M. (Soviet time—or 8 P.M. normal time). The martial law proclamation was posted only after dark, and many a citizen was arrested that night in consequence of this premeditated trick by the Soviet, which everybody considers quite natural for it.

March 9, 1921. Professors Zernov, Kakushkin, and Bystrenin[7] were arrested last night. Some time ago they gave a series of lectures at one of the largest city churches in which they stated their conclusion as scientists that natural phenomena could not be explained by the chemical and mechanical action and interaction of matter

6. As background, the Kronstadt Rebellion, calling for a revitalization of Soviet democracy, had broken out on March 1 and was not suppressed until March 17. Moreover, Communist leaders were involved in a heated dispute over the functions of trade unions, with Lenin and Trotsky taking opposing views. Although Lenin's views predominated in Saratov, Trotsky's position attracted some support, as did that of the so-called Workers' Opposition headed by A. A. Shliapnikov and A. M. Kollontai. Further, on March 8, Lenin announced the introduction of the New Economic Policy at the opening session of the Tenth Party Congress. In preparing for the Tenth Congress, Mensheviks and SRs agitated in town, and on March 2 workers at several Saratov enterprises struck, calling for a constituent assembly and establishment of a coalition government. Bitterly attacking the nagging food shortages, workers, undoubtedly influenced by moderate socialist orators, argued that the October Revolution had been premature. Their demands for better living conditions even brought M. I. Vasil'ev back to Saratov for a brief appearance (see note 62 to the 1917 entries).

7. N. M. Kakushkin, member of the faculty of medicine, 1912–30. I. N. Bystrenin taught in the same department, 1912–30.

 alone, and that some power as yet unknown seemed to be present in the world—unknown and unnamed—which might be named anything, might even be named God. This statement was found dangerous to the Soviet republic, and the lecturers were thrown in jail.

March 10, 1921. About five hundred persons are said to have been arrested last night as hostages, Borel among them.[8]

March 23, 1921. Peasants are said to have slaughtered every Communist in Khvalynsk, and Saratov is rumored to be surrounded by armed bands.[9] Factory sirens called Communists together last night after 11 P.M. This afternoon I met several workers armed with brand-new German Mausers and heading toward the suburbs. The workers are reported to be in ferment.

April 28, 1921. Moskvitin and his family[10] are out of bread again, with the prospect of staying without it during the whole Easter week since no bread is going to be made or issued to citizens by Soviet authorities during the holidays. Moskvitin himself was away from here in search of money when I called at the house—a loaf of bread costs now from 25,000 to 35,000 rubles. He seems to have nothing to sell. His excellent six-month-old puppy is a living skeleton. The city health authorities have refused to issue white bread, tea, and sugar for his typhus-stricken boy of six, disregarding a physician's prescription.

April 30, 1921. I just turned into a country road out of town on my way to my favorite woodcock patch at about 5:30 this morning, when a large automobile made me hustle out of its way in the dim light of dawn: it was the Cheka execution gang returning from its slaughter ravine lying about four miles from town and directly across the valley from my elevated hunting ground.

May 1, 1921. Famished Germans flee from their homes, camp on the banks of the Volga, and invade Saratov—many of them mere

8. I could not identify Borel, nor verify the number of arrests.

9. Probably referring to the Greens, whose activities throughout April preoccupied the provincial executive committee. Particularly active in Volsk, Pokrovsk, and Balashov, the different Green bands led by Popov, Vakulin, and Antonov had killed more than one hundred Communists.

10. A friend of Babine's. See his entry for December 24, 1920.

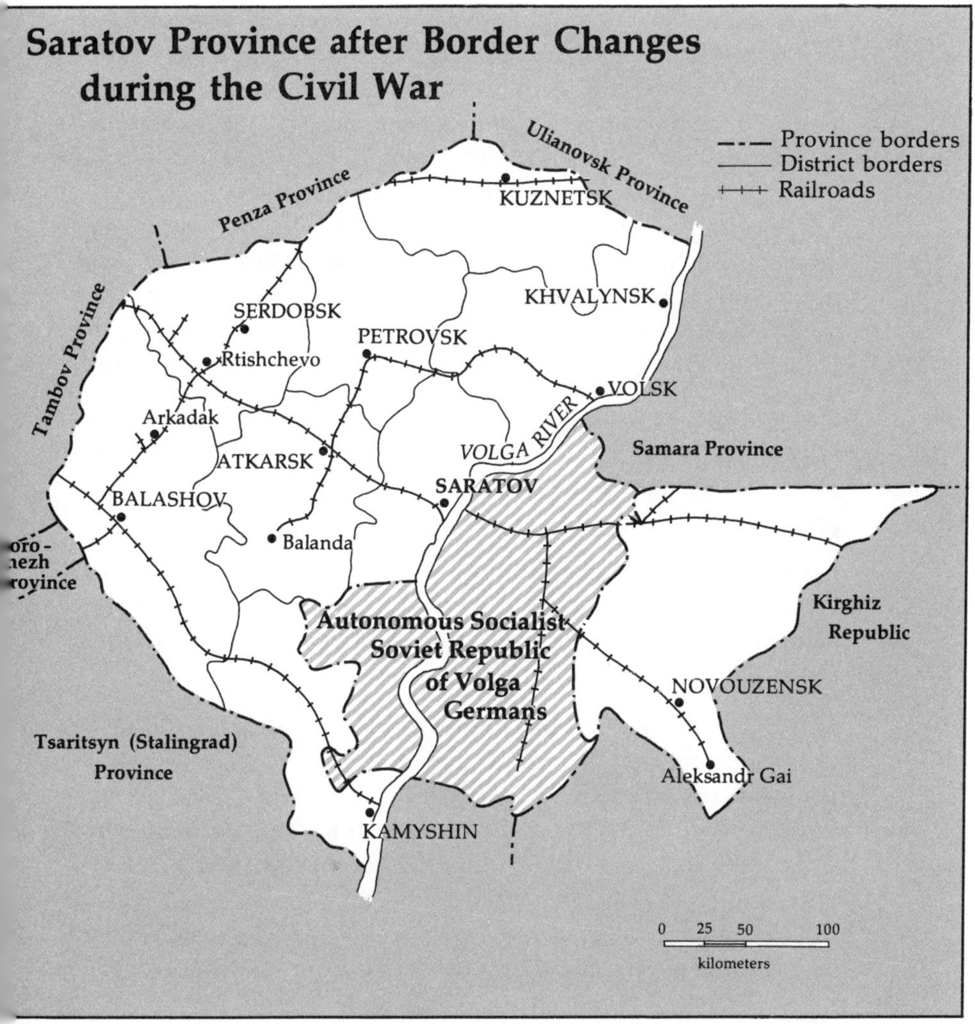
Saratov Province after Border Changes during the Civil War
Province borders
District borders
Railroads
Ulianovsk Province
Penza Province
Tambov Province
KUZNETSK
KHVALYNSK
SERDOBSK
PETROVSK
Rtishchevo
VOLSK
Arkadak
ATKARSK
VOLGA RIVER
Samara Province
SARATOV
BALASHOV
Balanda
Voro-nezh Province
Kirghiz Republic
Autonomous Socialist Soviet Republic of Volga Germans
NOVOUZENSK
Tsaritsyn (Stalingrad) Province
Aleksandr Gai
KAMYSHIN
0 25 50 100
kilometers

 skeletons hardly able to move around. Two small boys came to the Mitrofan Market this morning. A kindhearted milkwoman gave them a good feed, after which the boys dropped to the ground, and died.

May 3, 1921. Am entirely out of bread since none has been made or issued during this Easter week by Soviet authorities. I have to get by the best I can with the little millet I happen to have, and with lentils. To aggravate such bad luck, my salary for the second half of April has not been paid nor is going to be paid for some time owing to the absence of money at the treasury office.

Have spent several hours today washing and patching up my drawers. One pair deserves a place in a museum for the number of patches on it. But I cannot afford to buy a new pair on account of the terribly high prices, and so have to keep on adding patches to the old ones, till the garment has become one solid piece of patchwork.

May 13, 1921. Spent this afternoon cleaning lentils (Soviet, and awfully dirty) for my soup, and later on two and a half hours cooking them on my diminutive brazier.

May 17, 1921. Mrs. Stammenov, wife of a former high school principal (still engaged in educational work and starving), is making dung fuel bricks today for the coming winter, her little bare feet black with the dung juice oozing out of the wooden form into which she pluckily stamps the stuff.

May 21, 1921. At a birthday dinner given by Stadnitskii, our Communist professors (Vorms, Bogomolets, Mirotvortsev, Raiskii)[11] were severely attacked by their colleagues for their Bolshevik sympathies. Bogomolets insisted that in all epidemics many innocent lives were lost, and so justified the Bolsheviks' unprecedented cruelties.

Am entirely out of bread again. Could not receive my ration owing to the negligence of the medical dean's office, where red tape

11. A former vice-rector of Saratov University, V. V. Vorms taught chemistry in Saratov, 1909–30, and again in 1938–40. He had been vocally anti-Bolshevik back in 1918. A. A. Bogomolets, who later became a member of the Soviet Academy of Sciences, taught medicine, 1911–25 (see note 108 to the 1918 entries). S. R. Mirotvortsev also belonged to the faculty of medicine at Saratov University, 1914–30, and was elected to the Academy. M. I. Raiskii, later designated a "distinguished scientist of the RSFSR," worked in Saratov, 1917–30.

and indolence reign supreme. I have to live on lentils and cream of wheat.

May 27, 1921. The city is beset by beggars—German colonists who have fled from their settlements after the bloody suppression of their unsuccessful insurrection against the Soviets.[12]

June 5, 1921. Moskvitin called this morning, begging for a piece of bread. He and his family have been out of bread several days. Unfortunately, I was unable to help him out this time, being out of bread myself, and out of money.

June 6, 1921. Somebody has been telling of the manner in which the advent of the Bolsheviks has been received in various parts of Russia. In Tashkent the Turkmen, boozy and sober, would wager as to who could chop off a man's head the cleanest—and experimented on Russian heads at the marketplace. An eyewitness has described a procession at which the Sarts chanted "Airam-Bairam-Carla-Marla" ad infinitum, with their eyes half-shut. When asked what it meant they shook their heads and waved the question off, without discontinuing their singsong. In the auls [tents—Ed.] of the Caucasus the Bolshevik troops would find red ribbons and red flags everywhere—on men, women, children, horses, cattle, cats, dogs—and be greeted with "We all Bolshevik—I Bolshevik—she Bolshevik—my horse Bolshevik—pray, go away—sotsial-motsial no wanted—a tsar wanted."

June 16, 1921. Rumors of a peasant insurrection all over Russia are a common topic of conversation. A Tambov rebel leader, Antonov,[13]

12. Believing peasants were minimizing their resources in order to escape paying the requisition tax, the Soviet government had cruelly carried out grain requisitioning in 1920. Armed bands of hungry workers from Tula descended upon Saratov's German communities, seizing everything they could lay their hands on. The workers whipped and beat women who begged for food for their starving children. Disturbances broke out in January–February, and Vakulin, a leader of the Greens, urged the Germans to die fighting. They recaptured grain from the government, distributed it among the colonists, and repaid the Communists for their cruelty by slaughtering them. See "The Hardships of Our Co-Religionists in the German Volga Colonies," Hoover Institution, ARA Russian Operations, Container 99.

13. The Tambov uprising led by Antonov (see note 25, 1919) was part of a broader spate of uprisings in western Siberia and the North Caucasus. The movement broke out in August–September 1920 after requisition teams appeared in the villages to claim their share of the harvest.

 has become a sort of anti-Bolshevik hero. Having formerly worked for and in the party,[14] he knows all the ins and outs of Bolshevism, has many confederates among the leading quasi-Bolshevik officials, learns the plans of his enemies long before their execution, stops, derails, and loots Soviet trains, exterminates Soviet officials wherever found, and, having the peasantry on his side, successfully eludes all pursuit.

It requires a whole army of Reds to fight him. A student friend of mine has told me about one of the victories over the rebel about which the Reds boasted. The day after the "victory" 520 "victors" were brought to their village and buried.

June 18, 1921. We have not received any salary since last April and are told there is no probability of receiving any for another month or month and a half. Heartrending scenes are said to be taking place at the Local Bureau of Education, where starved women teachers bewail their fate daily.

June 21, 1921. Soviet bread now consists of a mixture of rye flour, lentil meal, and some other stuff (oil cake, I am told). I got so sick as a result of having eaten it today that I was even unable to go to the market to buy some white bread—after a thirty-six-hour complete fast.

July 10, 1921. A charge of extortion has appeared in the local Soviet paper against Professor Tsytovich.[15] A man called the professor to treat his boy. Tsytovich agreed to go only on payment of fifty thousand rubles down, and a cab both ways. Having examined the patient (a two-year-old boy) the professor found inflammation of the ear and said that unless an operation was performed within two hours, the brain tissue would be affected, and death ensue. At the father's request the professor consented to perform the operation at once, and they went to Tsytovich's house after the instruments. In the professor's dressing room the father was approached and informed by Mrs. Tsytovich that the operation would cost 1 million rubles. The man had no such sum, but offered his gold watch, chain, and wedding ring. These trinkets were declined, and the professor refused to operate. The child was taken to the city hos-

14. Antonov actually considered himself a former SR.
15. The local press did report on this episode.

pital the following morning and was immediately operated upon, but died, the operation having been put off too long.

The professor is out of town and cannot defend himself. His accuser is a Soviet official.

July 12, 1921. No bread or any other products have been issued by the Soviets since July 1. I am in difficult straits. Bread now costs from nine to ten thousand rubles a pound, and my salary is paid very irregularly (none has been paid for May and June as of yet).

July 20, 1921. In order to avoid possible delay in traveling by rail through Antonov territory—the environs of Tambov—I have decided to go home this time by the Volga and Oka steamers. I was fortunate enough to embark before a new tariff came into force, and paid only 385 rubles for my ticket from Saratov to Nizhnii-Novgorod. The once magnificent steamer was terribly dilapidated and dirty, but I hope to reach my destination in spite of all her shortcomings.

The Volga looks dead—hardly any boats in sight anywhere.

July 21, 1921. I had to share my very untidy stateroom with another passenger who had occasional visitors. Coming in and out, I apparently disturbed the company, and by dinnertime my mate had decamped, while I was fortunate enough to secure a key to my room through the courtesy of a steamer mechanic whose daughter, a student, happened to be aboard.

For breakfast I boiled a handful of millet in my camping can, making use of the steamer kitchen range, together with scores of other passengers whose female element often squabbled over the position of their utensils on the range. This thin broth, with a piece of rye bread, made a sufficient impression on me to enable me to wait patiently for my dinner. I took the latter at the steamer restaurant of three- or four-person tables in the middle part of the upper deck. Very few people patronized it owing to the high price charged—six thousand rubles for a plate of soup with a pretense of a very small piece of meat, and a very small slice of rye bread.

For supper I had only a little tea, without sugar, of my own concoction in the same steamer kitchen.

July 22, 1921. The air on the lower deck is sickeningly strong, and the general condition of the deck unsanitary. A cholera patient is said to be aboard. At every landing the banks of the river are swarming with famine refugees waiting—some of them for weeks—for a chance to get a passage to a more prosperous part of Russia. The condition of the refugees, their improvised, unprotected camps on bare ground, and their emaciated bodies are heartrending.

July 23, 1921. At some of the landings provisions are sold by peasants from nearby settlements. They charge 7,000 rubles for a pound of bread, 3,000 rubles for a pound of meat, 7,000 for a pound of sausage, from 9,000 to 10,000 rubles for a dozen eggs, 3,500 rubles for a jug of milk, and from 6,000 to 8,000 rubles for a cooked chicken. I bought 10 eggs in Kazan for 8,000 rubles and 5¼ lbs. of rice from a sailor aboard for 42,000 rubles.

One of the passengers said that on a Caspian steamer the crew had confiscated all their rice and other food supplies as contraband—and offered the same stuff for sale to them the next day.

Nobody seemed astonished.

July 24, 1921. The boat crew is doing a great business in salt, which is scarce everywhere and is carried by them in large quantities up the river from the lower Volga salt lake districts. At one of the landings the boat was swamped by women peasants who purchased quite a bit of the precious mineral for cash. But when they left the steamer, they were at once stopped by the soldiers and their salt confiscated on the ground that it was a state monopoly and as such represented a smuggled article in the hands of its buyers.

The passengers did not doubt for a single moment that the trick had been prearranged between the steamer's crew and the soldiers.

July 31, 1921. In Elatma once more. Only my unmarried brother and my stepmother[16] are living in the old house, my father having died in the fall of 1919. The house is in fair order. My rooms were looted last March 24–26, on a false report about concealed firearms (of which none were found). My motorcycle, McClellan saddle, riding equipment, a large number of tools, spare motorcycle parts, and sporting appliances mysteriously disappeared after the search. I have been advised not to protest against this robbery: the local brigands in power are arbitrary enough to throw me in jail with perfect impunity or at least to spoil my little vacation.

16. After Babine's death, $500 from his estate was sent through the Chase Manhattan Bank to his stepmother, who acknowledged its receipt. Unfortunately, Babine's papers reveal no trace of what had become of his family in Elatma after he fled Russia in 1922.

August 6, 1921. Am hunting with borrowed guns, and with varying success. My hunting costume is a sight to behold. My pants have gone through a number of seasons, each of which has left its mark in the shape of patches on them. Seeing that they needed some new ones, and there being no cloth whatever to be had, I cut up one of my American canvas gun cases, put four more patches on my garment (making a total of fourteen), and produced an article that for color scheme Joseph himself might envy. My shoes, too, are a wonderful piece of patchwork. But old as they are they have one great virtue: they fit me like a glove, which is an important item in my long tramps through marshy country.

August 15, 1921. Our diet has been black bread and coffee substitute for breakfast; potato soup or fish broth, fried potatoes with or without salted cucumbers for dinner, and the same soup and millet pudding with milk for supper. Never a bit of meat—except when I get a wild duck. After a night of fishing we usually have fried fish for two or three days.

August 17, 1921. Our fishing has been so successful that I have seriously considered giving up university work and following my father's profession, on which he always prided himself since it saved him from having ever been anybody's man. During the short time I tried it, I found that one good night's catch would give me more than nine months' university salary.

August 30, 1921. "The peasants in our village began to notice that four or five sheaves out of every row of ten would, after a while, turn empty without any grain being found nearby. After wondering for some time, they began to watch. One night a man and his wife came, stuck the head of a sheaf into a grain sack, beat it with a stick, put it back in its place, then went to another and another. . . . Our men killed the thief outright and tied the woman to a post to make her tell where the rest of the grain was. At first she refused, but finally disclosed a store under a grain stack. About fifty bushels were found—and the woman was killed, too. I am sorry for the kids she has left. . . . Four other men had been killed in our village before I came home on my visit from Baku, some of them for as little as a cluster of stolen potatoes." (Fellow passenger on a Volga steamer.)

September 2, 1921. The once magnificent Volga steamers are at present in a state of utter dilapidation, dirty, without mattresses or cushions, mirrors (stolen by the freedom-loving passengers, especially the ever-thievish low peasantry), without elementary sanitary facilities. The restaurants are poor and expensive. There are no keys to staterooms—with constant thefts as a result. The smell and dirt are indescribable among third-class passengers, especially the Tatars.

September 8, 1921. Our School of Modern Languages has been left without funds. It is necessary for somebody to go to Moscow to get money. It is said that nothing can be gotten there without bribes, that one-half percent of the sum granted always has to be presented to the official on whom the grant depends. Every agent that goes to Moscow from Saratov University takes along three gallons of pure alcohol. The university keeps a lawyer permanently in Moscow to look after the interests of the institution (Professor Iurovskii's brother).

September 11, 1921. Large crowds of people are camping on the square in front of our railway station, waiting for a chance to get entrained. I found them tonight sleeping on sidewalks, on the rough cobblestone pavement, singly and in families, covered with what rags and dirty quilt blankets they had.

September 24, 1921. When the English "Save the Child Fund" organization came to Saratov,[17] the Soviets, in order to accommodate them, turned Dr. Mordvinkin out of his comfortable house and lodged him somewhere in a single room (full of insects).

I put a patch on my hunting boots today: cobblers charge absurd prices, and I have not received my salary for over two months owing to the financial straits of the Soviets.

This is not my first experience with cobbling.

October 3, 1921. Sugar issued today on the university ration (2 lbs.) is not only damp, but positively and disgustingly wet. Professor Kaplinskii,[18] in charge of the university store and of the distribution of supplies, has carried sugar by the sackful to his wife out in the country, according to her neighbor's statements.

October 6, 1921. Got up at 5 A.M., had rice soup with a whole

17. The Save the Child Fund opened its Saratov office about the same time as the ARA (see note 19 below).

18. V. Ia. Kaplinskii, member of the department of philology at Saratov University, 1918–30.

woodcock in it for breakfast, and at 6:20 was off for the woods. Had tea at Raspberry Spring, with a piece of rye bread. Brought home eight woodcock and a hare, having covered during the day (I returned at 9 P.M.) a little over twenty-five miles according to my pedometer. Would have had a better bag had I had a dog.

October 14, 1921. Mrs. Osetrov, an old friend of mine, was arrested at the railroad station when she was about to board a train on her way to her husband, from whom she had been separated for two years under pressure of the Bolsheviks. As soon as she located him, she sold everything she had and with her aged mother and two children, three and five years old, was about to start on her journey when the Cheka appeared on the scene. She and her mother were taken to a separate room at the station, both stripped to the skin and searched, their baggage was rifled, my friend arrested, her money and the store of provisions she had with her taken away. Her mother and the two girls were thrown out into the street to shift for themselves. The old lady, widow of a wealthy landowner ruined by the Bolshevik revolution, was compelled to place the children in a Soviet orphan asylum to save them from death by starvation, and terribly suffered from want and anxiety for over three weeks, when her daughter was at last liberated without any explanation having been given her of the cause of her arrest and of the detention in the filthy Soviet jail. Her children came home with a skin disease that they had contracted in their temporary refuge and which will take a long time to cure.

October 26, 1921. Called on Ivan Ilich Nikiforov, a ruined, self-made printer and stationer, born and bred peasant. Only Mrs. N. was at home: the head of the family had left for the country in search of supplies. They had not had any bread for two weeks, and lived on potatoes, potato soup, pumpkins of their own raising, and the like. They had no money either. Out in the country, where they had been weeks before after provisions, they found peasants living exclusively on potatoes, too.

[Sometime in late October Babine went to work for the American Relief Administration, or ARA.—Ed.]

November 2, 1921. An old German farmer called at the ARA office[19]

19. The American Relief Administration opened its Saratov office in October and began feeding services the following month.

View from the ARA office, Saratov (Photo courtesy of the Hoover Institution)

and wanted to know if he could return to the U.S. "But can they make a mistake like this there?" he wanted to know. "The devil has made me come here," he grumbled. When Kinne[20] asked him about the cause of his destitution, he anxiously looked around and said: "May I talk. . . . *They* want to take everything away from you so as to make you come to them and beg for your own. . . . I used to have a big herd of cattle and many horses—now I have only two horses and two cows left, and am compelled to sell even them for lack of forage."

November 3, 1921. We keep our lodgings intentionally in a state of extreme neglect and dirt, with all ornaments, hangings, pictures, rugs, etc., out of sight, and with a stablelike kitchen, in order to scare the Soviet house hunters away from our house, which looks rather tempting from the outside. We have been successful so far.

November 7, 1921. The Maizul's, before starting on their return trip to Poland, hid their valuables in a feather bed, but had it confiscated at the border.[21]

November 9, 1921. American supply cars are regularly disabled and

20. David B. Kinne, district supervisor of the ARA, arrived in Saratov in October 1921.

21. By the fall of 1917, more than 20,000 Poles and an additional 6,000 Polish Jews had been evacuated from the front to Saratov province.

Saratov children fed by the ARA (Photo courtesy of the Hoover Institution)

ARA poster (Courtesy of the Hoover Institution)

detained at Kochetovka[22] or between Kochetovka and Tambov, and robbed. Neither the railroad authorities nor the Cheka have found (if they have sought) any means to check this abuse or to establish the present whereabouts of seven cars lost from American trains sent from Moscow on October 12, 14, and 18.

November 15, 1921. Our courier has brought a report that Pugachevsk[23] has been sacked by a band of "brigands" (anti-Soviet insurgents). Kinne had the report confirmed at the Gubispolkom.[24] The insurgents remained in town only about two hours, killed every Communist they laid their hands on, ransacked Communist offices, placed a strong guard at the American supply train, and left at the approach of a Soviet armored train. Assurance has been given by the local Saratov Soviet that it would find out all that is possible about Mr. Floete[25] and the American products at Pugachevsk.

November 18, 1921. The October university ration was issued only today. It contained 36 lbs. of rye flour, 7 lbs. of "meat" (which I had to throw away), 1 lb. of country butter, 1 lb. of damp granulated sugar, 2 lbs. of coarse dirty salt, 1 lb. of barley coffee, 20 lbs. of millet, 10 lbs. of lentils (unwinnowed), ¼ lb. of soap, and 2 boxes of worthless Soviet matches. This is the best ration we have had yet.

November 18 [28?—Ed.], 1921. Kinne and the Soviet provincial commissar (a Jew)[26] nearly quarreled this morning over admitting priests to local famine relief committees. The commissar bitterly opposed the priests as counterrevolutionaries and "bandit" (insurgent) spies. "Priests tell the people the relief has come from God. . . . God had nothing to do with this relief. It has come from the American people and the ARA."

November 30, 1921. Coleman[27] returned from Uralsk at 8 A.M. From fifteen to twenty corpses are dragged daily through that town, stripped of all clothing: their clothes are saved for the living. The

22. A settlement in Tambov province.

23. Called Nikolaevsk, 1835–1918. Landing on the right bank of a tributary of the Volga, now located in present-day Saratov oblast.

24. Provincial Executive Committee of the Soviet which governed the province.

25. I was unable to identify him.

26. The Soviet provincial commissar at this time was Stiksov.

27. Walter H. A. Coleman, an assistant with the ARA in Saratov.

500–600 children deported from Uralsk by the same train with Coleman to be forwarded to some point in Saratov were stripped naked and thrown on the straw in their boxcars: their rags and shoes were kept for those left behind. Eleven children died between Uralsk and Saratov.

December 2, 1921. The family doctor of a well-to-do typhus patient worried about the temperature not going down quickly enough to suit him and suggested a consultation. Professor Krylov[28] was decided on. His maid had to be given fifty thousand rubles before she admitted the patient's wife to the Presence. When approached, the professor grandly said he did not treat cases like that; but finally consented to see that patient for two million rubles. He examined him, pronounced the treatment correct, collected his fee, reminded his hosts that the cab was to be paid for by the family, and departed.

December 4, 1921. There is great mortality in the city from disease[29] and starvation. Dr. Uroda asked the drayman in charge of the removal of bodies to the cemetery about how many he would move in a day. "This is my thirty-fifth man, and my fifth trip, and I am not through yet. There are five of us, picking up corpses all over the city."

About fifteen to twenty corpses are taken daily from the railroad station, where people are dying of starvation.

December 7, 1921. The Soviet official in charge of potato distribution has told Kaplinskii that if he got some morphine for him again, he would give the university another lot of potatoes. Now K. is hunting for the dope—in order to get enough of it "to make him forget that we have already had our share."

December 12, 1921. An old German farmer from Gnadentan called at the ARA office this morning and asked if Kinne could not do something to deliver their neighborhood from bandits. Suppress-

28. D. O. Krylov, member of the faculty of medicine, 1913–25.

29. As of November 1, 1921, 28 percent of the province's population was classified as starving. By December 1 this figure had risen to 37 percent, and by January 22, 1922, had shot up to 68 percent. Cholera epidemics were a sorry complement to the lack of food and to the widespread filth. By March 1922 an estimated 81,000 adults and 425,000 children had been evacuated from the province. The famine was particularly devastating in those districts in which food requisitioning had been most successful and brutal.

 ing a smile and having cautioned Kinne, I translated the German's request. But the obtuse Yankee did not appreciate the humor of the situation, sent for Poretskii[30]—the Communist (and Cheka) factotum whom the ARA had very unwisely accepted, and told him to transmit the old man's application to the head state commissar. The German barely had time to say that there were good men among those bandits who wished to give up their raids but would not trust the Soviet amnesty proclamation—that indeed they would surrender if Americans had vouched for the Soviets, that there were "White bandits" and "Red bandits," and that both took away their cattle and horses—when Poretskii hurriedly spirited him away.

December 19, 1921. At a conference on medical relief it was suggested today that it would be a good idea to open a soap factory in Saratov to supply the surrounding countryside. A doctor from the German districts said that the necessary fats used to be obtained from dead animals. At present all animals are in bad condition, are killed for food, and no fats can be had. Even cats and dogs have been eaten. "Sometimes you enter a house, and see only one person at the tub—the rest hiding somewhere, as they stay naked while their clothes are washed and dried."

December 29, 1921. Kinne drunk yesterday and today—having received a good supply of imported liquor for Christmas. McElroy[31] is powerless to keep him from the booze, and Kinne himself has not will power enough to fight the devil. The relief work suffers badly —Clapp[32] and Uralsk were forgotten yesterday, the Mennonites[33] neglected today.

December 30, 1921. Distressing reports come from the once flourishing Dergachi country, across the Volga from Saratov. The mortality this fall has gone up to 324 per thousand of population. The Soviet kitchen rather irregularly issues to the starving some 320 calories a day. The soup it issues looks like a thin paste with pieces of unpeeled potatoes in it, which a doctor friend of mine could not induce himself to taste. The sick lying on the floor of their cabins,

30. I was unable to identify him.

31. Dr. Jesse L. McElroy, an ARA assistant and representative of the Red Cross, who arrived in Saratov in December 1921.

32. Paul S. Clapp, an ARA assistant, who arrived in Saratov in October 1921.

33. Refers to the German colonists.

swollen from starvation, with malodorous inflammation of periosteum, decomposing cartilage, and diarrhea, would have, besides this soup, a black half-baked pone of wild millet, with powdered chaff in it, and at times—but seldom—with pumpkin, potatoes, or flour added to it, or else a boiled piece of old rawhide. In some townships all rawhide had been eaten up before the cold weather set in, and people began to use old sheepskins for food, singeing off the wool. Cats, dogs, and gophers were eaten everywhere. A bloated old woman who had managed somehow to drag herself to a village dispensary (at Ershov) to get medicine for the family complained in my friend's presence that it was getting harder and harder to get a little kitty or a little doggy even in Christ's name. Whole families have migrated to town, live by begging, and lodge in abandoned houses and other buildings. The county hospital is daily besieged by starving humanity. The poor victims of Soviet spoliation would lie on the ground in front of it until given at least a small piece of bread. They eat all the garbage near the hospital and fight the few surviving dogs for it. Whole families die out. At one time the local relief committee had hired workers to dig graves for future emergencies before the ground froze, and paid them half a pound of flour and half a pound of potatoes a day. The good work, however, had to stop for lack of provisions.

December 31, 1921. I took Dr. McElroy to the university this morning and showed the university outhouses to him. It is hard to imagine a man more disgusted than the doctor was. The frozen excrement was piled up eighteen inches and two feet high above what were supposed to be seats. The floors were covered with excrement and thick ice that made the use of the place next to impossible. The place has always been a source both of contempt and disgust to me chiefly because the university authorities—our lights of learning and liberalism—have always tolerated these conditions and to my knowledge never took any steps to mend them.

I was especially sorry for female students who had to use these dirty sheds.

1922

Not surprisingly, Babine's last diary entries focus on the horrors of the Volga famine. The ARA *reports substantiate Babine's depiction of the suffering and provide even more graphic, firsthand accounts from other districts, where there were cholera and influenza epidemics, cannibalism, and packs of starving wolves and swollen humans roaming the steppes. Those in the city were undoubtedly better off than the wasted mass of humanity in the countryside. As* ARA *operations intensified, for instance, parcels of food, clothing, and medicines brought relief to the members of the teaching staff at Saratov University. By 1922 a new saying had entered into popular usage: an American package brought more than food and clothing, it "brought good luck."*

It certainly did for Babine. His survival and escape from Russia involved a stroke of good fortune and the aid of his American friends. As an ARA *interpreter, Babine was entitled to a life-sustaining ration. He also received timely food remittances from friends at Cornell, and he enlisted the support of the* ARA *office staff to assist him in fleeing Russia. James P. Goodrich, former governor of Indiana, met Babine while touring* ARA *facilities. Goodrich later recounted his adventures to Jerome Barker Landfield (1871–1954), who had befriended Babine at Cornell in the 1890s. Landfield, then associate editor of* The Independent, *contacted Cornell University's George Lincoln Burr to see how they might help Babine return to America. Both men consulted Dr. Vernon Kellogg, secretary of the National Research Council, who was associated with the* ARA *and who remembered Babine from his Stanford days. Although Kellogg believed that Babine, in his letters to Burr and Landfield, had exaggerated the danger he was in in Saratov and did not "limit his talking to the necessities of the case," the* ARA *files indicate that Russian employees of the* ARA *were indeed under constant threats by the local authorities. In a practical sense, the problem in helping*

 Babine was simply that he had not taken out American citizenship earlier. Still, he eventually managed to return to the States through the intercession of his American friends and benefactors and via a strategy he himself had suggested: he reached Riga and from there London "under the ARA *flag."*

Babine's observations during his short stay in Moscow in mid-1922 show how the famine had made Saratov a world apart from the national capital. The diary entries reveal the extent to which the New Economic Policy had revived initiative in Moscow and had begun to restore the economy. Finally, they expose a style of bureaucratic rule and lack of initiative, born during the Civil War, which would become a mainstay of Soviet political culture.

January 2, 1922. Cobb[1] and I went to Bishop Dositheos[2] of Saratov this morning to deliver Patriarch Tikhon's[3] note to him. We went to the two little rooms assigned to him in his former palatial residence, and were told that the bishop was in his office. The bishop's attendant took us there in our auto. We went up a flight of very dirty stone stairs, and behind a rough board partition found the bishop in an unheated room, sitting at a table, surrounded by a dense crowd of untidy, musty petitioners over whose applications the bishop was poring. I leaned toward the old man's ear (he is hard of hearing) and told him what our errand was, to which he said he would see us in another room. We were conducted through a hall to a door with a cheap padlock on it, and shown into a little cubbyhole in which three of us could not move without jostling. The bishop came immediately after us, asked us to be seated, remained standing seeing that there was no room for us to sit, glanced over the letter informing him of a shipment of some $500 worth of provisions for his clergy, observed it was very good for his people across

1. Russell Cobb, ARA Russian unit staff member.

2. Dositheos or Dosifei.

3. Patriarch Tikhon, V. I. Belavin (1865–1925), was the first patriarch of the Russian Orthodox church after the office was reestablished in 1917. Although a strong opponent of Bolshevik power, he had issued a circular in September 1919 calling for the clergy to end their opposition to the government. In late 1921 and early 1922, however, he directed local clergy not to hand over church valuables which the Bolsheviks began requisitioning, ostensibly to be used to feed the starving. U. S. organizations wishing to assist the Orthodox clergy in Soviet Russia addressed packages of supplies to Tikhon in January 1922. He divided the 300 packages among the seven bishops serving in the famine provinces, who saw to it that the ARA supervisors delivered the goods to needy clergy.

the Volga, thanked the ARA, and we left him in his narrow, cold, comfortless closet. Poor old man.

The ARA New Year supper party purportedly cost 12 million rubles. The music was good, the table inappropriately—almost indecently—sumptuous. My friends have said they had not seen a table so served and provisioned for many years. Kinne, dead drunk, had to stay at home. All Englishmen present got drunk. Two of them behaved improperly to the ladies. It is bounty, and not justice, that saved them from getting slapped in the face, and their besotted condition, too. Day[4] slept under Flynn's[5] office desk till noon.

January 6, 1922. (Pokrovsk) [We brought] a Christmas tree for the Pokrovsk children. Kinne and I were utterly disgusted with a ragged crowd of them in front of the city theater. The program was not badly arranged—with clowns, dances, sleight-of-hand performances that amused the children. Before the feast prepared for the Americans began, they were all invited to a little dark closet, where a demijohn of some strong concoction was produced. Kinne swallowed three tumblers of the stuff, liked it, but looked dazed at the table. I found out afterward that the mixture consisted of pure alcohol with some aromatic spirits of ammonia in it. At the table Kinne drank two more tumblers, and was quite drunk. After Cobb's speech, Kinne tried to speak, too, but could not get up, and spoke only sitting, while I stood up translating his incoherent sentences. With plenty of pure alcohol, champagne, wine, and beer under his belt, Kinne was finally unable to walk straight, and refused to go home at the time set, unable to make up his mind as to his movements when the time came. The Pokrovsk committee louts insisted on his staying. He was in a pitiful state when McElroy and I left for Saratov, leaving him in Cobb's care, who, though pink in the face, was in full control of his faculties, having only one tumbler of the nasty stuff inside him, and that forced on him.

January 9, 1922. The Soviets are highly displeased with Dr. McElroy's visiting the hospitals without being accompanied by any Communists: he, not properly and safely attended, may thus get the wrong impression from what he sees, and especially from what he may hear. The ARA courier has brought whisky, gin, and other bev-

4. Rush O. Day, ARA Russian unit staff member.
5. William E. Flynn, ARA Russian unit staff member.

 erages from Moscow. Last night Franklin,[6] of the English mission, came to the house, and Kinne, Franklin, and Cobb drank one bottle of Scotch and ¾ of a bottle of gin among them. Kinne is in bed today; Cobb is OK, on duty, but gloomy.

January 10, 1922. At the reception given last night by the English mission, Kinne, Webster,[7] and Birman[8] got disgustingly drunk. They joined in one brotherly embrace, hardly able to stand on their feet. Some of the English vomited. Kinne spent all night at the mission, and did not report on duty today, as he did not report yesterday. Cobb said this morning rather gloomily: "I'm getting tired of the damned thing. . . . I'll either have all of it or none of it," meaning the job he has to attend to in Kinne's absence.

January 13, 1922. Lord Robertson, Member of Parliament,[9] wished to see the Pokrovsk kitchens. Kinne and I met him and the rest of the English party of five in their car at the station and thence went to Pokrovsk in three autos—our worn-out Ford and the two brand-new English Fords. Mr. Bulle,[10] a Moscow Soviet representative, a Red Army man, and other individuals in Soviet service accompanied the party. Mr. Robertson is an elderly gentleman, keen, intelligent, thorough, well bred as are all members of the English party. Two members of it looked Jewish, and not in keeping with the rest. We went to the Pokrovsk committee's office, where Kinne spoke of the situation quite frankly, unmindful of Bulle & Co. "Then 75 percent of these people (in Dergachi and Novouzensk) are practically condemned, since your grain, your 36 million poods, cannot reach them owing to bad transportation facilities," was Mr. Robertson's conclusion. We visited two kitchens and went back to our Saratov office, where further details were given to Lord Robertson. "Today is the 13th—my mother's birthday, and Friday, too. Friday the 13th

6. Probably James H. Franklin of the Federal Council of Churches.

7. Webster was a British superintendent.

8. Birman was the local representative of Aleksandr Eiduk, the Soviet government's representative to the ARA and other relief organizations. See note 51 below.

9. Most likely Sir Benjamin Robertson, chairman of the British United Russian Famine Relief Committee. A member of the India Council, he had administered famine relief in India before bringing his experience and expertise to Russia.

10. I was unable to identify him.

—an unlucky day. . . . Something bad must happen," said Kinne, leaving the office.

January 14, 1922. Kinne returned home at 2:30 A.M. today. He was at his desk at 10:30, and quite fresh. McElroy came in, and they went together to his office. Then Kinne disappeared for about two hours. He returned with a wobbly gait, and fell rather than sat into his chair. I hurried the pending business, various office appointments and two or three other papers. A visitor or two strolled in, when Cobb called me to the side office and shut the door after me. "Tell this man," said he pointing to Kinne's chauffeur, "that I will kill him if he dares to get another drop of spirits for Kinne, will just kill him." I saw it was hard for him to keep his hands from the man's throat, all six-feet-two of him trembling with emotion. "I am not trying to scare him—I will actually kill him." When the chauffeur explained that he had refused three times yesterday and twice today to comply with Kinne's orders, and got the spirits under compulsion, unable to lie any longer, Cobb calmed down, and we began to make plans for getting rid of the chauffeur at least temporarily. Later on I learned that, considering the detriment to the work of the administration and the disrepute the personnel was falling into among the Russian employees and the Soviet through Kinne's inebriety, McElroy had sent a wire to "Moscow Lonergan confidential can you find a good job for Kinne in Moscow condition hopeless do you understand." Lonergan[11] was very intimate with Kinne and a great drunkard, too. After dinner McElroy and Cobb put Kinne to bed, and are going to send him to Novouzensk with the next shipment of supplies to that base—pending Moscow's action.

January 24, 1922. A letter dated January 21, 1922, came this morning to our ARA office from a Russian physician who had received one of the ten-dollar food packages sent to Russia for distribution among needy members of the medical profession. Overwhelmed with gratitude, the recipient of the gift immediately sat down and wrote a letter of appreciation—"An open letter to American physicians," which Kinne found impolitic to forward even to the Moscow office of the ARA. "In spite of the hardships of the old regime," says the writer, "of five years in Siberian exile, of eight arrests, I

11. Captain Thomas C. Lonergan, Colonel Haskell's deputy appointed "executive officer" of ARA operations in Moscow.

 was able to do the work I loved. Now our work has been ruined and entrusted to ignoramuses. My earnings never were so insignificant as they are now. I always had enough for myself and for my family. Under present conditions, my salary sometimes would not be paid for three months at a time, and we have to live by selling our belongings. For my whole family I get from the government less than 36 lbs. of rye flour and a few pounds of rotten potatoes a month, and no meat or butter. Even in our Siberian exile we were better off. Every day I had a two-course dinner, two pounds of black or white bread, tea and sugar, milk, butter, and eggs—and never imagined I would ever lack black bread. Now, in spite of my occupying a responsible government position, we have no meat or milk for weeks at a time, never can afford to buy butter, eggs, or sugar, and have to divide our black bread into small portions in order to make it last and go around. Formerly I was not afraid of illness; now illness (typhoid or pneumonia) twice compelled me and my family literally to starve. In Siberia I always could make my room as warm as I wanted even in the coldest weather; now, with a nursing baby on our hands, we have to live in a room where we can always see our breath. I lecture on hygiene and sanitation; I try to raise the people's culture, and at the same time use for my family of five only two buckets of water a day, do not bathe my children for months, have no kitchen, no city water, no sewage, not even an outhouse. The fact of my being a full-fledged citizen of the Soviet Socialist Republic is no comfort to me, since my service is a compulsory thraldom; *all* Russia is now under secret observation that is not regulated by any laws. The Cheka can break into my house any night, throw me without trial into an overcrowded jail reeking with typhus and governed more wantonly than any jail under the tsar had ever been. I cannot earn anything with my pen, since there is no press in Russia any longer.

"Now you have sent us white flour, rice, sugar, lard, tea, milk. It is long since we had any of these, and both my wife and myself, being very much undernourished, have already suffered from scurvy. Tea and lard shall be shared by all the family; but the rest of the products my wife and I have decided to save for our two children, eight years and two months old. They will last them two months, and we shall use our earnings for ourselves alone. . . . My wife is a physician, too. In olden times she alone used to earn enough to support our whole family. Now she has to nurse the baby, to take care of it, there being no servant to cook our food, to scrub the floors, to do our washing and all other housework, to make our linen and to alter our old costumes into something fit to wear. She, of course, cannot do any hospital work, since it would take her away from home for hours at a time. My daughter is to graduate from medical school in a year. She already has done hospital work, has had cholera and typhus cases on her hands. At present she cannot help the family with any earnings of her own since she must hurry to graduate. Besides, she would lose her student ration if she took up some employment. Thus our family of three efficient workers and only two small children cannot support itself owing to the conditions of utter confusion in the country. Such is ours, and such is the general situation in Russia. Nothing is being built here; everything is being destroyed—houses, factories and mills, schools, social order, and all in this Russia of ours. During the second year of the Great War I had occasion to be of service to some Austrian and German refugees whose condition here was truly dreadful. When some of them asked me what they could do for me in return, I said self-complacently at the time: 'Give me Goethe's and Schiller's works—that's all.' Now I have received some daily bread from their side of the border. It is a fair compensation. Once more, I thank you."[12]

January 26, 1922. Water is again freezing in my washbowl. But this year I stand the cold of my unheated room much better than I did last or especially the one before last when winter seemed so terribly cold. I get better food owing to my work for the ARA. I also come home only to sleep and to get my breakfast and supper, staying the rest of the time either in the ARA office or at the university.

January 27, 1922. Miss K. P. Kamenskaia, a very promising student of mine, has to be on duty at her office at 9 A.M. She goes to the university immediately after the office and gets home at 9 P.M. on weekdays. Only then she starts the fire in her little firebox and cooks her potato soup or millet gruel, and sometimes coffee, never having time to eat in the morning or during the day. She "really washes" only in the evening, too, when she has hot water, only wiping her "little mug" a little in the morning "like a kitten," the

12. The original letter can be found in the Babine Papers, Manuscript Division, Library of Congress.

 water is so cold. For her irregular mode of life she looks quite healthy and is always cheerful. The only time I saw her moody was after she got news from home of their house having been raided and looted by the Soviets and a friend of the house murdered right in the house and without any provocation. She has not received her salary for months, though entitled to two rations that have only flour in them of any value.

At Poretskii's suggestion a "shashlyk" party was held in an Armenian dive last night. Having lectured at the university, and distrusting Poretskii, I declined to take part in it. The spree was over at about 10 P.M. After it, Kinne and Cobb, both quite full, went to the theater, where they were to join McElroy and his company. They found all doors closed. While looking for an entrance, they got separated, Cobb losing Kinne. Cobb returned home at about 11 P.M., staggered first into Flynn's room, then went to his own. Kinne appeared much later. Having lost Cobb, he started for home, but walked in such a tortuous way that a cabby who knew him offered to take him home. Just as he got into the sleigh, two men appeared, laid their hands on him and declared him under arrest for intoxication. Kinne was taken to the Cheka office and thoroughly searched in spite of his protests. Only after his pockets had been rifled did the officials condescend to look at his American passport, profusely apologized and set him free. Both Kinne and Cobb are terribly sick today and confined to their quarters. Cobb got sick in bed last night without knowing it. Dr. McElroy says they must have been drugged. Cobb went to the party in order to look after Kinne, was on his guard all the time, and drank Kinne's glass, knowing his own capacity to stand liquor. But it burnt his insides like fire, and quickly affected him beyond expectation. He drank only four glasses, and Kinne apparently less. Cobb has no doubt that the thing had been framed up by Poretskii—this seems perfectly natural to me.

January 29, 1922. Sending Mukhannov[13] out of the room on some errand, Kinne told me this morning of his having been warned that charges had been proferred against me of hostility to the Soviets, that I was to be called up before the Cheka to be told that I was to be shot unless I mended my ways. "Have your story ready, should

13. Apparently a Soviet employee of the ARA.

they dare to touch you while we are here," said he. Knowing the Soviet's unfailing efficiency in these matters, I immediately wrote brief farewell letters to my American friends, stating the facts and asking for help on their part if any could be rendered.[14]

February 2, 1922. Speaking about a leading Uralsk Bolshevik, Clapp, the ARA local supervisor, writes: "He has a heart of gold. He has killed fifteen men with his own hands."

February 3, 1922. Dr. McElroy left Saratov this P.M., disgusted with the work conditions here—dirt, incapacity, pettiness, and the formalism of Soviet officialdom.

February 4, 1922. Dr. Morehead,[15] of the Lutheran Church in the U.S., is here to examine the field—several times closeted in our office with local Lutheran clergymen, all of them Germans. Kinne is sick again, but Cobb keeps him under lock and key and out of Dr. Morehead's way. Today Kinne all of a sudden disappeared from the house and was not to be found anywhere. At 7 P.M. he was discovered in his office with a streetwalker. He did not even look ashamed, but merely laughed in a silly, defiant way.

February 9, 1922. Mukhannov has brought a letter from Moscow from McElroy to Cobb, which says that both Haskell[16] and Lonergan stand by Kinne—"the best man they have."

February 10, 1922. The 27th Division of the Red Army has received a secret order to go to the Rumanian frontier in a few days.[17]

One of the city hospitals has refused to accept medical supplies sent by the ARA, owing to a Soviet secret order not to deal with the ARA except through the Soviets.

February 11, 1922. People have been undressed by footpads in this frost right in the streets, and without clothes and shoes, in their

14. The Department of Manuscripts and University Archives, Cornell University Libraries, contains letters Babine wrote to George L. Burr, requesting assistance.

15. J. A. Morehead of the National Lutheran Council. The Lutheran Church in America also set up famine relief, especially in Russia's German community along the Volga.

16. Colonel William N. Haskell, Director of ARA operations in Russia.

17. Soviet-Rumanian relations were strained throughout this period. By this time the major problem concerned Rumania's occupation of Bessarabia.

 underwear alone, forced to speed home the best way they could. A lady friend of mine got pneumonia this way. A priest (St. Sergius Church) has been robbed on his way home from the evening service.

In Novouzensk a Soviet commissar removed the ARA warehouse manager without consulting the ARA, contrary to the Riga Agreement[18]—of which Kinne rather sharply informed Birman.

Cobb went to Pokrovsk this morning and found a man at the ARA warehouse—a Soviet agent—keeping tabs on what and to whom supplies were being issued. Cobb took the man to his office, examined his "mandate," told him whose warehouse it was, and who was running the show, and turned the man out without much ado. Arnhold[19] was instructed not to let any outsiders interfere with the ARA work in any way whatsoever.

February 12, 1922. An old woman doctor, Mrs. Harizomenova, returning home from a professional call, found two burglars in her lodging one afternoon, called the police, and had them arrested. Her rooms were found turned upside down. The thieves searched every nook, every pocket, and found all her money, wherever hidden—about 800,000 Soviet rubles. The money and the thieves were taken to a police station. Two hundred thousand of it melted away in transit to the station—"sausage was bought to feed the thieves," and two or three days later Mrs. Harizomenova met the burglars on the street looking for more loot.

February 14, 1922. Having run out of supplies, a woman in one of the famine-stricken districts began to use the body of her husband who had died of starvation for food. When local authorities got on to the fact and tried to remove what was left of the corpse, the wife and children of the dead man stuck to it in a state of wild frenzy shouting: "We won't give him up—we will eat him ourselves, he is ours."[20]

18. Signed between the Bolshevik government and the ARA, the Riga Agreement regulated the operations of the ARA within Russia. See Benjamin M. Weissman, *Herbert Hoover and Famine Relief to Soviet Russia, 1921–23* (Stanford, 1974), especially pp. 52–64.

19. D. A. Arnhold was an inventory taker at the Pokrovsk warehouse.

20. The local press and other contemporary sources carried other reports of cannibalism.

February 17, 1922. Rye bread is 50,000 Soviet rubles a pound at Pokrovsk, and up to 100,000 rubles in the famine-stricken surrounding countryside. There is no chance for the starving population to earn anything, all industrial life having become extinct under the Soviets.

February 20, 1922. Our woman mail-carrier has begged for a piece of bread. They have not received their salary for some time and have nothing to live on.

Mr. Landy[21] and his interpreter arrived today from Samara via Pugachev-Ershov-Pokrovsk. Their trip from Samara to Pugachev cost them 18 million Soviet rubles. They went through villages devastated by the famine. In Marievka only about ten houses out of seven thousand houses were inhabited: the rest is a cemetery. At Pugachev kegs of salted human flesh is brought every day from the outlying districts—and confiscated by the Soviet authorities. Mr. Landy took two day's provisions for his trip to Ershov (sixty miles from Pugachev). But it took them five days to cover the distance on account of a blizzard, and they were nearly starved. At Ershov the stationmaster, a Communist, said: "Let me show you what we do with your Pugachev people." He led the American guest to a barn where there lay seventy-five bodies of people starved to death and frozen stiff. He cried ("a Communist cried," repeated my informant) when he said that villagers had come and begged him on their knees, and kissed his hands, to let them have the corpses—to be used for food. Landy was three days on his way from Ershov to Pokrovsk, about 120 miles, and thinks he did well. He had a railroad inspector along with him who helped to expedite the travel. There are perfect mountains of snow between Ershov and Uralsk. When a train got stuck in the snow a few days ago, a snowplow was sent to its rescue, but got stuck, too. Then a train from Uralsk joined those. At present there are twelve engines between Ershov and Uralsk buried in the snow up to the top, cars and all.

Kinne is not on duty: he returned from last night's theater party only this morning at seven, and slept all day. After the theater he, Poretskii, and Perlov (a Jewish Soviet spy) went to a dive. Kinne managed to tank Poretskii up. Poretskii phoned for women, and

21. Louis A. Landy, ARA Russian unit staff member.

 in no more than three minutes, three of them appeared. He took a red-haired one. He, too, failed to show up this morning. His wife phoned for him several times, and finally went to all police stations looking for him—to Kinne's joy and amusement.

February 21, 1922. Robberies of supplies from our trains are so frequent, the transportation so bad, cooperation on the part of the railroad authorities, employees, and the Soviets in general so lukewarm and inefficient, that both Kinne and Cobb feel very much discouraged and want to leave the country as soon as they can. Our town transport agent (a young German-Russian) has been reported as removing, with the connivance and cooperation of the railroad service, supplies from the care of ARA before making out his statements of shortages. He is being watched by Soviet secret service men—who know too well on which side the bread is buttered.

February 22, 1922. Someone told me about Professor Stadnitskii's statement in his lecture this afternoon to the effect that a country doctor had been eaten up by the starving peasants in one of the outlying districts. Dr. Uroda has corrected the statement: it was a feldsher (a trained male nurse) that had been eaten, at Balakovo. He was a big, portly man, and his patients did not want him to go to waste when he died from some cause or other.

A medical friend of Dr. Uroda's has had an occasion to taste human flesh. Lost in a blizzard in the boundless Novouzensk prairies, he and his companion came across some frozen bodies, probably victims of the same blizzard and, to save themselves, they carved up, cooked, and ate part of them. The doctor stated that the worst part of that experience was the insuperable and uncomfortable craving he and his companion had acquired for human flesh.

February 22, 1922. A medical inspector of ours, driving through a German village, caught glimpse of a couple of little girls running toward the road. He looked back and saw the girls pick up the fresh, warm horse dung and eat it.

February 23, 1922. Our interpreter has been told at Pugachev that persons who have tried human flesh acquire a peculiar craving for it, and stop before nothing to get it.

In Pugachev children are not allowed to go out after dark—to safeguard them against being waylaid, killed, and used for food. To protect Americans against attacks, the Pugachev Soviet has issued revolvers to them with twenty-five shells apiece.

February 24, 1922. Kinne is still spreeing. He eats nothing. He is so weak that half a bottle of weak wine lays him flat. Poretskii has offered Mukhannov a bottle of pure alcohol for Kinne. But the youngster was willing enough to tell the lout, at my suggestion, that Kinne was already well supplied with liquor.

It is certainly to the Soviets' advantage to keep Kinne drunk and out of their way as much as possible.

February 25, 1922. During their carousal of a few days ago, Poretskii got hold of Kinne's pocketbook. This explains how a check for 1.3 billion Soviet rubles turned out to be in Poretskii's hands when Kinne had given it up for lost. But besides this check, Kinne was missing a copy of a confidential letter to Haskell on conditions in Saratov. Last night at the ARA house Cobb actually grabbed Poretskii and demanded surrender of the letter, but Poretskii denied all knowledge of it. At midnight Poretskii came to the house again and said he could not sleep. But Cobb still wanted the letter.

February 27, 1922. Kinne sent in his resignation yesterday by wire. His nerves are badly shattered. His heart gave out, and a doctor had to be sent for last night to pull him through.

Before leaving Saratov, Dr. Morehead intimated that he was not going to tell any tales in Moscow. He actually has told Haskell that Kinne was the best man for the job he had seen in Russia. I hope it was a mere courtesy and Christian charity on his part.

February 28, 1922. Kinne is at his desk, and his own man, again, working as of old. He called in Poretskii and told him to return the copy of the confidential letter to Moscow abstracted from his pocketbook in a dive a few days ago when the pocketbook was passed to Poretskii to pay the bill. (We knew that the letter had been taken to Aksanova[22] for translation and that Aksanova had been threatened to be shot if she squealed.) Poretskii denied all knowledge of the paper. But Kinne would not give in, knowing all the facts: "There is no use talking about it. You know all about it.

22. Probably a Soviet interpreter employed by the ARA and by the local Cheka.

 So do I. I know it was in this building. I know where it is now [meaning the Cheka of course], and I want you to return it to me for my files. You need not assure me that you know nothing about it since I know that you do. And I want it back. That's all. Moreover, if you cannot return it this afternoon, you need not report on duty tomorrow."

I wondered if Poretskii ever as much as dreamed that he had been given away by a Cheka rival of his?

March 2, 1922. It has turned out that a waiter found the paper on the floor. Not knowing what it was about, he finally decided to show it to Poretskii—who returned it to the owner.

March 7, 1922. Colonel Haskell came last night with Mrs. Haskell, Miss Gardner,[23] and Mr. Mitchell.[24] Today he inspected the Medical and Food Remittance Sections in the morning, went to Pokrovsk with all of his following in the afternoon, and to the opera in the evening. Ammonia keeps Kinne in shape, with three moderate drinks a day administered by Hand,[25] who keeps the liquor locked up in his trunk, and though Kinne smells of rum, he manages to hold his ground—and to save Haskell from learning too much.

March 8, 1922. Kinne is down again, having taken just one little drink too many this morning. He went to the colonel's car, but was soon sent back to the house with an order to go to bed. The colonel remained at Kinne's desk all morning and afternoon, and I kept my seat in the office, acting as his interpreter when needed. Just before leaving the office, Haskell dictated a wire to Moscow ordering to relieve Kinne "as soon as possible" and to send Jones[26] or any other good available man to Saratov. Ten minutes before going to the house he sent Hand there to put Kinne in shape.

Kinne has given the colonel his word of honor to abstain from liquor until relieved.

Mr. Mitchell is a Stanford graduate ('10), and has given me his latest news about Newsom, the Marxes, Pierce, and others.[27]

23. Nellie E. Gardner, ARA staff member.

24. Mowatt M. Mitchell, assistant director of the ARA's European Headquarters.

25. Harry V. Hand, an ARA assistant who arrived in Saratov in February 1922.

26. Dr. Glenn G. Jones replaced Kinne in March 1922.

27. Friends and colleagues of Babine from his Stanford days, 1898–1902.

Just before Haskell left, I asked to be transferred to Moscow owing to the undesirable and dangerous complications in Saratov. He found it inadvisable to take me from Saratov immediately, with a new man coming in, but promised to consider that matter at a future date.

March 10, 1922. Kinne was drunk at the theater last night and this afternoon, unable to keep his promise to Haskell.

March 11, 1922. Kinne drunk as ever. I had a hard time rousing him this afternoon to go to the direct wire as per appointment with Cobb at Rtishchevo.

March 12, 1922. Finding the door of my restaurant closed today, I looked at a note on it—which read: *Po sluchaiu godovshchiny Sv. monarkh segodnia zakryto*. Officially, for the Soviet authorities, it would be interpreted to mean: "because of the anniversary of the overthrow of the monarchy closed today." To faithful Russians, however, it meant: "In memory of the anniversary of our sacred monarch closed today."[28]

March 16, 1922. A dead horse has been lying for several days in front of our neighbor's house. Returning home this afternoon, I saw a dog's tail sticking out of the animal's belly and nervously twitching: the rest of the dog was belaboring the interior of the carcass.

March 17, 1922. The spring sun was playing on my windows for all it was worth this morning, and the ice that had accumulated on them during the winter began to melt and flood the windowsill, which is also a book shelf. To save my books, I temporarily moved them to my couch and, armed with a table knife, scraped the ice off the panes. Thoroughly warmed on the sun side, it came off quite readily, so that after an hour's work on my two windows I filled two horsepails with it to the top, and threw it out into our yard. I never suspected my lungs could make so productive an ice plant.

March 18, 1922. Received a telegram from John Newsom, % ARA, in answer to my letter of January 29:[29] "Am taking matter up immedi-

28. The abbreviation *sv.* could mean "overthrow" (*sverzhenie*) or "sacred" or "holy" (*sviatoi*).

29. Letter to George L. Burr, dated January 29, requesting assistance in fleeing Russia.

 ately can you make any further suggestion as to needs answer." I feel very happy indeed.

Took my first sponge bath today since last October. I had forty-eight degrees Fahrenheit in my room, and an afternoon to myself for the first time in a long while.

April 2, 1922. A battalion of starved soldiers from Uralsk looted the Mitrofan Produce Market yesterday.

April 4, 1922. Black bread is 120,000 Soviet rubles a pound.

April 12, 1922. For the last two days the ARA mess hall workers have been finding fine broken glass in their food and coffee. A deliberate effort to harm the staff is suspected, and my attempt to treat the matter as a joke proved unsuccessful, especially in view of some very interesting recent tilts with Birman, and his tools.

April 14, 1922. Price of products per pound: black bread—140,000 Soviet rubles, granulated sugar—500,000, rice—350,000, American lard—1,000,000, butter—800,000, meat—500,000.

April 21, 1922. Among other things, Dr. Jones has issued to Professor Kakushkin's clinic a number of blankets, sheets, and woolen socks. These the medical staff divided among themselves. But someone did not get enough and reported the matter to the Soviets. When an official investigation got under way, Kakushkin and Professor Markov[30] (who had a reputation for being a regular swindler) came to beg Jones for exculpation. Jones was indignant. After his sudden departure for Moscow, they called on Toole,[31] stating to him that Jones had found no fault with their conduct, which was an impudent lie. Markov was so disgusting that Pogorelova,[32] acting as interpreter, remonstrated with him on the impropriety of his conduct. The matter was hushed up owing to Spiridonov's[33] subservient intercession.

April 27, 1922. An order has been forwarded by mistake to the

30. V. N. Markov, department of pedagogy.

31. Dr. John J. E. Toole, an ARA assistant, arrived in Saratov in April 1922.

32. N. S. Pogorelova worked as chief clerk in the office's medical division.

33. F. I. Spiridonov, a Soviet employed as "workman" in the Saratov ARA office.

ARA office, directing all office employees to report at the May 1 demonstration and implying penalties for absentees.[34]

May 4, 1922. Waiting for a lecture, I noticed that a female student was picking up something from the desk she was sitting at and putting it into her mouth. I began to wonder if she was not picking up crumbs of bread left on the desk by one of her predecessors (everybody eats everywhere nowadays—when he is lucky enough to get something to eat). She caught my look, laughed, and said she had not had anything to eat for two days—the issue of the student ration having been unexpectedly delayed—but that she had been promised her ration in a couple of days. Their monthly ration at present is 26 lbs. of rye flour—and they are the favored medical students.

May 5, 1922. "We three lived together last summer, all by ourselves. We taught in a German school the year before, but the school had to be closed for lack of funds and food supplies for the teaching staff, and of fuel, and of books, like everwhere," chirped the sweet Asya Arapova on our way home: "and all three starved. We had one dinner card for the three of us, and ate a Soviet dinner in turn—once in three days, and all three entered the university together. . . . Yes, we were in the same school. I taught history and geography. Irma taught mathematics, and Lena—Russian and German."

May 11, 1922. The city housing committee has called at the new neat little house of N. I. Benderov,[35] an Armenian businessman, who holds an important position under the local Soviets. He is an enthusiastic sportsman, who keeps two fine bird dogs and two fine pups, an excellent foxhound, decoy ducks, and a fine sports library. He now is to be evicted because, though not belonging to the unemployed idle element, he does not live up to workers' standards: when the Soviet committee entered his house, they saw white bread and butter on the dining room table.

May 12, 1922. The British have opened a student kitchen in Saratov city. Communist students were the first to get admission tickets, and the rest of the students got what was left.

34. This document can be found in Babine's papers, Manuscript Division, Library of Congress.

35. I was unable to uncover any additional information about Benderov.

May 14, 1922. Mme. Iumatova, vice-president of the Saratov Conservatory of Music, has applied for a food package, pleading that her need was great and means scant. At a restaurant a plate of soup costs from 50,000 to 60,000 Soviet rubles, and a small piece of meat 100,000 rubles. The lady considers herself more entitled to a free food package than Dr. Martens, for instance, who has received several packages merely because he entertains Kinne, and his daughter enjoy's Kinne's attention. Moreover, the doctor, as a skin disease specialist, is the most successful practitioner in Saratov, and is in no need of American relief.

May 16, 1922. At a meeting of the Auditing Office employees last Saturday a resolution was proposed to the effect that in spite of a new Soviet decree to the opposite, every Soviet employee should still belong to some union.[36] One simpleton rose to defend the new decree, and invited all present to abstain from voting. About twenty sided with him. The simpleton is already in jail, and the abstainers have been turned out of office.

May 17, 1922. A report from Atkarsk on distribution of the American corn (delivered by mistake to the ARA instead of to the Soviet office) shows that Soviet institutions, labor unions, and Communist bodies have received the corn contrary to the Riga Agreement. Mr. Gaskill[37] only laughed when I told him about it: he had not had any doubt it would be so.

The Soviets have certainly turned Kinne's drunkenness to their advantage.

May 19, 1922. Horses and other domestic animals refuse to eat "bread" prepared from various food substitutes and issued by the Soviets to the starved human bipeds.

May 20, 1922. An ARA medical inspector has just returned from Serdobsk. He states that the ARA medical supplies were about to

36. After the introduction of the New Economic Policy, unions were instructed not to be so militant. Placed in a weak bargaining position, the unions were directed to think in terms of national interests rather than those of their memberships. It is interesting to note that Saratov authorities appear to have interpreted the new directives in their own way.

37. Charles S. Gaskill, ARA district supervisor, arrived in Saratov in March 1922.

be placed in a local Soviet drugstore and to be issued to patients for money, according to the "New Economic Policy"[38] of the ruling party. With the inspector's arrival and under his direction the drugs were distributed among hospitals and other institutions.

May 22, 1922. Poretskii had made an agreement with his ARA coachman (a surly Hungarian)[39] to plant about twenty-five acres of land. Sabo contributed 130 million Soviet rubles toward the enterprise. They purchased seeds, etc., on the money. Now Poretskii has turned Sabo out, and the poor dullard has no proof of having ever advanced anything toward the undertaking, as all business had been transacted on faith.

May 23, 1922. University professors have received an "American present" consisting of 4 lbs. of cocoa, 2 lbs. of tea, 20 lbs. of dry soup, 20 lbs. of powdered potatoes, 6 tins of pork and beans, 1 tin of shoe polish, 2 cakes of good soap, and three yards of woolen fabric for a costume. The food is a great blessing to those who have not had an ARA ration or food packages from the U.S.

May 25, 1922. Dr. Toole, on a pleasure ride out of town this afternoon, ran into a decomposing corpse of a man near the Gusyloka bridge. The body was swollen up and black, the face eaten by flies, all in rags, and in bast shoes. The man is said to have died of starvation. Dr. Toole took a couple of photographs of the corpse.

May 26, 1922. On the day of his resignation from office (very nicely effected by Mr. Gaskill) Poretskii came at midnight to the ARA stable and asked for Sabo, the coachman. Sabo happened to be out at the time. Later on Poretskii came again, and ordered Sabo to hitch up. Sabo refused in view of the late hour. At that Poretskii pulled out his Browning automatic, and Sabo had to hitch up and to take the horse to Birman's stable, the horse that belonged to the ARA.

May 28, 1922. My landlord, a high school teacher, and his wife, a

38. The New Economic Policy (NEP), economic policy of the CPSU instituted after the Civil War, which ended grain requisitioning and replaced it with a tax in kind. The state monopoly of small and medium-scale retail trade and services manufacturers was abolished. The government maintained control over heavy industry, banking, and foreign trade.

39. Probably a former Austro-Hungarian prisoner of war who had remained in Russia.

 physician, still have to cook their meals, split wood, do their laundry work, etc., etc., without any time left for reading. The lady particularly complains of the forced discontinuance of all special periodical publications during the Soviet regime, and of the compulsory separation from the Western European world of science and literature.

June 9, 1922. Left Saratov for Moscow at 8 P.M., in a special car, with Colonel C. S. Gaskill, now on his way back home. This is my very first railroad trip since 1918. There are only two of us in the sumptuous saloon car, with our conductor. The train is making good time. Birman, who came to see the colonel off, must have told the engineer that there was an American railroad man aboard his train.

June 10, 1922. Have not slept so comfortably for a long time. We had fresh bedclothes, as in the good old times, and a good attendance. The colonel cooked flaked bacon and eggs on gas himself for breakfast, which was simply gorgeous, and we did not eat again till our dinner at the Pink House,[40] to which we were taken in a Cadillac from the train that arrived in Moscow exactly on time—at 5:15 P.M. It is a wonder to us that we were not searched as soon as we got out of Saratov and of Birman's jurisdiction: we were prepared for it, and had nothing with us that might have compromised us in any way. Some of my valuable papers were left in Saratov, to be forwarded to Moscow later on.

June 10, 1922. The Pink House is a palazzo of a former millionaire, with excellent pictures, crockery, many pianos, and rich furniture. It is such a rest after my hole in Saratov. Hutchinson[41] and Golder[42] are here.

June 11, 1922. It is curious to return to civilized conditions of exis-

40. The ARA took over six large houses in Moscow to house the fifty Americans engaged at the ARA headquarters in the Soviet capital. They were known as the Pink, White, Blue, Brown, and Green houses, and the Hermitage.

41. Lincoln Hutchinson, special investigator, ARA operations, Russian unit.

42. Frank A. Golder, special representative of Herbert Hoover. Born in Russia in 1877, Golder came to the United States in 1880 and was educated at Harvard. Following his tour of duty with the ARA, he taught at Stanford. Among his publications on Russia is (with Lincoln Hutchinson) *On the Trail of the Russian Famine* (Stanford, 1927).

tence, with hot water ready for you in the morning, your clothes brushed daily by a valet, your shoes shined, and your meals waiting for you in due time, while your nails no longer get jet black in your struggle for existence.

June 12, 1922. Called on Col. Haskell this morning. He wishes to keep me in Moscow for a few days or even weeks. I have been detailed to the medical warehouse at Boinia for duty, to be quartered there with the rest of the medical warehouse staff.

June 14, 1922. Searles[43] and I were already in bed when Farraher[44] entered our room hardly able to stand on his feet. Leaning on Searles's table, he explained to us that they had four women in their room and only three men, that he had so-and-so, and could we not come and help them, etc., etc., of the most disgusting character. We suggested his trying our neighbors, which he did.

June 16, 1922. Searles, returning from the Brown House, said he found everybody sick, with a slop pail by his bed after yesterday's spree, and the floor in awful condition, with stench in the house beyond description.

June 18, 1922. Driving in our ARA car purposely to a women's swimming beach in Moscow, some of our men stopped on the bank and studied the female anatomy through a field glass, to the wonderment of the uncouth Russian passersby. Tourtillot[45] was especially hungry for the sight: the bathers wore no suits.

June 20, 1922. Tourtillot invited me to his room to help him out with one of his girl callers that could not speak English. She wondered if all Americans were like those who came with the ARA to Moscow. "Our Russian young men are not much on morals, I mean about women, but they are angels in comparison with you Americans." She was a frailish looking high school graduate, and had to do the work of a male laborer in order to support herself and her family.

June 21, 1922. One of the Russian servants at our Boinia quarters has told me how amusing it was to watch from an outside window

43. Babine may well mean Charles W. Surles from the ARA.
44. Thomas J. Farraher, ARA Russian unit staff member.
45. I was unable to identify him.

 as the Americans had a good time in their room with wine bottles and streetwalkers.

June 25, 1922. "Of course, some of them behave disgustingly. One afternoon, it was Sunday, too, I was ordered to call on X at his quarters. When I entered the room I saw two women without a stitch on them, and X in his bathrobe, drunk as a pig. . . . Of course, Americans have helped us very much, but we might have a soberer lot sent here." (I. P. Volkov, Russian assistant at the ARA medical warehouse.)

July 5, 1922. American ARA employees are criticized for speculating in furs and diamonds. One of the Americans is said to have smuggled out of the country a 5-carat stone (with a little flaw in it).

July 7, 1922. Botek, the medical warehouse chief's right hand, is said to have opened a drugstore in a partner's name and to be getting rich at the expense of the American medical stores. His conduct is much talked about among Russian employees, and looks suspicious to everybody, while his influence is explained by his sister-in-law's intimacy with one of the leading Americans.

July 9, 1922. Large quantities of American products and medical supplies are stolen daily. Russian workers are badly underpaid, and work only for what they manage to steal, in spite of constant watching and searches among them. Stimulants like cocaine are particularly favored by them. "It would be perfectly easy to stop it all, and it is a wonder that you Americans don't know how to do it," philosophized one of the senior Russian employees this afternoon.

July 23, 1922. Dr. Davenport[46] is said to have made an embarrassing proposal to our stately and lively Miss N. K. Benson, who has not reported on duty for a few days. However, being the only wage earner of a now ruined but formerly well-to-do family, she is not in a position to give up her job at the ARA warehouse.

July 24, 1922. It is next to impossible to find a room in Moscow. An acquaintance of mine has received 10 million Soviet rubles for the privilege of settling in one of his furnished rooms rented for 30 million Soviet rubles a month. I changed several places since I came to Moscow (the ARA warehouse; Urusov's; Pianowski's; Iasu-

46. Dr. Walter P. Davenport, ARA Russian unit staff member.

ninskii's; and a night at Kalinin's—when I found myself within an inch of spending the night at large in the streets of the great Russian capital).

July 31, 1922. The signatures on Voronov's and Volkov's "poruchitel'stva"[47] had to be certified by the institution employing them. So I had to go to Mangan,[48] and was on Spiridonovka at 9:10 A.M. He asked me to come an hour later, when he told me that it was necessary for me to go to Boinia to get the "poruchitel'stva" initialed by Dawson.[49] "Then you will come back to me, and I will sign the papers." Before the next Boinia car I had time to go to my district "militia" to have my domicile document certified, which took about ten minutes and cost only one million Soviet rubles. I reached Boinia only at 1:30 P.M., the ARA bus having been delayed by something or other, got Dawson's initials, and returned to Spiridonovka by 2:30 P.M., having skipped my lunch today. I had to wait twenty minutes for Mangan, who was out for a walk with a pretty young Russian woman. He signed the *poruchitel'stva,* but consulted Quinn,[50] by phone, when it came to stamping them. Quinn's answer was: "We do not put our official stamp on foreign passports." Senseless as the plea was, there was nothing to do about it: Quinn looked sober when I met him in the morning, while Mangan's face was the very picture of a Sunday spree. To argue with the contemptible cur was useless. I only pointed out to him that my documents were of no value whatever without the ARA seal. Then the idea came to him of having them signed and stamped in Eiduk's office[51]—the last place I wanted to go to, and the worst one. But there I went, and Bartoshevich (very busy that afternoon) stamped and countersigned my precious scraps of paper that were to deliver me of the Soviets. I took the very next bus to Boinia and was at my desk at 4 P.M., having lost a whole day because Mangan's boozy brain would not conceive the senselessness of his suspicions and

47. "Guarantees."

48. John J. Mangan, chief of the ARA's Moscow Division.

49. John M. Dawson, ARA staff member.

50. Cyril J. C. Quinn, executive assistant to Haskill, who replaced Lonergan. Quinn was in charge of ARA operations during Haskill's absence.

51. Aleksandr Eiduk, a hero of the revolution who served as the Soviet government's humorless representative plenipotentiary to the ARA. He was empowered to issue whatever orders were necessary to facilitate work of the ARA.

 fears. It was rather fortunate that Bulle did not recognize me with my moustache off and in my American costume that I have managed with much difficulty to save from Soviet robbers (in Saratov he saw me only in my Soviet rags), when he ran into me in Eiduk's office. Else my game might have been badly spoiled.[52]

August 1, 1922. Went to the foreign passport office, on Spasskii Pereulok 4. At 9 A.M. the door was not yet open. Only at about 1 P.M. was I able to hand in my application for a foreign passport, together with my autobiography, which I made as detailed as possible and from which I omitted only one point—a point that would have prevented my getting a passport. I was told to call again on September 1, the Soviets in the meantime gathering data about me, and deciding upon the advisability of letting me get out of their clutches. Most of the applicants for foreign passports were Jews fleeing Russia from the slaughter of the innocent Jews that is sure to take place in case of the overthrow of the Soviets, for which all Russia is known to be fervently praying.

August 10, 1922. Am living on Bolshoi Znamenskii Pereulok, within a few steps from the Cathedral of Christ the Saviour, and enjoy the Kremlin chimes every morning. I get up at 6 A.M., shave, cook my bacon and cocoa, and at 8 A.M. leave for Granatnyi Pereulok, where I catch the ARA Boinia bus. I eat only a little piece of dry bread at noon—all I can afford—and, leaving the office in the same bus at 5 P.M., stop downtown for dinner on my way home, paying for the dinner from two to four million Soviet rubles. White bread is 650,000 Soviet rubles a pound, and that not of the best kind. Coal oil is 140,000 rubles a pound, eggs 1.2 million rubles a dozen, a pound of apples 400,000 rubles, a small bun—200,000 rubles.

September 1, 1922. Called at the passport bureau, found there the usual crowd of anxious and nervous Jews, and was told to call tomorrow.

September 2, 1922. After two hours of nervous tension, I got a scrap of paper at last, which directed me to the Foreign Office for my passport—my present scrap serving as a certificate to the effect that the Cheka does not object to my leaving Russia. This is an immense step forward on the road to freedom and safety.

52. Babine is referring to his plans to escape.

September 4, 1922. Another, though smaller, mob of Jews at the Foreign Office. With some use of wits, and with the assistance of a Soviet guard at whom I looked fixedly for some time, I was permitted to present my Cheka document without wasting too much time waiting. All went well until the very obliging young Jewish official asked me for my certificate that I was going abroad under ARA instructions. As I was going abroad on my own, I had no such paper—though the ARA clerk in charge of passports seems to have made the impression on a corresponding Soviet clerk that the ARA was interested in me—with the view of facilitating the issuance of a passport to me. My present well-meaning youngster saw no way out of it except my going and talking it over with "Tovarishch (comrade) Markus." This I did. As I made my way toward the tovarishch's desk, five or six young men entered the room unannounced and headed me off in getting to my tovarishch, who turned out to be a comely and fairly young Jewess. They occupied her attention for at least half an hour with theater and picnic plans, and when at last she turned to me with a faint smile of "Young men will be young men" I smiled back a faint assent and sympathy, briefly stated my case, and had the pleasure of seeing her OK my application. With this I flew back to my doubting youngster, who furnished me with a little scrap of paper directing me to call for my passport on the 16th of the month.

September 16, 1922. These were a nervous two weeks of waiting. I was at the Foreign Office at 2 P.M. The room was already filled with anxious humanity, looking for a chance to escape from the Soviet paradise. A friend of mine, familiar with the interior workings of this office, has told me that my passport was ready, and I immediately bought the necessary stamp for it, which cost seventy-three million Soviet rubles. After two hours of anxious waiting I was told that my passport was not yet ready, and that I was to call on the 18th. I began to fear that an important little secret of mine had been discovered after all—and to be prepared for the worst.

September 18, 1922. I got the passport after all, and it only remains to get out of the country within the two weeks during which it is valid in Russia. It has been suggested at the ARA that I go to Riga in the Latvian diplomatic car that is available twice a week. I therefore immediately called at the Latvian Consulate, armed with a note from the Liaison Division of the ARA, obtained my Latvian visa without any difficulty, and was promised a reservation on the nearest train possible.

September 19, 1922. Having come across an old acquaintance of mine, a former well-to-do landowner, I was told that he was still getting food supplies in Moscow from an old peasant neighbor of his way in the country to whom he had entrusted much of his property, before his flight to Moscow under pressure from outside agitators.

September 20, 1922. In response to my letter to a dear old friend I received today an answer from his wife beginning: "Peter died yesterday morning of the typhus he came down with in a railroad car between Moscow and home. He went to Moscow in order to intercede for my brother, who had been sentenced to death for anti-Bolshevism. My brother has already been shot."

September 25, 1922. Have not been able to secure my car reservation yet. Were I not in Soviet Russia, this would be only annoying.

September 29, 1922. Riga. Left Moscow on the 27th. Our train was several hours behind time when we reached Sebezh.[53] This enabled our Latvian diplomatic courier in charge of the train to secure the services of a lenient Soviet customs inspector instead of the regular Cheka man (a lowly Jew) who always holds trains four or five hours at the border. The examination was by no means annoying, though I had to plead for my English Bible (no books are allowed out of Russia without a special Soviet dispensation) and for my alarm clock since I had a watch in my pocket and since only one piece of each commodity was allowed to be exported. The number of Soviet pamphlets I had in my possession made the inspectors infer that I was a Communist, which resulted in a rather superficial examination of my baggage. ("Are you a Communist?" whispered one of the inspectors to me. I glanced around in a frightened way and whispered somewhat tartly back: "This is no place to talk about it.") Had I foreseen this, I would have taken with me quite a number of things that it seemed wiser to leave behind under the ordinary conditions of Soviet existence.

53. City and administrative center of Sebezh district, Pskov province, located on a lake with the same name. Sebezh has a railroad station on the Moscow-Riga line, 189 kilometers south of Pskov. In 1922 it was still part of Vitebsk province.

Our train left Sebezh after dark. It stopped for a few moments before crossing the line—to change guards, we were told. Immediately after crossing the line, we heard three or four shots fired in rapid succession, and our train pulled up again. At a distance I could see a flashlight wending its way toward our train. Soon it stopped about fifty yards from us, below the embankment, and illuminated a figure in a leather jacket lying on the ground with its right hand thrown out, and its left resting on its heart. Four Lettish soldiers were grouped around the figure. It turned out that a Soviet agitator had crossed the line hanging under a car, dropped on the track before the car had gained speed, ran for the brush, refused to halt, and was killed by a Lettish sharpshooter.

September 30, 1922. They have been waiting for me at the American Consulate in Riga. I had my photographs taken today, and shall get my visa as soon as the pictures are ready.

October 3, 1922. Bought a book this morning by B. Sokolov[54] on the terrible condition of school and homeless children in Russia[55] under the Bolshevik regime. A namesake of the author, a university professor, was kept three months in jail in Moscow before it was established that he had nothing to do with the defamer of the Bolsheviks—though everything in common so far as his opinion of the Moscow bloody despots went.

October 11, 1922. Reached London this morning, via Libau and the Kiel Canal. Our steamer moored just below London Bridge. After a superficial customs inspection I drove to the Waverly Hotel, which had been recommended to me by a fellow passenger. Am somewhat bewildered by the immense traffic, and cannot see bookstore window exhibits enough to suit me.

Here I feel absolutely safe, and out of reach of the Soviets.

October 14, 1922. My first bundle of laundry was properly done for the first time since 1918. I sent to the laundry absolutely everything I had rescued from Russia. When the wash was returned, I understood why the late empress of Russia used to send her linen to London, instead of having it done at home.

54. B. Sokolov, author of *Spasite detei* (Save the Children) (Prague, 1921).

55. *Bezprizorniki* or *bezprizornye* were an estimated four million destitute, shelterless waifs, orphaned casualties of war, revolution, civil war, and famine, who roved the country by the winter of 1920–21.

 October 15, 1922. Rode to Whitechapel in a bus, and saw a small crowd on a street corner around an orator. I got off the bus. A youthful Jew was preaching Moscow Sovietism to a circle of English workers who apparently were already well informed about the Soviets and pressed the lout with questions that made him very uncomfortable. Among other things, the Communist quoted Trotsky's maxim about dealing with the bourgeoisie: "It is easier to shoot them than to argue with them."

November 16, 1922. The steerage and the second cabin of the *Berengaria* are full of Jews. Many of them are fleeing from Russia, where life at present is impossible and where pogroms are expected of all the Jews for the sins of a few criminal anarchists who are Jews only in name, but who bring a curse on the entire Jewish race.

November 18, 1922. Landed in New York, after a pleasant trip on the *Berengaria*. The customs examination was a protracted affair owing to a large number of passengers. After my many previous experiences with the New York Customs House my inspector did not waste much time on my baggage.

SELECTED BIBLIOGRAPHY

Unpublished Material

Department of Manuscripts, University Archives, Cornell University. Papers of George Lincoln Burr, Charles Henry Hull, and unpublished memoirs (1890) of Edwin Emerson.

Gosudarstvennyi arkhiv Saratovskoi oblasti (GASO), f. 521, op. 1, dd. 556, 14, 12, 16, 75, 80, 89, 117, 122, 133, 138, 159, 304, 333, 392, 394, 401. Saratov.

Hoover Institution on War, Revolution, and Peace. Documents of the American Relief Administration, 1918–1922. Stanford, Calif.

University Archives, Indiana University, Bloomington. Babine's correspondence with Joseph Swain and Swain's "President's Report to the Board of Trustees," June 10, 1896, Nov. 1, 1896.

Manuscripts Division, Library of Congress. Papers of Frederick B. Ashley. Manuscript, "History of the Library of Congress."

Manuscripts Division, Library of Congress. Papers of Alexis V. Babine (six boxes).

Tsentral'nyi gosudarstvennyi arkhiv Oktiabr'skoi revoliutsii (TSGAOR), f. 393, op. 3, dd. 80, 327, 328, 330, 331, 332, 333, 334, 335, 336, 337, 338, 340, 618. Moscow.

Documentary Materials

Alekseev, A. "Polozhenie narodnogo khoziaistva Saratovskoi gubernii (Vpechatleniia po ob"ezdu severnykh uezdov gubernii)." *Narodnoe khoziaistvo Nizhnego Povolzh'ia*, no. 4 (1920): 1–3.

Alekseev and Kul'manov. "Otchet uchetno-statisticheskogo raspredelitel'nogo Otdela Gubkoma s 15 noiabria po 15 ianvaria 1921 g." *Vestnik Saratovskogo Gubkoma RKP*, no. 1 (1921): 14–16.

Antonov-Saratovskii, V. P., ed. *Saratovskii Sovet rabochikh deputatov, 1917–1918: Sbornik dokumentov*. Moscow and Leningrad, 1931.

———. *Sovety v epokhu voennogo kommunizma: Sbornik dokumentov*. 2 parts. Moscow, 1928–29.

Chislennost' naseleniia Saratovskoi gubernii po dannym demograficheskoprofession-al'noi perepisi 28 avgusta 1920 god. Saratov, 1921.

Dubitskaia, P. A., et al., comps. *Kul'turnoe stroitel'stvo v Volgogradskoi oblasti, 1917–1941 gg.: Sbornik dokumentov i materialov*. Volgograd, 1980.
"Dvizhenie chlenov professional'nykh soiuzov Saratovskoi gubernii za 1919–1921 gg." *Biulleten' Saratovskogo Gubernskogo Statisticheskogo Biuro*, no. 1 (1922): 29–31.
Ekonomicheskaia zhizn' Povolzh'ia: Sbornik statei. Part 1 (3). Saratov, 1919.
Gerasimenko, G. A., et al., eds. *Khronika revoliutsionnykh sobytii v Saratovskom Povolzh'e*. Saratov, 1968.
Kokshaiskii, I. N. *Gorod Saratov v zhilishchnom otnoshenii*. Saratov, 1922.
———. *Predvaritel'nye dannye perepisi naseleniia goroda Saratova i ego prigorodov*. Saratov, 1916.
Kratkii otchet i rezoliutsii IX-go s"ezda sovetov Saratovskoi gubernii. Saratov, 1921.
Malinin, G. A., and Z. E. Gusakova, comps. *Kul'turnoe stroitel'stvo v Saratovskom Povolzh'e: Dokumenty i materialy*. Part 1, *1917–1928 gg*. Saratov, 1985.
Mal'kov, A. S. *Estestvennoe dvizhenie naseleniia Saratovskoi gubernii za period 1914–1925 g*. Saratov, 1926.
Materialy po statistike g. Saratova. Vyp. I. Saratov, 1921.
N. A. "Dvizhenie naseleniia Saratovskoi gubernii (1920–1925 gg.)." *Administrativnaia zhizn'*, no. 18–19 (1925): 3–4.
Naseleniia gorodov Saratovskoi gubernii v 1923. Saratov, 1924.
Novinskii, V. "Sotsial'nyi i professional'nyi sostav naseleniia goroda Saratova." *Nizhnee Povolzh'e*, no. 1 (1924): 82–85.
Obzor deiatel'nosti Saratovskogo gubernskogo soveta narodnogo khoziaistva za 1919 god. Saratov, 1920.
Odinnadtsatyi gubernskii s"ezd sovetov rabochikh, krest'ianskikh i krasnoarmeiskikh deputatov Saratovskoi gubernii 16–17 dekabria 1921 goda: Stenograficheskii otchet. Saratov, 1921.
Osipov, B. A., ed. *1917 god v Saratovskoi gubernii: Sbornik dokumentov, fevral' 1917–dekabr' 1918 gg*. Saratov, 1957.
Osobaia komissiia po razsledovaniiu zlodeianii bol'shevikov. *Bol'sheviki v Tsaritsyne*. Rostov-on-the-Don, 1919.
Otchet Prezidiuma Gorsoveta i Gubispolkoma. Saratov, 1921.
Otchet Saratovskogo gubkoma RKP k XI gubpartkonferentsii (s 10 iiunia po 12 dekabria 1921 g.). Saratov, 1921.
Piatiletie Saratovskogo gubernskogo Soveta narodnogo khoziaistva (1917/18–1923 gg.): Sbornik statei i vospominanii. Saratov, 1923.
Plenum Saratovskogo Gubkoma RKP (Doklady i rezoliutsii). Saratov, 1921.
Poliantsev, N., et al., eds. *Saratovskaia partiinaia organizatsiia v gody grazhdanskoi voiny: Dokumenty i materialy, 1918–1920 gg*. Saratov, 1958.
Polozhenie o kommunisticheskikh iacheikakh. Saratov, 1919.
Protokoly Saratovskogo gubernskogo s"ezda sovetov krest'ianskikh deputatov, proiskhodivshego v g. Saratove s 25 maia po 2-e iiunia 1918 g. Saratov, 1918.
Sbornik instruktsii i polozhenii Saratovskogo gubernskogo komiteta RKP po rabote v derevne. Saratov, 1920.
Statisticheskii sbornik po Saratovskoi gubernii. Saratov, 1923.
Sviatogorov, V. "1918 god. Sovetskoe stroitel'stvo v uezde (Po gazetnym materialam)." *Kommunisticheskii put'*, no. 9 (34) (1923): 63–71.
United States. *Russia: The Volga River and Caspian Sea*. Confidential report. Washington, D.C., 1919.

Vtoroi Saratovskoi gubernskii s"ezd Kommunisticheskogo Soiuza Molodezhi 11–14 fevralia 1920 g. (Rezoliutsii i tezisy, priniatye s"ezdom). Saratov, 1920.

Newspapers and Periodicals

Biulleten' Saratovskogo gubernskogo statisticheskogo biuro.
Bor'ba. Organ of the Tsaritsyn Bolshevik Committee and later of the Tsaritsyn Provincial Committee, 1919–20.
Golos anarkhii. Saratov Anarchist paper published in the fall of 1917.
Gornilo. Bolshevik literary and sociopolitical journal, Saratov, 1918.
Iunyi kommunist. Saratov Komsomol publication, 1920–21.
Izvestiia Balashovskogo Ispolkoma Soveta. Balashov, 1918.
Izvestiia Ispolnitel'nogo komiteta Soveta Vol'skogo uezda. Volsk, 1918–19.
Izvestiia Saratovskogo Soveta rabochikh i soldatskikh deputatov. Official organ of the Saratov Soviet.
Izvestiia Soveta Kamyshinskogo uezda. Kamyshin, 1918. Later, *Nabat*, 1919–21.
Krasnaia kommuna. Organ of the Atkarsk Soviet, 1918. After 1918, *Izvestiia Atkarskogo Ispolnitel'nogo komiteta.*
Krasnoarmeets. Saratov Red Army paper, 1918.
Proletarii Povolzh'ia. Newspaper of the Saratov Menshevik Organization.
Prosveshchenie. Saratov educational journal, 1918–19.
Saratovskaia krasnaia gazeta. Saratov Bolshevik newspaper, 1918–19.
Saratovskii listok. Saratov daily associated with the Kadet party, 1917.
Serp i molot. Organ of the Serdobsk Uezd Executive Committee, 1920–21.
Sotsial-Demokrat. Saratov Bolshevik paper, 1917–18.
Sovetskaia derevnia. Weekly paper for peasants put out by the Saratov Communist Party Committee, 1920–21.
Znamia revoliutsii. Organ of the Saratov Revolutionary Communists (Left SRs), 1918–19.

Memoirs

Antonov-Saratovskii, V. P. "Oktiabr'skaia revoliutsiia v Saratove." *Kommunisticheskii put'*, no. 34 (1925): 77–86.
———. "Otbleski besed s Il'ichem." *Proletarskaia revoliutsiia* no. 3 (26) (1924): 183–91.
———. *Pod stiagom proletarskoi bor'by*. Moscow-Leningrad, 1925.
———, ed. *Godovshchina sotsial'noi revoliutsii v Saratove*. Saratov, 1918.
Babushkin, A. V., et al., eds. *Za vlast' sovetov (Sbornik vospominanii starykh bol'shevikov)*. Saratov, 1968.
Bogdanova, E. N. "Uchastie zhenshchiny v stroitel'stve sovvlasti Saratova (Iz vospominanii)." *Kommunisticheskii put'*, no. 23 (85) (1927): 45–47.
Bunarov, V. "Oktiabr'skaia revoliutsiia v derevne." *Kommunisticheskii put'*, no. 9 (34) (1923): 72–75.
Chebaevskii, F. "Volzhskaia voennaia flotiliia v grazhdanskoi voine (1918–1920)." *Istoricheskii zhurnal*, no. 2–3 (1944): 22–27.
Istpart Nizhne-Volzhskogo kraikoma VKP(b). *V boiakh za diktaturu proletariata: Sbornik vospominanii uchastnikov oktiabria i grazhdanskoi voiny v Nizhnem Povolzh'e*. Saratov, 1933.

Lalova. "Kusochek vospominanii (O krasnykh dniakh oktiabria 1917 goda v gorode Saratove)." *Kommunisticheskii put'*, no. 58 (1926): 48–49.

Lebedev, P. A. "Fevral'-oktiabr' v Saratove." *Proletarskaia revoliutsiia*, no. 10 (1922): 238–56.

Levinson, M. "Kontr-revoliutsiia v Saratovskoi gubernii v 1918–21 gg. (Po dokumentam i vospominaniiam)." In *1917 god v Saratove*, 82–98. Saratov, 1927.

Martsinovskii, A. "Pervye mesiatsy Oktiabr'skoi revoliutsii v Saratove." *Kommunisticheskii put'*, no. 20 (1927): 126–30.

———. *Zapiski rabochego-bol'shevika*. Saratov, 1923.

Minin, S. K. *Gorod-boets: Shest' diktatur 1917 goda (Vospominaniia o rabote v Tsaritsyne)*. Leningrad, 1925.

Piat' let proletarskoi bor'by, 1917–1922. Saratov, 1922.

Radus-Zen'kovich, V. A. "O rabote Saratovskogo gubispolkoma letom 1919 goda (Vospominaniia)." *Istoricheskii arkhiv*, no. 5 (1958): 151–58.

Ruban, D. "Oktiabr'skaia revoliutsiia i bor'ba za sovety v Novouzenske." *Vestnik Saratovskogo Gubkoma RKP*, no. 5 (30) (1923): 79–80.

Shchegol'kov. "Na zare: Sovetskaia vlast' v Serdobske (Vospominaniia ob Oktiabre)." *Kommunisticheskii put'*, no. 9 (34) (1923): 51–62.

Shklovskii, V. *Sentimental'noe puteshestvie: Vospominaniia 1917–1922*, 208–25. Moscow, 1923.

Sorin, I. "Saratovskoe vosstanie 1918 g. (Po chernovym zametkam). *Letopis' revoliutsii*, no. 5 (Kharkov, 1923): 219–24.

Sukharev, G., et al., eds. *Za vlast' sovetov: Vospominaniia uchastnikov revoliutsionnykh sobytii 1917 goda v Saratovskoi gubernii*. Saratov, 1957.

Sushitskii, V. "Oktiabr'skaia revoliutsiia v Vol'skom i Atkarskom uezdakh." *Kommunisticheskii put'*, no. 20 (1927): 102–11.

Sviatogorov, V. "1918 god. Sovetskoe stroitel'stvo v uezde." *Kommunisticheskii put'*, no. 9 (1923): 63–71.

Tomarev, V. I., and M. Ia. Kleinman, comps. *Za sovetskuiu vlast' (Sbornik vospominanii uchastnikov revoliutsionnykh sobytii v Tsaritsyne)*. Stalingrad, 1957.

Vasil'ev, M. I. "Proletarskaia revoliutsiia v Saratove." *Sovetskoe stroitel'stvo*, no. 10–11 (1927): 119–41.

Vladimirova, Vera. "'Rabota' eserov v 1918 godu." *Krasnyi arkhiv*, no. 20 (1927): 153–74.

Zenkovich, V. A. *Dva goda vlasti rabochikh i krest'ian*. Saratov, 1919.

Secondary Works

Airikh, A. K. "Trudiashchiesia nemtsy Povolzh'ia v bor'be za sovety." *Nizhnee Povolzh'e*, no. 5 (1933): 7–20.

Antonov, S. P. *Bol'sheviki Saratova v bor'be za sotsialisticheskuiu revoliutsiiu*. Saratov, 1947.

Babine, Alexis V. *The Yudin Library, Krasnoiarsk (Eastern Siberia)*. Text in English and Russian. Washington, D.C., 1905.

Barkov, B. *Zhizn', izbrannaia serdtsem*. Saratov, 1967.

Barminov, F. I. "Bor'ba partiinykh organizatsii Nizhnego Povolzh'ia s golodom, 1921–1922 gg." In *Istoriia partiinykh organizatsii Povolzh'ia: Mezhvuzovskii nauchnyi sbornik*, vyp. 7, pp. 138–54. Saratov, 1977.

Belokopytov, V. I. *Likholet'e (Iz istorii bor'by s golodom v Povolzh'e, 1921–1922 gg.).* Kazan, 1976.
Biggart, John. "The Astrakhan Rebellion: An Episode in the Career of Sergey Mironovich Kirov." *Slavonic and East European Review*, no. 2 (1976): 231–47.
Blinov, M. "Saratovskaia organizatsiia za 4 goda." *Vestnik Saratovskogo Gubkoma RKP*, no. 12 (1921): 23–25.
Bugaenko, P. A., et al. *Saratovskii universitet, 1909–1959: Kratkii ocherk.* Saratov, 1959.
Ezergailis, Andrew. *The Latvian Impact on the Bolshevik Revolution: The First Phase, September 1917 to April 1918.* Boulder, Colo., 1983.
Fisher, Harold H. *The Famine in Soviet Russia, 1919–1923: The Operations of the American Relief Administration.* New York, 1927.
Gerasimenko, G. A. "Ustanovlenie Sovetskoi vlasti v uezdakh Nizhnego Povolzh'ia." In *Iz istorii Saratovskogo Povolzh'ia*, edited by V. A. Osipov, 71–102. Saratov, 1968.
Gross, E. *Avtonomnaia sotsialisticheskaia sovetskaia respublika nemtsev Povolzh'ia.* Pokrovsk, 1926.
Gubenko, P. T. "Iz istorii kolkhoznogo stroitel'stva (1917–1919 gg.)." *Trudy Saratovskogo instituta sel'skogo khoziaistva*, vyp. 12 (1958): 17–34.
———. "Iz istorii sovkhoznogo stroitel'stva v pervye gody Sovetskoi vlasti (1917–1920)." *Trudy Saratovskogo instituta sel'skogo khoziaistva*, vyp. 2 (1958): 3–16.
Gusev, S. I. *Trudovye mobilizatsii i trudovye armii v Saratovskoi gubernii. Materialy k 9-mu s"ezdu RKP.* Moscow, 1920.
Iakorev, N. A. "Iz opyta politicheskoi raboty v massakh v gody grazhdanskoi voiny (Po materialam Saratovskoi partiinoi organizatsii)." *Uchenye zapiski Saratovskogo universiteta* 59 (1958): 231–47.
Ionenko, S. I. *Likvidatsiia staroi armii v tylovykh okrugakh. Oktiabr' 1917 g.–aprel' 1918 g. (Po materialam Kazanskogo voennogo okruga).* Kazan, 1982.
Kadiksov, P. "Dvizhenie vol'nykh tsen na tovary v gorodakh Saratovskoi gubernii v 1919 godu." *Biulleten' Saratovskogo Gubstatbiuro*, no. 1 (1920): 30–38.
Kalashnikov, N. N. "Saratovskaia organizatsiia kommunisticheskoi partii v bor'be za ukreplenie soiuza rabochikh i krest'ian pri perekhode k NEPu." *Uchenye zapiski Balashovskogo pedinstituta* 2 (1957): 3–44.
Kasinec, Edward. "Alexis V. Babine (1866–1930): A Biographical Note." In *Slavic Books and Bookmen: Papers and Essays*, 73–77. New York, 1984.
Kenez, Peter. *Civil War in South Russia, 1918: The First Year of the Volunteer Army.* Berkeley and Los Angeles, 1971.
———. *Civil War in South Russia, 1919–1920: The Defeat of the Whites.* Berkeley and Los Angeles, 1977.
Kennan, George F. *Soviet-American Relations, 1917–1920.* Vol. 2, *The Decision to Intervene.* New York, 1967.
Khodakov, G. F. *Ocherki istorii Saratovskoi organizatsii KPSS. Chast' pervaia, 1898–1918.* 2d ed. Saratov, 1968.
Kliuev, L. L. *Bor'ba za Tsaritsyn (1918–1919 gg.).* Moscow and Leningrad, 1928.
———. "Rol' krasnogo Tsaritsyna v operatsiiakh Iuzhnogo fronta Sovetskoi respubliki v 1918–1919 gg." *Krasnaia armiia*, no. 13 (1922): 26–32.
Leggett, George. *The Cheka: Lenin's Political Police (The All-Russian Extraordinary*

Commission for Combating Counter-Revolution and Sabotage, December 1917 to February 1922). Oxford, 1981.

Lukov, N. "Sel'skoe khoziaistvo Saratovskoi gubernii s 1917 po 1924 g." *Kommunisticheskii put'*, no. 9 (34) (1923): 81–89.

Malinin, G. A. "Saratovskii Sovet v gody inostrannoi voennoi interventsii i grazhdanskoi voiny." In *Nauchnyi ezhegodnik SGU*. Saratov, 1954.

Mints, I. I., et al. *Grazhdanskaia voina v Povolzh'e, 1918–1920*. Kazan, 1974.

Na strazhe revoliutsii (Iz istorii Saratovskogo gorodskogo Soveta za 4 goda). Saratov, 1921.

Ocherki istorii Saratovskoi organizatsii KPSS. Vol. 2, *1918–1937*. Saratov, 1965.

Radkey, Oliver H. *The Agrarian Foes of Bolshevism: Promise and Default of the Russian Socialist Revolutionaries, February to October 1917*. New York, 1958.

———. *The Election to the Russian Constituent Assembly*. Cambridge, Mass., 1950.

———. *The Sickle under the Hammer: The Russian Socialist Revolutionaries in the Early Months of Soviet Rule*. New York, 1963.

———. *The Unknown Civil War in South Russia: A Study of the Green Movement in the Tambov Region, 1920–21*. Stanford, 1976.

Raleigh, Donald J. *Revolution on the Volga: 1917 in Saratov*. Ithaca, N.Y., 1986.

———. "Revolutionary Politics in Provincial Russia: The Tsaritsyn 'Republic' in 1917." *Slavic Review* 40, no. 2 (1981): 194–209.

Rashitov, F. A. "Osnovnye etapy Sovetskogo stroitel'stva v Saratovskoi gubernii v pervoi polovine 1918 goda." *Aspirantskii sbornik*, vyp. 1 (Saratov, 1965): 1–48.

Rigby, T. H. *Communist Party Membership in the USSR*. Princeton, 1968.

Rodionov, V. A., et al., eds. *Saratovskaia oblastnaia organizatsiia KPSS v tsifrakh, 1917–1975*. Saratov, 1977.

Rosenberg, William G. *Liberals in the Russian Revolution: The Constitutional Democratic Party, 1917–1921*. Princeton, 1974.

Shestak, Iu. A. "Bankrotstvo partii 'revoliutsionnykh kommunistov' v Povolzh'e." *Povolzhskii krai*, no. 4 (1975): 24–38.

Shido, V. G. "Iz istorii sozdaniia Saratovskoi komsomol'skoi organizatsii." *Povolzhskii krai*, vyp. 6 (1979): 47–58.

Sokolov, S. A. "Iz istorii bor'by za khleb v 1918 godu (Po materialam Saratovskoi gubernii)." *Uchenye zapiski Saratovskogo universiteta* 39 (1954): 3–26.

———. "K voprosy ustanovleniia prodovol'stvennoi diktatury v 1918 godu." *Povolzhskii krai*, vyp. 6 (1979): 26–46.

———. "Organizatsiia upravleniia narodnym khoziaistvom v 1918 g. (Po materialam zheleznodorozhnogo i vodnogo transporta Povolzh'ia)." *Povolzhskii krai*, no. 4 (1975): 121–34.

Stishov, M. I., and D. S. Tochenyi. "Raspad esero-men'shevistskikh partiinykh organizatsii v Povol'zhe." *Voprosy istorii*, no. 8 (1973): 15–28.

Sushitskii, V. A. *Saratovskii universitet i N. G. Chernyshevskii*. Saratov, 1934.

Taubin, R. A. "Iz istorii bor'by s menshevistskoi esero-kulatskoi kontrrevoliutsei v period grazhdanskoi voiny v Saratovskoi gubernii." *Uchenye zapiski Saratovskogo universiteta* 14 (1938): 3–46.

Terekhin, S. V. "Prodovol'stvennye zagotovki v rabote Saratovskoi kommunisticheskoi organizatsii v 1918–1920 gg." *Trudy Saratovskogo ekonomicheskogo instituta* 4 (1954): 20–49.

Tochenyi, D. S. "Raspad levoeserovskikh organizatsii v Povolzh'e." *Nauchnye trudy Kuibyshevskogo gosudarstvennogo pedinstituta* 165, no. 2 (1975): 54–62.
Utkov, V. G. "Sud'ba odnogo knigokhranilishcha." In *Knigi i sud'by: Ocherki*, 108–129. Moscow, 1967. 2d ed. (1970), *Liudi i sud'by, sobytiia*, 41–57.
Vasina, E. *Banditizm v Saratovskoi gubernii*. Saratov, 1928.
Vas'kovskii, O. A. "Rabota partiinykh sovetskikh organizatsii Saratovskoi gubernii po sozdaniiu prochnogo tyla letom 1919 goda." *Uchenye zapiski Saratovskogo universiteta* 47 (1956): 27–47.
Vodolagin, M. A. *Krasnyi Tsaritsyn*. Volgograd, 1967.
Wade, Rex A. *Red Guards and Workers' Militias in the Russian Revolution*. Stanford, 1984.
Weissman, Benjamin M. *Herbert Hoover and Famine Relief to Soviet Russia, 1921–23*. Hoover Institution Publications, no. 134. Stanford, Calif., 1974.
Wheatcroft, S. G. "Famine and Epidemic Crises in Russia, 1918–1922: The Case of Saratov." *Annales de démographie historique* (1983), 329–51.

Dissertations

Iakovlev, P. F. "Komitety derevenskoi bednoty Saratovskoi gubernii." Candidate dissertation, Saratov University, 1952.
Rashitov, F. A. "Sovety Nizhnego Povolzh'ia v pervyi god diktatury proletariata." Candidate dissertation, Saratov University, 1968.
Skibinskaia, S. B. "Kritika burzhuaznykh fal'sifikatsii istorii grazhdanskoi voiny v Srednem Povolzh'e." Candidate dissertation, Kazan Pedagogical Institute, 1981.
Sokolov, S. A. "Bor'ba za khleb v Saratovskoi gubernii v 1918 godu." Candidate dissertation, Saratov University, 1951.
Strel'tsova, A. I. "Partiinaia organizatsiia Saratovskoi gubernii v bor'be za provedenie politiki partii v derevne v vosstanovitel'nyi period (1921–1925 gody)." Candidate dissertation, Moscow University, 1953.
Tomarev, V. I. "Bol'sheviki Tsaritsyna v bor'be za ustanovlenie i uprochenie Sovetskoi vlasti, mart 1917 g.–iiun' 1918 g." Candidate dissertation, Moscow University, 1961.
Vas'kovskii, O. A. "Sovety Saratovskoi gubernii v bor'be za organizatsiiu tyla v period pervogo i vtorogo pokhodov Antanty." Candidate dissertation, Saratov University, 1953.
Vorob'eva, V. Ia. "Krakh men'shevistskoi kontrrevoliutsii Povolzh'ia i Sibiri v grazhdanskoi voine i interventsii." Candidate dissertation, Moscow Pedagogical Institute, 1969.

INDEX